FAMOUS ANUS

FAMOUS ANUS

Stories From a Decade Under the Sinfluence

JORDAN POWER

A COLE JAMES BOOK

FAMOUS ANUS
Published by Cole James Books

First paperback edition June 2020

Cover design by Abz Hakim
Book design by Sue Balcer

ISBN: 978-1-7771625-0-4

www.jordanpowerwrites.com

Contents

Author's Note:

This memoir is based on my experiences over a period of approximately 10 years. It includes true versions of events written to the best of my recollection. I was very inebriated for a lot of it, so keep that in mind. Dialogue between characters has been recreated from memory and by using journals and early drafts. At various points, time periods have been compressed. Names, locations, and other identifying details have been changed to protect the anonymity of individuals.

To Britt

My soulmate in "Simu"
You make me feel unstoppable

INTRODUCTION

"You need to make a stop before you come over to my place," said my boyfriend, Patrick.

"A stop?" I balanced the phone between my ear and shoulder. "A stop where?"

"At the grocery store," he replied. "I want you to grab a cucumber."

"For what?" I was on my way out the door and totally stuffed from a 20-piece McNuggets meal. "A salad? I'm *very* horny and definitely not hungry."

"No, you dirty little slut," he cooed into the phone. "You're the salad. I'm going to shove it up your ass."

It was the summer of 2009. I was 23, maybe 24, maybe a little too young to be scraping the bottom of the barrel for a level of acceptable sexual gratification. I blame Internet porn. It is insidious, an assault on your dopamine receptors that comes so slowly the changes are imperceptible.

The first time I downloaded porn it was on our family computer at 2 a.m. I was 14 years old. It was a grainy, 43-second clip of an oiled-up Hungarian twink with dead eyes and overdue rent. But it. Was. Spellbinding. When my older sister, Lisa, found it buried in the temp files of our Windows 98 operating system, I unconvincingly shrugged and told her we had been infiltrated by a computer virus of European origin. But nowadays, you could show me a furry fisting Zac Efron and I would ask you, deadpan, what your point was. God, I miss dopamine like a dead friend.

Anyway, I digress. It happens a lot, so you'd better get used to it.

I had never purchased a cucumber for the sole purpose of producing sexual pleasure. It was kind of exciting. Patrick had given no indication as to the type of cucumber he wanted. I went with the English variety because they were the only ones on sale. Colour also was not a major factor in my purchase decision. In fact, neither was size, surprisingly. I did however make sure to avoid those with sinister, bulging growths on their sides. I was looking for an orgasm, not a bowel perforation.

I grabbed the fifth cucumber I saw, which prioritized length over girth, and charged the $0.70 to my Visa card. As I walked out of the grocery store, I debated if it would be kosher to use it in a chopped salad after our depraved activities concluded.

You're probably wondering why I'd resorted to members of the gourd family in my rectum when there were BPA-free, dishwasher-safe, reasonably sized dildos at a sex shop mere blocks from my house. Well for one, I was broke. The kind of broke where you finish a $7 sandwich and briefly debate whether you should also eat the plastic wrapper to justify skipping your next meal. The kind of broke that makes you walk 50 minutes home from the gym because a monthly subway pass sounds like a distant pipe dream. So you can take your dildo privilege and shove it up *your* ass.

And well, I lied about Patrick. He wasn't technically my boyfriend at the time. We had broken up months prior, though we were still sleeping together on the regular, even as we both dated other people. I pretended not to notice his love for me still ran deep. Perhaps mine did, too, but that was quickly eclipsed by the intoxicating prospect of unrestrained singledom after five years together. I soon learned that being single is actually pretty great—that is, until the sun starts to set.

After we'd make love, about once a week, he'd roll over with yearning eyes and utter veiled phrases which always meant he was still in love with me. I would pretend not to hear him, rebuke his intimate advances, toss my clothes back on, and saunter off for a sale at H&M. I would later learn that pretty much every day is a sale at H&M, but it was a hell of an excuse. Truthfully, I do not really recall any of this, so I went straight to the source. Patrick himself filled me in on the details when I told him I was writing this book:

"I'd basically pour my entire heart out to you each time and then you'd roll your eyes and make up some sort of social commitment. 90% of the time they did not even check out! It was pretty ruthless, Jordan."

My bad.

I commenced my singledom post-Patrick by first moving out of his apartment. We had only been living together a month, which was a terrible idea in the winter of our relationship. Six months prior, we were already flickering like a dying ember, so you can only imagine how much worse it got once we were crammed together into 540 square feet. I started to hate everything about him: his idiosyncratic routines, his affinity for Hilary Duff music, and the sound of his turds hitting the toilet water as I tried to perfectly poach my eggs.

When we finally knew it was over, I started a furious search on Craigslist for a roommate. On my third viewing, I connected with a straight, effusive woman whose parents gifted her an industrial loft, two blocks from the Eaton Centre. The only stipulation they gave her was that she needed a roommate to support the carrying costs. A week after her ad went live, I moved in.

Her name was Lois. She was a trust-fund baby slash failed actress without an IMDb credit to her name. When she was not bombing auditions, she dated a revolving door of men like it was her day job. Sometimes two or three different suitors a week, which to me seemed a near guarantee that quality was being sacrificed. Lois was blonde, blue-eyed, and 5'10", with an uncharacteristically deep voice. I can still hear it bouncing off the walls as she rehearsed a monologue for each commercial audition.

Every week she would pick at her salad and recap her dates, reciting a laundry list of reasons why men weren't into her. She was too powerful, they were threatened by her family's wealth, she did not drink. Blah, blah, blah. In truth, she was a typical actress, a borderline megalomaniac who pranced around the city as if a director was always watching and could yell, *"Cut. That is absolutely brilliant Lois,"* at any moment.

Sometimes she would ask, "Do you have any ideas why they're not into me, Jordan?"

Many!

"I don't know," I'd reply with a shrug, heating my spicy-chicken-flavoured Mr. Noodles. But what I really meant to say was, "I would try a back shave."

My job at the time was a personal injury law clerk, despite having no formal legal training and an unrelated bachelor's degree in business studies. Do not ask me how I landed it, because frankly I do not know. I pulled out all the stops obtaining it because I needed an excuse to move to the big gay city. I think I made less than $39,000 a year and kept a staggering credit card balance every month. When you're that poor, you become extraordinarily comfortable with constantly asking friends at lunch, "Hey, are you gonna finish that?"

And I hated that job, so I unintentionally transferred my simmering disdain onto our roster of gravely injured clients. I would sit at my desk, picking at a Starbucks scone and reading a $50,000 lawsuit for "loss of sexual enjoyment," and scoff and scoff and scoff.

"Everyone wants a payday!" I would yell over the barrier to Carol, the 55-year-old admin assistant. "I haven't been properly satisfied in years and this whiner wants 50K. Buck up, pal. What about you, Carol? Are you getting a lot of sexual enjoyment?"

"Um, do you want cake, Jordan?" she would reply, ignoring me. "It's Sandra's 40th birthday today. It's banana chocolate."

"No Carol, I told you. I don't want cake. I want a jawline."

She sighed. I continued, "Homosexuals of my ilk do not participate in these antiquated rituals. It's absolutely brutal out there for us. I have got max 10 years of sexual viability left in me. Maybe 12 if I religiously apply sunscreen."

My boss at said law firm was a manic philanderer named Roger. He was in his late 30s and on the fast track to running the whole damn place. This guy would cut his mom's throat if it got him an upgraded parking spot. He filled every room he entered with the unrestrained freneticism of a coked-out squirrel.

He always had a fresh tan from a weekend in St. Barts or something adjacent. He had a wife, but we never saw her or heard her mentioned by name. I caught a whiff of gossip in my second week that he tended to mack on first-year associates at a few of the upscale watering holes in the financial district. Predictable. Ugh. Men, amirite?

Roger filed formal HR complaints when I was two or three minutes late in the morning. It was peak petty. The man—who routinely billed upward of $600 an hour—would take 15 minutes of his time to complete the paperwork in its entirety, all just to prove a point. Well, I had already proven *mine*, which was that I didn't care about him or his Prada loafers. I loathed the routine of indentured servitude that had become my life. By the third HR report, I was summoned to the office manager's desk for a verbal lashing.

"And what do you say to all this, Jordan?" The HR rep lowered her reading glasses.

I looked back at her, completely unfazed. "Um, get used to it?"

A week later, she told me I was on "very thin ice." You see, Roger was a partner, in addition to being a self-important piece of shit who made over $500,000 a year. And as much as I was playing the tough-guy routine, I was riddled with anxiety at the prospect of losing my job. Without a paycheque, I couldn't party and it was my sole habit at the time. Some people do arts and crafts; I sucked last-call dick.

When I realized my days were inevitably numbered, I actually became even more negligent. It was as if my arms could not bring themselves to participate in such a soulless existence. Sunday-night panic was no longer sporadic, it was inevitable and downright crippling. I surmised I had mere weeks before the guillotine dropped right on my cock. Luckily, I had nothing to worry about because two weeks after my "final warning" from HR, I suffered a complete mental breakdown and went on paid medical leave.

Yes, that's right, a mental breakdown. Have you ever had one?

I don't quite know how I feel about them. On one hand, they do a wonderful job of breaking up the monotony of the work week. On the other hand, you wave goodbye to your faculties and any sense of reality.

Something inside me always knew I was destined for a mental breakdown, but truthfully, I thought I might save a couple for my geriatric golden years. Maybe then I would decide to fling feces, make a dress solely from paperclips, or blow my wad in my 91-year-old neighbour's mashed potatoes. Come to think of it, mental breakdowns in the winter of your life are kind of a gift from your mind. Who the hell wants to be fully present as a spectator of their own demise? Me? Fuck no. I want to believe I'm the empress of Candyland until I flatline.

On the day of said mental breakdown, Roger told me to grab him lunch at the food court three blocks from the office. It was just after 1 p.m. and overcast. I was wearing a purple Le Chateau dress shirt and size 30 grey pants from H&M. My black shoes were spit-shined hand-me-downs from my dad. I was only a block from the office, carrying his fiesta burrito, when the bones in my chest felt like they were violently melding together, squeezing my rapidly depleting oxygen reserve. I dropped the burrito and bent over, thinking I had to vomit, and for a brief second I realized I had no clue where I was geographically situated. Not just in Toronto… on the whole planet! I started rapidly inhaling and exhaling while grabbing the sides of my head and fighting the unrelenting spins.

A woman saw my panic and hailed me a cab. I basically threw myself into it and lay strewn across the leather seats in the back. Then, like any homosexual with an affinity for obscene histrionics, I yelled, "TAKE ME TO THE MENTAL HOSPITAL. YA BOY IS GOING CRAY-ZEEEE."

"What?" The cab driver was clearly annoyed.

"THE MENTAL HOSPITAL, SIR!" I said. "WE HAVE LITTLE TIME LEFT!"

He shrugged and punched the gas. "I don't know what the fuck you're on, man."

Fifteen minutes later, he dropped me at the door of the Centre for Addiction and Mental Health (CAMH). I sprinted up to the front desk and yelled through the hole that had been etched into the glass partition.

"Help. I'm losing my mind! Call the big guns!"

The receptionist looked like she was doing everything in her power not to roll her eyes. She had seen much worse in her day. I was dressed in business casual. I imagined she'd seen young men dressed only in shaving cream and buttons. She barely blinked as she pushed a clipboard toward me. With feigned concern she asked, "Sir, are you thinking of harming yourself?"

"No."

"Are you thinking of harming others?"

"No." I chuckled. "Why would I do that?"

"OK." She seemed almost disappointed. "Take a seat in the grey chairs. We'll call you when we're ready for you."

What a letdown! I thought. I had almost romanticized the idea of a mental breakdown, probably after seeing Mariah Carey storm MTV with an ice cream cart almost a decade earlier. Or well, Mariah Carey in all interviews since then.

Where were the men in lab coats smothering my mouth with a rag of chloroform?

Where was the man blowing a whistle, demanding I calm down, telling me we could "do this the easy way or the hard way"?

Who did I need to piss on around here to earn a vial of milky tranquilizer violently shoved into the side of my neck?

I sat on the grey chair closest to the window and started shaking. I sent a text message to Patrick and my best friend Lara, providing them with an update.

A moment later, Lara replied. *Oh my God,* she said. *Do you want me to come over? I can leave work.*

No, I texted back. *It's fine. I've got this.*

After maybe an hour, a nurse summoned me to a side room with a female, twenty-something master's student by her hip. They asked me a series of repetitive, banal questions about my mental state. I was barely listening. I continuously peppered the conversation with questions about drugs I could possibly place sublingually or rectally. You know, in my money holes.

"Jordan, what were you thinking about the moment before you hailed the cab?" asked the oddly cheerful master's student.

"My family and my parents' divorce. They are all driving me nuts! Everyone continuously leans on me because I'm the most resilient. They think I'll just laugh it off or make some joke but the bank is dry. I'm spent! I'm getting it from all angles. And I think I just snapped," I replied. "Also, I'm about to become unemployed so that is not ideal. Write that all down."

Once the questions stopped, it was time for my homework. I was given a mental health assessment questionnaire and a pen. I had to respond to each statement using a range of 1 (strongly disagree) to 5 (strongly agree).

This is some remedial BS, I thought. But just the prospect of a small distraction helped to soothe my breakdown.

1. I have trouble trusting others.

Response: 5

Then I wrote in the margin, *I would also like to add as a footnote that my trust issues stem from the day I found out James Corden is actually not a homosexual.*

2. I get angry easily.

Response: 4

3. I have a high opinion of myself.

Response: 5, but in fairness others also share this opinion.

OK, that one felt like a trap.

I finished the questionnaire and sat tapping my foot while surveying the poorly lit room. What a joke. I could easily strangle myself with that phone cord or freebase the debris between the letters on the keyboard. *What kind of an operation were they running here?*

The nurse returned to tally the results of my questionnaire with the master's student. They both left minutes later and returned with a doctor in his 70s. I couldn't wait for what Father Time had planned for me. He would have real solutions to my problems. I rubbed my hands together in excited anticipation.

"Jordan," he began. "Your questionnaire shows evidence of a very high level of anxiety along with medium depression."

"OK," I said. "Not surprised. What else?"

"We also think you may have had a panic attack on the street today, so we are recommending a series of twice weekly sessions with a therapist."

I looked around the room, as though said therapist would jump out from behind a curtain. "And where is he or she?"

"We'll give you a recommended list of providers based on your medical condition."

"OK," I said. "I should note I am very broke. Not too broke to buy vodka, but most certainly groceries or a Sunwing vacation."

"I understand. Therapists can be very accommodating in terms of sliding scale payments."

I mentally calculated the balance of my checking account. "How much, do you think?"

"I'll have to check, but I believe the sliding scale starts at $70 a session," said the doctor. "It can vary widely depending on the provider."

"Doc. Let me level with you. I am paying the minimum on my Visa card. Not to mention, I have been using cucumbers for both sustenance AND sexual pleasure. Do you really think I'm in any sort of position to pony up thousands of dollars?"

"Well," he said. "Your workplace benefits can assist. We are highly recommending you start this treatment as soon as possible."

"I'm sure you are," I said. "Anything to pass the buck around here. And what about drugs?"

"We can't prescribe you anything at the moment." He smiled apologetically. "But I'm sure your family doctor or a psychiatrist can assist with that."

"So, no drugs and you're referring me elsewhere?" I asked. "Not even an emergency session on the house?"

He stared at me with a deep vacancy often reserved solely for Ms. Universe pageant contestants proffering solutions for geopolitical conflicts.

"OK." I stood and wiped the top of my pants. "Congratulations to you all… I feel worse!"

Then I lifted my finger at them and said, "When you people find me in the alleyway out back next week, still crazy, and munching on the macaroni from my first-grade art project, well, it will be a REALLLLL wakeup call to upper management."

He stared at me with the same vacancy.

Then I left in a gay huff so pronounced it must have left a blinding trail of glitter and fireflies.

I hailed a cab, and as it pulled up to my apartment, I saw Patrick sitting on the curb outside. He was holding the tiniest potted plant under his arm with a disconsolate expression on his face. He was slouched over, wearing a wrinkled white shirt and black jeans. When we caught eyes, he smiled so unnaturally I knew he was shrouded in undeniable pain.

"Jordan!" he yelled as I stepped out of the cab. "Are you OK?"

"Hi," I said, hugging him like it was his last day on Earth. "Yeah, I'm OK. I mean, I'm not. I think that's kind of the point."

"I've been so worried about you."

"Well, that's a normal reaction to a person checking into a mental hospital."

"I'm going to stay here tonight," he said. "I'll go get my stuff and come back."

"No, no," I said, surprising myself. "Please don't. I need to do this whole healing thing on my own."

As I said it, I realized the truth of my words. I had to stop holding on to Patrick. I started to cry on his shoulder, deeply inhaling the scent of his shirt. Tide Coldwater and Calvin Klein cologne. I knew these were the last moments he would be mine. The five years we'd spent together clicked in front of me like a slideshow on my childhood viewfinder until the images slowed and dissolved, along with the future dreams I'd sketched in my head. I cried with more vigour.

We were no longer a lifetime and, in that moment, I learned that every love, no matter how it begins, comes with no guarantees. They should teach you about impermanence in kindergarten; the fact that they don't is downright cruel. They read you fairy tales about love that will span a lifetime and beyond, but as it turns out, it doesn't. Not all love lasts a lifetime, and sometimes instead of a happily ever after, all you get is a $13 plant as a parting gift.

"What can I do to help?"

My head still lay on Patrick's shoulder. "Let me jump off the cliff," I said.

I could feel him tense under me. "Don't be stupid."

"I don't mean an actual cliff, idiot." I rolled my eyes. "It's a metaphor."

"For what?"

"I don't know. Life, love, sex, people, places. Everything?" I paused. "Don't you feel like our relationship was the only thing keeping us from going off the deep end?"

"No. I don't."

"Well that's where we differ," I said, shrugging. "I feel like it's all I had."

It has been 10 years and that day would serve as a single bookend marking the start of the next decade of my life. I carried with me such certitude that unmistakable love would come knocking again. So much so that I kept journals with the intention of documenting its arrival. I would become the next Nicholas Sparks. I would write a love story that ended with a candlelit proposal on a sandbar. I'm not sure why I always pictured it on a sandbar. That's just impractical.

I was a dreamer back then, a hopeless romantic with no reason to feel the nagging doubt that drags behind me like a peg leg today. From my perspective, I met a man I loved for half a decade after only searching for two months. Why couldn't it happen again?

But here is the problem. The decades before Patrick carried with them such scars that I had buried entirely with the healing power of his unconditional love. And when he was gone, it all came flooding in like a hurricane. I had never realized how much I needed him just to survive. His cuddles and kisses that took my breath away were a safety blanket from the dark horrors of my undeveloped mind. Sadly, I was never taught how to fully love anyone, including myself. I was what the kids today would call "a hot mess." And as fast as I ran this past decade, my pain always seemed to beat me to every finish line.

Make no mistake of it, self-destruction is a sideshow very often worth the price of admission. All the stories in this book are true and some are so seemingly far-fetched that you'd think they were conjured in a writing room. Truthfully, I wish most of them were. Some were the result of bad luck and timing, while some I orchestrated simply to entertain my friends at brunch. I was taught from a very young age that if I performed for people, they would shower me with love.

Some people have an angel on their shoulder, or a devil. I have a monkey. You'll hear from him sporadically throughout this book. His name is Otis. He paws at me daily, asking me to cultivate chaos or amplify it once I find it in others or situations. Sometimes he leaves, and life gets kinda stale. Even to this day, when Otis the monkey is gone, he leaves me sitting alone with myself in uncomfortable silence until I feel like I might start shaking.

I'm an addict. A humour addict. It's a colossal shield that protects me from the full range of my own emotions. When I stop performing, people get uncomfortable. Like clockwork, they'll ask me if I'm feeling OK.

I wonder what value I bring to their lives besides entertainment. I wonder who I am without humour, but I can't let it go because it's all that saves me at times. I can't imagine life without it, especially now that I've started using it to earn a living.

Humour isn't all bad. It can be a reliable coping mechanism. I cleave to it like a life raft through the darkest hours of my life. And because I've relied on it so often, I started to master parts of it. Some people journal; I laugh to repel my tears. And I know I am not the only one. That's why I'm filled with uncontrollable fury when moralistic types move to censor any kind of comedy, thinking they know better. Comedy has been my oldest friend, a refuge from the chaos that comes with trauma, betrayal, and abandonment, sometimes by those I loved dearest.

Parts of this book are a cautionary tale. My behaviour is not to be revered but it will surely be repeated in different derivatives, by millions. And that's kind of OK. We're all a work in progress, and we all should be given some time to experiment with trial and error.

Lots and lots of trial and error.

I've written the comedy book I needed back then to pull me out of my many emotional floors. Gift it to someone who needs a frivolous escape from political correctness, bereavement, a fresh breakup, or even just to escape themselves for a couple days. I don't care if they're laughing at me or with me. Maybe I should?

But keep in mind I wrote these stories exactly as the self-involved, careless, loveless person I was at the time. These pages include my missteps, false starts, and my inability to take myself or anyone else seriously. And it has been kind of tough looking through old journals and first drafts. Because as much as we hear people don't change much, I know I have. Not entirely, but still profoundly.

In editing the final copy of this book, I resisted the urge to write a new tale from the therapized vantage point of my current self. Doing so would change the story and erase the essence of who I was at the time including both the good and the bad.

Any publicist worth their weight would tell you this intro is ill advised. I should know—I used to be one. The school of thought is to assume the brand in its entirety. I could tell you I am still a party boy disposing of men like straws. But I'm not a brand, and I'm not 25 anymore. I'm just a guy trying to figure out life one day at a time, like you. If my "brand" is anything it's that I'm the most honest guy you'll ever meet. "Authentic to a fault," as someone once called me. I'll never apologize for calling the world as it is, but I will try to soften my edges along the way.

And before we get this show on the road, can I let you in on a little secret about the past decade?

I wouldn't change any of it for the world.

Whaddup Big Sur.

CHAPTER ONE

CALIFORNIA

BEFORE WE GET INTO the horror that was (and largely still is) my life, I would be remiss if I didn't tell you a little more about Patrick.

He is the only man I have ever genuinely loved. We met on a now-defunct website called Face Party, a pre-Facebook dating site trolled mostly by heteros, Christian closet cases, and miscellaneous other closet cases, like yours truly.

Neither of us had the balls to post a photo. My profile interests at the time were textbook uber-bro, with themes most commonly found in any Budweiser commercial: muscle cars, beer, fist bumps, and of course, farm fresh pussy. (Hey, I was a faux bisexual at the time.)

At the time, I was 19 and he was 21, both of us fragile, closeted messes. I would chat with him until the sun came up on MSN Messenger as my grade point average tumbled further and further to the depths of future underemployment. It took us a whole month to gather up the courage to send each other a photo. I snapped mine on a first-generation webcam in my green polo shirt with a popped collar. The final photo looked like a still from an ISIS video against the white background of my university dorm room.

At 10:06 p.m., two days after my 19th birthday, I apprehensively dragged the photo file into the only chat box I was paying a smidgen of attention to. My clammy hand trembled as I looked down at my Britney Spears mousepad. At the time I owned Britney everything. Pens, T-shirts, and even a six-foot cardboard cutout of her beside my bed. Everyone thought I wanted to fuck her. I just wanted to *be* her.

My inner monologue was filled with irrational worst-case scenarios. *Well done, idiot. Everyone is going to know you're gay. You're toast, buddy.* I didn't think anyone could be trusted. I'd heard of many a gay being outed well before his time because people thought speculating on someone's sexuality was a fun pastime. They still do.

But my fears were unfounded.

Wow, he typed seconds after opening the photo. *You are so hot, man. Thank you for sending.*

Thanks. Your turn, I said. *Don't leave me hanging here.*

He was openly hesitant. *I am so scared to do this. Promise you won't out me.*

Why would I do that? The thought had never crossed my mind. *Just promise me the same!*

OK, he typed, as the waiting file notification glared under my last typed sentence.

I took a deep breath and opened the photo. He was sitting on a brown couch in someone's cottage, a woman on each arm. Quite the modern Casanova if you asked me. Dark brown hair with piercing blue eyes. He was gorgeous, but with an aura of trustworthiness. He was going to be my first boyfriend. I was totally sure of it. My heart fluttered as I felt the corners of my mouth stiffen into a frozen smile. My fingers were shaking as I composed a reply. His photo had confirmed what we had been building up to for weeks. I typed, *I am very attracted to you, Patrick. Can we please meet?*

I received a response immediately. *I would LOVE to. How about tomorrow?*

The next night, Patrick drove to my university campus to pick me up in his mom's green Malibu. I told my best friend (and roommate at the time) that my cousin was in town from Buffalo.

"On a Monday?" he asked.

"Dunno, must be a long weekend thing," I said with a shrug as I laced up my shoes. "Don't wait up."

I walked 10 minutes from my university dorm with a hoodie deep set over my face like I was about to enroll in a rap battle showdown. My legs wiggled, disjointed every time they lifted and returned to the ground. I saw his car and bright headlights parked under a set of trees on the east end of the lot. As the lock flickered up on the passenger side door, panic rattled the entirety of my chest cage.

"Hello," I said with a laugh as I jumped into the passenger seat, avoiding any semblance of eye contact.

"Hi." His eyes were locked on his steering wheel. "This is so awkward."

I extended my hand. "Let's shake. Hi, I'm Jordan."

His hand clasped mine and I felt unyielding electricity shoot up my arm. Then our eyes met and locked, like the most reliable mechanism on a piece of heavy machinery. CLICK. BOOM. It was true love instantaneously, the kind you'd be an idiot to lose even once in this glint of time we call our lives.

We drove 30 minutes to a parking lot on the edge of Hamilton, our hands intertwined the whole time. By the time we got there, our palms were gushing with anxiety-fueled sweat. Damned if I even noticed. He put the car in park and grabbed the side of my freshly shaven face with a restless inhale.

"Let's try this," he said, as his lips met mine.

God, it was like floating.

Listen, you may have felt love, but gay love has such a higher ceiling. Despite all the odds against you, you found it in its purest form, in the bottom of the haystack. It's the ultimate antidote to a life of inexpressible anguish. That love has the power to make you realize why you suffered in silence all those years, and you immediately value it like you'd die for it.

Patrick and I were two misfits in perfect unison, and I was willing to go wherever he led me. As time suspended that night, we started to spiral on an expedition into the unknown.

Three months later, I told him I loved him at a stoplight four blocks from my house. I couldn't contain myself—it poured out of me like blood from a gushing chest wound. Over the term of our relationship I wrote him a slew of love letters, and let myself fall with a youthful pureness of heart that we all only get one shot at. Man, if that newness was a candle, I'd burn it every night.

Here's one letter (Give me a bit of a break, I was 19):

Patrick,

It's 12:00 a.m. and there's no way in hell I can sleep.

Today was probably the worst day ever of not being able to get you out of my head. It was total insanity. This 'being apart' jazz blows the big one. I kept dreaming of living together and how I don't think anyone on planet earth would be happier than me. Like seriously man, I dunno how I'd be able to go to work cause I'd just wanna cuddle or talk or chill all day long. I can't see myself ever falling out of this. It's gonna be the worst thing ever if we break up... no pressure, punk. ahhah... Again, I state the obvious—don't leave me, P...

I'm really looking forward to March. I know man, 'what a loser,' *ur probably thinking, but complete freedom for a week is amazing. Maybe it's the real test to see if this could work out in the long term.*

I'm starting to care less and less every day bout what people think. I just kinda know that no one else is better than you... more special... more loveable. I guess that's all that matters, right? Ahaha, I can't believe I'm saying all this. I can't even tell one person. I think in like a year or so we'll know. Don't wanna make up stupid ideas. I'm drunk with love I guess...

Miss your smile and the way your eyes light up when you see me, or your laugh or the way you make me feel like the most special person on earth. I guess nothing is better than that. I couldn't ask for someone better. What have we done? We're entering the red zone with no turning back. Just wanted to say thanks for being so special. I feel like any day you are gonna be like, "Jokessss..." cause this is too good to be true. I NEVER thought in a million years I could love a guy so much. guess you changed it all, eh? Thanks so much.

Love you tons,

Jord/Jor

For years, Patrick was the emotional Band-Aid smothering the deep-seated shame I held about being gay. He was what made sense after years of searching for something to believe in. Love did save me from myself when we were together.

The entirety of our relationship took place in the closet. It was an endless loop of lies, faux stories and late-night secret rendezvous. We lived nocturnally, sneaking out while family and friends slept. There is an unintentional, undefinable romance that comes with total secrecy. No third parties weighing in on your relationship with their own biases. No one trying to understand something they never could. We were isolated from the world in what was both the easiest and hardest battle I'd ever fought. I still remember how the moon lit up his sanguine face when he told me we would make it through anything.

We fucked in corn fields, dorm rooms, and cheap motels in neighbouring cities out of necessity. Once, a cop shined her light into his car while Patrick's nuts were in my mouth. I don't know all my rights as a citizen, but I don't think there is one that says you have the right to remain ball filled in a public park at 1 a.m.

But it was a testament to the pureness of our love that we persevered with a daunting secret that nearly ruined us. I mean, trust me, there were missteps. Once, my sister caught us half a second from a passion-fuelled makeout on my bed. (She says she doesn't remember it.) Then there was the placeholder girlfriend, "Sarah," whom I invented to throw my best friend Lara for a loop. But through it all, Patrick and I were incorrigible warriors. Day in and day out, us against the world. And as stressful as it was, it gave me a purpose and a reason to believe as I opened my eyes every morning.

There are many reasons we eventually burned out. I wanted to see my restless ambition reflected in him. I wouldn't rest until he fulfilled all the potential he had living inside him. But then he pushed back. He withdrew affection. He became short and callous, and I'd spiral, reminded of my father.

Once we were both living in Toronto, a gay epicentre, we raced to make up for lost time. As new fish, we sopped up every drop of attention from gay men at parties. We were no match for the onslaught of external validation which countered the many messages of our youth. We thought attention meant guaranteed love. Even the smallest fragment of a compliment left us strung out for hours. It was sick.

I'm sure there are larger reasons why we never lasted, but they remain intangible to this day. I just know it felt like a blink—

one day, my brain had remodeled him into a best friend. I'd kiss him and nothing would register. The electricity had dispersed elsewhere. After that, there was no going back for either of us. So, after many ill-fated attempts, we called it quits at a sushi restaurant three blocks from Dundas Square.

And now it was his 26th birthday and I was all alone. Despite how strong I pretended to be, I didn't know how to live without Patrick's love. He was my safety net and I had underestimated how much I needed him to survive. I had lived a stunted adolescence and the tools I needed to mature weren't there. Even worse, my father had just packed up his life and left, leaving my mom standing in the driveway holding our baby pug. (We'll save that story for another book.) I was destined to spiral in the years to come.

Luckily, there was another pseudo patch on the horizon.

I was standing by the makeshift bar at Patrick's birthday, probably still praying my asshole would snap back to normal post-cucumber coital. I had arrived at said party with my relatively new friend, Jesus, whom Patrick had met on a website called Manhunt (what's in a name?!) months earlier. Patrick told me he had only created an account on the site to "meet someone platonically," and after meeting up for drinks, he knew Jesus "would be our new best friend." There was no denying it. Jesus was a barrel of monkeys, living a fast life by the seat of his pants. He had come to Canada on a vacation from Mexico earlier that year and decided to let his tourist visa expire and grab an apartment instead. Within weeks of hanging out, it was clear Jesus had no plans to leave Canada anytime soon.

Despite Patrick's pleas, Jesus and I had ordered a stripper. Jesus had taken the reins when it came to making the call, and had specifically requested "the grossest one you have on staff."

"Sir, that's not a category of dancer," said the woman to Jesus, on the phone over brunch.

"Sure it is. You know, overbaked, dead eyes, we want it all," said Jesus in reply, winking at me. "Just do your best."

At 9 p.m., the male stripper arrived, pushing 50 with an ass like a sundried tomato.

"Perfect," said Jesus, as we clinked red Solo cups.

"OK, what is that outfit? I said cop," I yelled over the music, wrinkling my brow. "Cop! Not co-working-space security guard."

The stripper pinned Patrick to a chair and ripped off his tearaway pants to reveal yellow silk briefs. "Pony" by Ginuwine blasted through a Bluetooth speaker perched on the ping pong table as he started to gyrate his crotch across Patrick's chin. Then he swung his briefs around his finger and into the cheering crowd. This guy was old school Deuce Bigalow, exactly the right flavour for the evening. After only a minute of his routine, he seemed incandescent.

"Wooo!" screamed Jesus. "Keep…it…on!"

"This is just sad," said a 6-foot-tall redhead to his right. "They should honestly have retirement pensions just for strippers."

"I like you," I said to the redhead, extending my hand. "I'm Jordan."

"Ben," he answered. "Hi."

"And this is Jesus from catering," I said, pointing.

Jesus shook Ben's hand. "I am NOT catering."

"I'm kidding," I replied. "He works at Subway as a sandwich artist, you know, like Picasso and Michelangelo."

"You having good time, Ben?" said Jesus, in his uber thick Mexican accent.

"Yep. I'm actually new to the city as of this week, so I don't really know what to expect. It's a lot to take in for sure. I'm more of an outdoors guy." Ben turned to me. "I did not expect a stripper tonight, though, so that's commendable. A nice touch."

"Wasn't he?" I said. "I am *such* a good friend. Jesus had to call four companies to figure it all out. These stripper rental companies aren't known for having all their ducks in a row."

"Dicks?" asked Jesus.

"No, ducks," I said. "Ducks in a row. It's like a common saying."

"You've never heard that saying, Jesus?" asked Ben.

"No," I interjected. "He hasn't been here long. He came from Mexico on a tourist visa months ago and, well, let's just say our boy here is currently off the grid. An extended vacation, if you will. But don't let the substandard English fool you, he is assimilating very well."

"Yes," said Jesus. "I love this country."

"Show him what I taught you, Jesus."

"*O Canada, our home and native land,*" sang Jesus, proceeding to recite the first three lines of the Canadian national anthem.

"Nailed it," said Ben, refilling his vodka soda. "I think I just found my first two friends in Toronto. I mean... if you two will have me?"

"We'll definitely take it under consideration," I replied.

Our new buddy Ben soon became a permanent fixture in our cabal of faggots, mostly consisting of Patrick, Jesus, and myself. It had been four months since my mental breakdown, and Patrick and I were finally on a solid foundation as friends. Sure, he'd cheated on the next two guys he dated with me. *Big whoop*. You know me... always the depraved whore, never the bride.

But by the time his birthday rolled around he had found someone more substantial, and the thought of fellating him felt incest-adjacent. We had mostly healed, and adding Ben into our little family felt like the next logical step to lessen our reliance on one another. Like addiction recovery theory goes, to get over one dependency, you swap in another.

Let me paint you a picture of my friend: If there was ever a gay party-doll mould, I would 3D-print the shit out of Ben. He's a redheaded financial analyst who very casually skips out on office meetings to have his asshole waxed on a biweekly basis.

We bonded fast, a recipe that included a thirst for adventure, adulation for non-white cock, an insatiable taste for emotionally unavailable, toxic men, and heaping amounts of alcoholism. Speaking of alcoholism, his, unlike mine, barely made a dent in his productivity. I've seen him slam down 15 drinks, sniff four key bumps of coke, suck face with a 19-year-old Asian, and then get up at 7:30 a.m. for a Bikram yoga session. I've also oddly never seen him with a semblance of a hangover. In fact, sometimes when I'm in the depths of a bad one, he'll tell me to "grow up" and that hangovers are merely "a stupid urban legend."

Ben is a great dresser; his wardrobe is adorned with impeccably pressed Club Monaco shirts, Cole Haan shoes, and blazers retrofitted to conceal various sizes of disposable flasks. He's also the most responsible, deliberative person I know. No matter where I release him into the night at 3 a.m., he always finds his way home. Picture a homing pigeon doused in Grey Goose. Ben has many other wonderful attributes, but this is my top criterion: I'm not a babysitter of drunk people. I'd rather just end the friendship on the spot.

Six months into our friendship, I decided he'd make the *most* perfect travel companion. I googled "gayest place on earth," and the city of San Francisco registered as top billing. I immediately composed a text to Ben that read, *Hey I think we should go on a trip to San Francisco. It looked amazing on Full House. We are young and basically professional whores so it should be a blast.*

He wrote back, *K, when? And we should also do LA too. How are you going to pay for this?*

I'll figure it out, I replied, which was code for 'draw monies from my student loan account.'

You see, post mental breakdown, I never did return to that fated personal injury law firm. In order to delay the inevitable 9-5 fate, I had enrolled in journalism school. I deemed it to be an excellent vehicle for my loud mouth, especially as I had already been published in *The Chicago Tribune* a year earlier. I quickly learned journalism is not a field for people with inviolable opinions. In fact, the very profession is built on a foundation of impartiality. This is a fact that neither my parents nor any of member of the admissions team mentioned once.

Three weeks in, I had already received two academic warnings for getting into verbal arguments with the professors, a group of "industry veterans" noticeably absent from a basic Google search of their own names.

And I certainly wasn't making any friends at school, mostly because post-breakup I was becoming a depressive, guarded recluse. Plus, gay friends were way more fun, and I had limited bandwidth. My classmates were like nerdy aliens. I'd sit in the corner and write jokes about them as the foundation for a future book. I was awestruck by their ability to survive on carb-only diets while avoiding energy lulls. I couldn't relate. When it comes to dieting, I am every stereotype of a gay man. The last time I ingested a carbohydrate was my First Holy Communion.

I booked the San Francisco/Los Angeles combo trip a mere week before midterm testing. That fact alone should illustrate the level of investment I had in both the program and my future career trajectory. I could tell Ben had reservations about the adventure, but he knew it would be better to uproot his life, empty his savings account, and fly to the opposing coast than try to initiate any sort of argument with me. Plus, we both knew that with Otis the monkey on my shoulder, no one could stand in the way of anything I wanted.

Otis is an impulsive, short-term thinker. But you have to give him credit for forcing me to always live in the moment. He's a primate with an unquenchable thirst for untamed adventure.

You can always make money. You have the rest of your life to make money, he cooed into my ear. Then he hopped into my lap and looked up at me with adoring eyes. ***But no-strings, youthful, gay gallivanting? That's going to pass you by in the blink of an eye.***

I scrunched my face, hesitated, then gave him a fist bump.

In preparation for California, I decided to go on a Hollywood diet. My life post-breakup had produced dramatic ups and downs on my bathroom scale. Months of maniacal discipline and CrossFit would inevitably lead to me falling off the wagon and then crying directly into a jar of Nutella. That is still the binary in which I live today.

So, I tried to starve myself. I even asked a Muslim student for diet tips when I noticed she hadn't eaten lunch for days. She said it was something called "Ramadan," and she was fasting while the sun was up.

"Well, someone's willpower is *very* trendy!" I said, during a class lecture on defamation. "Hey, can I Muslim, too? I'm already fasting, right now."

"I guess," she replied, contorting her body away from me. "You're weird."

"I get that a lot," I said.

Ben and I meticulously planned our upcoming adventure to

California to be the gayest 10 days possible. We would stay with two of his close friends in Berkeley and, we figured, journey to San Francisco on a nightly basis, like alley cats trolling the tech capital of the world. We would look for rich men that owned something, preferably with VC funding.

After we lured them into matrimony, we would immediately obtain green cards and retire at the ripe age of 23. I'd go to Pilates on Mondays with all the other tech wives, while Ben would cycle through multiple livers he'd buy via a Nigerian black market dealer. As he recovered from each of his transplants, I would refill his cocktails dressed in a sarong—but a nice Jennifer Lopez sarong. With these dreamy visuals in mind, we clinked our martini glasses in the Toronto airport lounge before our flight.

"I'm sick of working," said Ben. "I've been in the workforce for almost two years and I'm completely spent."

I lifted my martini class to clink his. "To tech husbands, and a short respite from anorexia."

From my shoulder, Otis chimed in, ***And to stories, Jordan. Lots of stories. You can never run out of stories. Life is an adventure, my friend.***

I smirked, already imagining the shenanigans I could share with my friends over brunch. ***I'll drink to that, Otis.***

"Cheers!" yelled Ben as he drank the martini in one gulp.

Unfortunately, our dreams of prized tech cock were squandered the second we got off the BART at 16th St. Mission Station in San Francisco. It was our first gander at the city and our dreams of becoming Mrs. Elon Musk (x2) were immediately dashed by the sight of a homeless man jerking off into a paper bag. Let me tell you, my friend. When you see something like that, it will change you as a person forever.

"Wow," said Ben. "This city is a real shithole."

"I really was not expecting this at all." I stepped carefully over the heaps of trash and broken syringes that littered the sidewalk.

"That guy in the corner is making sounds like the audio CAPTCHA on Gmail."

"I think that's a death rattle," I said.

"OK, don't make fun of me for this, but a couple of those homeless guys are kinda hot, no?" Ben winked at me. "I mean, if the homeless are attractive in this city, things are looking up."

"They are. I wouldn't judge them too hard, though. Their tech start-ups probably went under."

"You're probably right."

"Also, where did he get *those* biceps from?" I pointed to a man on a blanket. "Does he have a gym membership?"

"Probably just plyometrics," said Ben with a shrug. "I do them all the time."

Living off Ben's work phone as a Wi-Fi hotspot, we opened Grindr to spark some trouble. If you're a heterosexual reading this and not familiar with the dating app Grindr, you're probably better off. It's the only place on Earth where a photo of someone's gaping asshole is a widely accepted salutation.

It's largely for hookups and works off geographic proximity, sometimes offering men less than 10 metres away. Each profile is presented in a grid format with the boxes at the top being the closest to you. It's a fun tool in the office if you have nagging questions about Carl in accounting's sexuality.

Dating apps are, by their very nature, incredibly impersonal in that they cause us to treat each other as disposable. This is very similar to how Ben and I tend to treat men we meet on vacation.

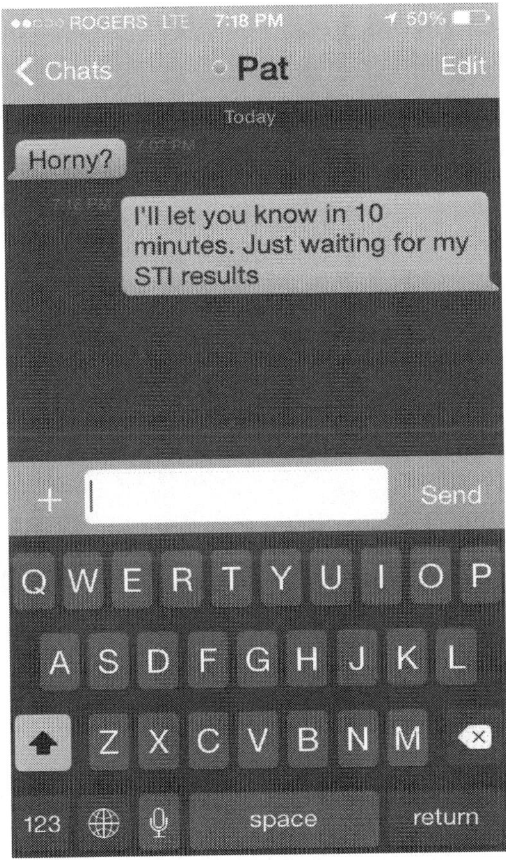

A vintage Grindr conversation. I'm the second message, obviously.

We think of them less as human beings and more as a type of seat-filler. I don't think we've ever really had a forthright conversation with any of the men we've collected during our travels. We've had fake occupations, fake children, and have been "saved" by Jesus more times than I can remember.

Ben quickly chatted with the third-closest guy on Grindr. We agreed to meet him at a gay sports bar eight blocks south of Hotel de Homeless. His name was Archie. He was 24 with four roommates, which we learned was par for the course in a city with one of the highest monthly rents in North America. He had a handsome face, perfectly parted hair and a skinny-fat exterior. Speaking from experience, this body type can be quite perplexing during fornication. It often arises after gay men enter a metropolitan city and develop an eating disorder so fast their muscles atrophy.

Archie also had a friend named Jack who immediately became my catch of the day, largely by default. He was textbook manic masquerading as extroverted. Like looking right in the mirror. I chatted with him for the better part of 20 minutes and thought he was kind of fun. At one point, he kissed me on the cheek and told me I was the sexiest man he had ever met.

"What do you do for work?" he asked.

OTIS: You're a happiness co-ordinator for Nutella.

"Uh, I'm a happiness co-ordinator for Nutella," I said. "You?"

"I'm between jobs."

"Cool." I shrugged. "Wanna French?"

"Sure." We proceeded to make out beside the ATM machine to Madonna's *Like a Prayer*.

After 20 seconds he paused. "I gotta tell you, Jordan. I find it so refreshing how honest you are. Do you get that a lot?"

"Thanks. I do," I said, my twelfth lie of the day. "It must be because I'm a Buddhist and a Mormon."

Jack looked fascinated. "I didn't know you could do that."

"Oh, sure you can."

I was a gay black widow spider, drunk on myself and highly enamoured with my elaborate web of lies. I was so excited for the inevitable chaos that I failed to see Ben motioning to me that he wasn't interested in Archie.

"Let's go to another bar," yelled Ben. "Please, Jordan! Come on."

We walked four blocks north with our respective dates' arms around our shoulders. While Jack described his unemployment period of "self-assessment," Ben struggled to break loose of Archie. It was quite entertaining. I pretended not to notice, but I don't miss any potential entertainment sources that I can spin into doses of attention.

The second bar was a dive bar with stained glass windows and a small 20x20 wooden patio out back. The patio was entirely lit with red lighting, which clashed against a wall of neon signs. Palm trees drooped softly over the wooden fence as reggae pulsed over the speakers.

Ben motioned me to the bar in the corner and punched my shoulder. "Did you not get my text?"

"Ow! No, why?"

"Just fuckin look," he said, waving the bartender over.

I opened my phone to a text that read, *Mine has moobs. We're outta here.*

"Did you cup them?" I asked, laughing. "Or just see them through his shirt?"

He waved me off, annoyed. "We need an escape plan pronto. What ya got?"

Just then, Jack appeared behind us and fondled my ass. "Where's my drink, Jordan?" He kissed me on the cheek.

"OK, chill out, Romeo," said Ben, shoving him back. "Jordan, I'm not even gonna be discreet about this, so I'll just say it. You better have a fuckin plan."

"A plan?" asked Jack.

"Nothing," I said. "Drinks?"

I waved down the bartender and ordered Jack a double, knowing that due to his precarious employment status I would be funding the evening. Otis assured me it would pay huge dividends sexually, even in the face of the crippling U.S. exchange rate, and I prayed he was correct. At the time, I could barely stomach a monthly subway pass, so I was in no position to be footing the bill.

I handed a drink to Ben, then Jack, then put mine on the bar. By the time the bartender brought me my change, Jack had killed his entire drink.

"Slow down, intervention," I said. "Do you want another?"

He nodded.

Archie ran into a few of his friends and sauntered off with them to the danc floor inside. I told Ben I had to pee and asked him to babysit Jack in the meantime.

On the way back from the washroom, I ran into a drag queen who asked me who "did my lips." I assured her they were real and she said, "Yeah right, and I might be getting a pussy in the fall." So casual. Like she was buying a painting. I love shit like this. We chatted for maybe 20 minutes about plastic surgery. When I returned to the bar, Jack had taken a turn for the worse. He sat double-fisting by himself under a heat lamp with booze spilled down his shirt. Ben was shaking his head in disapproval as I walked over, looking at him incredulously.

"Well, looks like he will be in no position for the naked cobra pose I was stretching for in the washroom," I said.

"Yes, Jordan. That is because he is an alcoholic!" yelled Ben. "He told you this."

"He did? When?"

"You're not serious." Ben narrowed his eyes. "OK, you're serious."

"I guess I need to start listening to what people say to me, not just the sound of my own voice," I said with a shrug.

"Well, if you'd take the puppet strings off people for a hot second you would learn a lot," said Ben.

But what fun is that? Otis asked, his tail coiling around my shoulder like a feather boa.

You're so right, I thought.

"Oh, and quick update, Moobs came back and is quite pissed that we provided Jack with alcohol."

"Who cares about him?" I replied. "He's dead to me already."

Ben looked relieved. "Now *that's* the attitude I wanna hear tonight."

Jack's glass slipped out of his hand and smashed on the floor, startling him awake. "Oh God, is Jack foaming at the mouth?" I asked, squinting. "Doesn't it look like he's foaming at the mouth or something?"

Then the bouncer came over to converse with him.

"An opening! We're outta here." Ben grabbed my arm and maneuvered us toward the front door. "Quickly, before they notice us!"

As we ran onto the street, a full moon glowed above us amidst a smattering of stars.

"Great start," said Ben.

"Not great." I glanced around us. "There must be better prospects."

"Well, I've been doing enough yoga lately that I can easily blow myself as a backup if we don't find any," said Ben.

"Do you honestly think I would let it come to that?" I asked, putting a hand over my heart like he'd wounded me. "I would never allow that sadness in our lives."

"No, I figured you would blow me if necessary."

"Of course, Ben," I said. "You're like a brother to me."

Once we found the Castro strip, we walked into the first open gay bar we could find and immediately ordered a round of drinks. Then another, then another. We were playing catch up. I like to bail on full shitfaced if I've only had four drinks or less, an hour within last call. It's not worth the caloric overabundance. But we had time, so that night, I leaned in entirely. Then we hit the dance floor to rip it up, a vodka soda in each hand.

Only five songs in, a jacked-up Asian man in an Ed Hardy shirt started to grind up on me. I tried to move away but he pulled me back by my underwear band, giving me a wedgie. I yelped and smacked his hand away, which only caused him to become even more aggressive. It was a #metoo moment before Rose McGowan had even created a Twitter account. I was dealing with an unrelenting predator. Then the man poured the drink in my right hand into his mouth in one shot. I resourcefully tried to purse my lips into a makeshift rape whistle. *Nothing.*

I casually began to dance away, gaining about six inches at a time. I seemed to be gaining ground until I realized I was in the middle of an unplanned prostate exam, but way too violent to feel any lumps or nodules of note. Someone (I'm sure you can guess who) had shoved a finger into my no-no slot and removed it within seconds. As I stood in awe, dumbfounded, the lights in the bar snapped on and reality came rushing back in. Beefcake was nowhere to be found. Bouncers immediately began ushering us out of the bar and Ben turned on the histrionics.

"Oh great. It's 2:01 already?" said Ben. "I was just ramping up."

"I think that beefcake just fingered my butt," I said, white as a ghost.

Which finger? asked Otis, with genuine concern.

Does it matter?

Of course it matters.

I considered for a second. ***OK fine, it felt like an index.***

That's hot. Otis put his arm around me as Ben and I descended the club stairs. ***That's actually my favourite one.***

Back at the Berkeley house, Ben and I battled through a sleepless night of fending off our hosts' cat, which would jump onto my stomach to elicit my bloodcurdling screams. It happened at least four times throughout the night. When Ben's friend Kristina entered the room at 9 a.m. to check on us, I lifted my head from the protective barricade I had constructed and yelled, "Hey Kristina, do you mind getting that fat, hairy pussy out of here?"

"OK, sure," she said. "No problem."

"Oh, and can you please also take the cat?"

I tried to fall back asleep to prepare myself for the nine-hour drive to L.A., but Ben was up and asking Kristina for a funnel to refill his boot flask. And he's loud. He doesn't do inside voice at all. I quickly folded my clothes in my suitcase, still feeling Beefcake's phantom index finger in my booty hole. Then I joined him in the kitchen to see his boot flask affixed to his leg.

"I think it defeats the whole purpose when you're wearing shorts, Ben," said Kristina, with a scrunched brow.

"Oh whatever." Ben waved her off. "Let's not get technical here."

I smacked him on the ass. "Come on, let's hit the open road."

Ben and I hopped in our rental car, a white Ford Mustang, and started down the long highway to Los Angeles. Determined to get the full convertible experience we paid for, we agreed to ignore the brisk San Francisco weather that loomed over our day. People stared incredulously as we drove with the top down, fully bundled, with the heat on full blast. It was ridiculous, even for us. This continued for nearly six hours, including through a light rainstorm and four complete cycles through a Taylor Swift album.

God, I love Taylor Swift. Not really the person or the brand but the musician. How could you not? For her next single she could honestly queef into a microphone for three minutes and I'd immediately ask if I could order 10 copies on vinyl.

"I feel like the gay version of *Thelma and Louise*," I screamed through chattering teeth.

"Remember these moments, child. These are the days of our lives," declared Ben as he sipped from his $6 flask, a ripped towel wrapped around his legs.

"Did I tell you I joined an underwear club last night when I was drunk?" I asked.

"What the fuck is an underwear club?"

"They mail you new underwear every month. Like a book club, but for whores," I explained. "It's a pretty good deal."

"Sounds like it," he replied. "Send me the link."

"Are we going out tonight? I was thinking maybe we could stay in. I'm kinda wiped." Even as I said it, I could feel Otis grumbling. ***You're no fun at all.***

"No," said Ben. "We didn't drive nine hours and get immunized against multiple strains of HPV for you to just pass out in the Airbnb. Vacations are for partying. That's it and that's all."

"OK, fine," I said. "You had me at vaccine. It wouldn't be fair to my mom."

My mom, a family physician, had urged Ben and me to get our vaccines after she attended a conference claiming HPV was now the second leading cause of throat and mouth cancer, behind smoking. *Bananas.* After telling her I was more of an oral sex receiver than giver, she failed to laugh and told me she would pay for it if I agreed to get the injections. So I did, in three injection rounds, and made Ben do it too. Whorishness must be mitigated.

"From here on out be careful, Jordan," she said after my third injection. "And if you contract anything ever, like any STI, it's important from a public health perspective that you call your past partners right away."

OTIS: And write about it in a book.

"I don't have any of their phone numbers, Mom," I said. "I think that's the whole point of hooking up. You have a lot to learn about this whole medicine thing."

As the sun set over the Pacific Ocean, I raised my hands to the sky and screamed, "Woohoo, L.A.! I'm unstoppable!"

"Days of our lives, my boy," yelled Ben with a fist in the air.

It was our final day in Los Angeles and I had experienced pretty much all I needed to see. Let's keep it real—L.A. is a shithole. Plastered around the city are billboards exclaiming Los Angeles leads the U.S. in gonorrhea infections. Umm… congrats? I guess you have to remember to celebrate the small victories.

Gonorrhea seemed to be the only thing we hadn't yet encountered on our trip, but don't worry, we very quickly found a way to eliminate any degrees of separation: an orgy.

You always hope the morning of your first orgy will mimic a Folgers commercial. Bright sun rays bouncing along a charm of dancing hummingbirds as you brew a steaming pot of morning joe. The best part of waking up is an orgy in your cup.

The previous evening, I had received a rather unorthodox message from a faceless Grindr profile:

"Hey man, cute pic. I'd like to take the opportunity to invite you to

an exclusive party in West Hollywood. Only high-level gentlemen. Only whites. We play together. No drugs, no camera, no bareback. Under 30 only. Please send me a shirtless photo of yourself holding today's date on a piece of paper to this email address XXXXXXXX@gmail.com. The group votes on all members and only the hottest get the arrival details."

Ben said I should at least send a try-out photo.

"Do we even have time for an orgy?" I asked him. "Our flight is tonight."

"We'll make time," Ben responded. "You always make time for an orgy."

I've been posing my entire life for, besides myself, absolutely no one. At that point I could easily have taught a seminar at the Barbizon Modeling School. But the debauchery of the past week had done an aggressive number on my body, and I didn't have much to work with. On a regimented diet consisting largely of sushi, soy sauce, pork rinds, and vodka sodas, my morning eyes were puffy and incredibly deceiving. In fact, my entire face had begun to retain water like a body pulled from the Atlantic Ocean.

I was up 15 pounds, 14 of which were probably water weight. And something menacing was wrong with my tongue. It was spotted and lined with a thick white film. I responsibly googled "oral cancer photos" and pulled up the image results. Yes, I definitely had oral cancer. I figured it would be best to share this info with a professional, so I immediately sent a text to my mom, who was knee deep in the middle of a hectic workday at her physician's office in Canada.

JORDAN: Mom, there is something seriously wrong with my tongue. I suspected oral cancer and was proven right on Google Images. Should I wait until I get back to Canada to begin chemotherapy? Can you drink with oral cancer? This is not a test.

Within four minutes, my mom called my cell phone. She had seen decades of my immobilizing hypochondria and knew exactly how to deal with me.

"Honey, you don't have cancer. Do you have any other symptoms?" she asked.

"Yes, I have a headache."

"Are you hungover?"

"Oh yeah," I said. She was good.

"Right, and did you try scraping your tongue?"

"No, I hadn't even thought of that. Does that cure cancer?"

"Please just scrape it."

I scraped my tongue back to front three times and stared back in the mirror.

"Yeah, it seems to be gone. That ol' cancer. Incredible," I said. "You're Suzanne Somers!"

"She's a fraud," said my mom. "So, what do you boys have planned for the day?"

"Well we were going to go shopping but I feel like I've gained new perspective as a cancer survivor. I should probably go for a hike in the fresh smog or something."

She sighed. "That's great, honey. Have fun. Love you."

Cancer scare aside, I did my best with what I had to take a selfie suitable enough for an L.A. orgy. Luckily, the photo passed, which was rather shocking in a city of models and actors. The orgy administrator wrote back, *Very cute, man. You half Filipino?*

After Ben and I agreed to RSVP "yes +1" to the orgy, we spent the day driving around L.A. (doesn't everyone?) and walking through Runyon Canyon as vigorous physical preparation for the evening's sexual circus. Around 7 p.m., we returned to our Airbnb to google the phrase "orgy etiquette."

I myself was no stranger to the multi-person sexual

experience. Months earlier, I had sparked up a relationship with a couple I met on Grindr for encounters on a scheduled biweekly basis. They were professional group-sex directors. This wasn't the sort of low-grade schmaltz you'd come across around last call on a Thursday. We'd chat politics, eat fresh quiche, share a vintage Chianti and then get to work turning me into a human pretzel. But this was different—I had never extended the party to more than three.

As the clock struck 9 p.m. in Hollywood, Ben began to experience an orgy-related panic, pacing across the condo and gesticulating wildly.

"Would you please simmer down?" I popped open my third tin of Pringles and surveyed my half-packed suitcase.

"No," he said. "I will absolutely not. You are not the boss of me."

"Please," I replied. "I'm trying to get centred. I need to be on my A game here."

"I can't CALM DOWN, Jordan. It's my first orgy!" he yelled. "What will I wear? Whose cock will I sniff first? How many times do you cum? There are at least a million variables at play here."

"Well it's my first orgy, too," I said. "How about a drink? Or three? You're being very annoying."

"I can't drink, I have to eat something first. I'm starving," he said. "Let's go to Ralph's for takeout. Go get your shoes."

"We don't have time," I said, idly folding a shirt and placing it into my suitcase. "If we don't leave soon for the orgy you know we're definitely going to miss the national anthem."

Ben grabbed my shirt and, with all sincerity, looked me straight in the eyes.

"Jordan, I don't need your jokes right now, man. I can't go to an orgy on an empty stomach. We need to carb load. I don't know much but I definitely know you are not in the right mindset for an orgy. Get your head in the game."

"Oh, so now we're athletes?" I shook Ben off and opened another bag of pork rinds. "Hey, how do you even dress for an orgy? Like, business casual?"

Ben threw his hands in the air and went to the bathroom to have one of his "anxious poops." Three minutes later, I walked up to the door and knocked twice. He didn't answer so I decided to get changed. I popped on my bright pink shorts and a slim-fitted Zara T-shirt I had copped for $9.

Five minutes later I knocked on the door again, struck by a concern of my own. "Hey Ben, sorry to bother you but, umm, do you think there will be time to stretch with the others before we start the orgy? I have an excitable sciatic nerve."

"Yeah probably," he yelled back.

At around 10 p.m. we walked five blocks to the address on the orgy invite. I don't want to give away any details because, well, not to brag, but I'm still on the email list. Let's just say it's right in the centre of where you would expect it to be in West Hollywood. We stopped in front of the building and looked up to the top. Ben gulped audibly, and we embraced in a tight hug.

"This is it, amigo," I said. "We've graduated."

"OK, now remember what we talked about," Ben said. "Don't look anyone in the eye during any sexual encounters, ESPECIALLY me, and don't take drinks from anyone."

From my shoulder, Otis made a sound like, ***Pfffft.*** He advised me, ***Take drinks—and fluids of all kinds—from everyone***.

"I'm shaking," Ben said.

"Me too," I said. "I'm sure it will all go away once we're cock-filled."

In Malibu, hours before the orgy.

"It always does."

We were buzzed up to the condo and took the elevator to the 9th floor. Both of us were pale and visibly trembling. We paced back and forth in front of the door waiting to see if we could hear something from inside. Nothing. I put my ear to the door. Still nothing. Was it a trap? I surveyed the risk and gathered up a final injection of my remaining gusto. The invite had said not to knock, so I turned the knob and entered the condo with Ben.

Listen, there is nothing that could ever prepare you for the sight of 25 stark naked men stuffed into 600 square feet, banging like wild turkeys. Immediately we saw that this was certainly not a group of guys spending the evening playing Clue, unless it was the version where Colonel Mustard finds the candlestick in Professor Plum's anus. If they were playing any board game it would be more along the lines of Connect Four, and damn they were good at it.

I bent over and untied my shoes on the door mat, mere feet from a *very* young bleached blond on his knees performing fellatio. We locked eyes as his partner's balls daintily grazed his chin. Then he turned, removed the penis from his mouth and said, "Nice to meet you," before resuming his work.

"Wow, manners," said Ben. "Even in L.A.!"

"Well, his mother clearly raised him right," I said. "Take notes."

The condo was clearly prepped for the evening's festivities. Sheets were laid across furniture and most of said furniture was pushed to the periphery of the room. Space was limited but cock was not. Certain areas, like the hallways, were so dark it was tough to make out faces. At the front of the condo was a single bedroom that seemed to be overflowing with activity. The first thing I saw in the main room was a man with two cocks in his ass, bouncing up and down on the couch. Call me old fashioned but this was a sight I would have enjoyed building up to gradually. It was like starting Super Mario and immediately facing the final boss.

I needed a drink to palliate my rapidly ascending anxiety. The host of the party, an Asian man evidently drowning in self-loathing (remember the 'only whites' rule), offered me a gin and tonic. I gladly indulged, as did Ben, breaking one of our rules in the first five minutes. Then I nursed it as I watched three men bukkake on a dark-featured twenty something, spilling half the contents of their nuts onto the white carpet.

"Well *that's* gonna stain," I said to Ben.

"It's like an OxiClean commercial," said Ben in his faux British accent. "Should I assist with cleanup?"

"I don't know about this whole orgy thing," I said. "It's overly sexualized. I feel absolutely nothing. Not even a half chub. I think my brain has shut down in panic."

Ben laughed. "What would your parents—namely your dad—think if they saw us right now?"

Then two very hairy arms came from behind me and pulled me into a tight bear hug. The stench of terrible cologne hit me like a tidal wave. I tried to wrestle free like a slippery seal locked in the jaws of a shark.

"Did someone say *Daddy*?" the hairy-armed man asked, tightening his embrace around my midsection.

I turned around to confront a man who most definitely did not adhere to the under-30 rule. He also had the one feature I can never seem to get past—the chinstrap. Talk about a disqualifier. A chinstrap is not for me because we all know deep down it is just a jawline mirage. It's up there with shoe lifts, padded underwear, and other artificial constructs. I love to judge others who buy these products even though my own laundry list extends well beyond the carving of facial hair. I strip my hair of its natural pigment with hydrogen peroxide, inject neurotoxins into the corners of my eyes, and blast the hair follicles on my shoulders with high-priced laser beams. And this is all just last year.

Next to me while I struggled, Ben downed the rest of his drink. "And here we go."

"I'm not interested, thanks," I said, trying to squirm out again.

"Oh, you're not?" said Daddy, kissing the back of my neck. "Well I think you're making decisions a little too quickly. I'm an experience in bed."

"Yes, the experience of you cumming in 30 seconds," I replied. "Who calls themselves an experience in bed?"

Ben cackled.

"Listen, you're just a bit old for me," I said to Daddy.

"Really? I'm 30." He released me from the hug, frowning.

"Is that BC or AD?"

"If you're 30, I'm a fucking embryo," muttered Ben, rolling his eyes.

The man walked away.

We drifted to the back corner to take a good gander at the full extravaganza taking place before our eyes. I began to realize that orgies are quite anxiety-inducing. At the bare minimum, I like to know the name and horoscope sign of whoever's penis ends up in my hand. Here, there was no order to the kingdom. It was a free-for-all of bodily fluids spraying in multiple directions. If there ever was any doubt that we all descended from unbridled apes, this was it.

I watched one guy finish on two different men's faces and then saunter past me to the fridge to grab a bottle of water and towel off. I wasn't sure how to interact with him so I awkwardly high-fived him like I was his high school football coach.

"Good game," I murmured.

"Thanks," he said with a laugh. "I'll be back at it shortly. You have to stay hydrated."

"Absolutely. You totally seem like someone who makes your sexual health a priority."

"Right?" He walked over to the couch, ostensibly to violate someone else's face.

"Someone is gonna get the flu or staph… definitely staph," I said, turning to Ben only to find he had disappeared. I panicked and paced around the condo, trying not to interrupt anyone's flow. I found him several minutes later in his underwear, coming out of the front bedroom.

"I can't believe you abandoned me, ass face!" I yelled. "And where are your clothes?"

"I couldn't tell you," he said, white as a ghost. "I was standing by myself when some sort of magical man came behind me and undressed me in about six seconds."

"OK, but where are your actual clothes?"

"I think they're in the bedroom but it's vicious in there and I'm staying away."

"Vicious?" I peered inside. "What do you mean, vicious?"

"Let me put it this way, Jordan. It looked like when a pack of hyenas aggressively attack and eat a live animal," he said. "I wish I was exaggerating."

"Oh my God, who is the hyena?"

Ben shrugged. "I'm not sure, I could barely see his face."

"Well, *I* don't want to be a hyena," I said. "So that's a big no from me."

"And I don't want to be a baby emu," he said.

"A baby emu?"

"I dunno. I'm experiencing an orgy-related assault on my cognition," he replied. "Also, I love baby emus, they are super cute. Have you ever petted one?"

"No, Ben, I haven't had the luxury of petting a baby emu," I said. "I'm not a Rockefeller."

"Well that's your problem then."

I glanced back into the bedroom one more time. "Let's get out of here."

"OK," Ben said, nodding. "Let me just put my clothes back on."

As we started to move toward the door I said, "I thought we were going to be able to leak stories to *Us Weekly* about Neil Patrick Harris getting fist fucked, but not one of these whores even has an IMDb credit."

Just before we got to the door, I noticed a man standing by the kitchen, still clothed and not dripping in semen. A diamond in the cum. Like a lady, I audaciously shined my iPhone light in his face.

"Whoa," he said, shielding his eyes. "Am I under arrest or something?"

"Sorry," I said. "I was evaluating your hotness. I'm Jordan and this is Ben."

"Hey," he said. "I'm Kristoff."

"Kristoff, we've seen enough and we're overwhelmed," said Ben, waving his hands wildly in the air. "You coming with us or what? Our flight leaves soon."

"Coming? Um, sure," he said. "Let me just grab my shoes."

"It might be better if you left them, Kristoff." I put my hand on his shoulder. "Crabs can jump."

We found Kristoff's shoes along with our own, and tied them at the front door before proceeding to leave. As we did, we saw the same twink of dubious sexual legality, back on his knees, blowing another gentleman by the front door. It seemed he had an undeniable fetish. I turned to Ben and said, "Take a mental picture of that face. You might see it on an Amber Alert later."

We took Kristoff back to the Airbnb and downed a few cocktails. Ben passed out on the couch while watching *Wives with Knives*. I, on the other hand, was watching Kristoff fall madly in love with me. He really had no clue who he was dealing with. I had the emotional availability of a shoehorn. I pulled him into the bedroom and initiated the first stages of heavy petting.

Five minutes later as he softly bit my ass cheek he said, "I just finally feel like I've met someone amazing. You know?"

"Well, that's why they call it the city of dreams, Kristoff." I didn't even try to conceal my sarcasm. "Umm, a little to the left, please."

"My mom would love you," he said.

OTIS: Gross.

JORDAN: The Grossest!

"I'm sure she would absolutely NOT love me," I replied.

Not long into the action, my phone screen flashed with a text from Ben. *We gotta go. We board in 95 minutes. COME ON, WHORE.*

I turned to Kristoff. "I'm sorry, I gotta get out of here."

He laughed. "Are you serious? You are brutal."

"Yep, my flight to Canada—or whatever country I told you I'm from—leaves in two hours. Can you help me finish packing?"

"Sure, let me put my number into your phone first for when my mom and I come to visit sometime," he said. "She would love you."

I cringed. "Would she, though? You shouldn't have said that, man. My hidden superpower is disappearing once a man mentions meeting his mom." I handed him my phone. "Here, you can put your number in this."

We packed up my clothes in two minutes and went down to hail a cab. Ben and I hauled ass through LAX completely wasted and stumbling through airport security. I couldn't even figure out how to empty my pockets of metals. Before the plane even left the tarmac, my phone exploded with a slew of texts from Kristoff, who registered in my phone as "Prince Charming a.k.a. Soulmate."

Only a month later, I was home for Christmas vacation at my

mom's house. In order to neutralize the never-ending assault of carbohydrates, I decided to take a run on the treadmill. I turned on the TV and watched my favourite nutcracker, Patti Stanger, lay into an older gentleman on *Millionaire Matchmaker.* One of the potential suitors for said millionaire was Kristoff, bright-eyed and bushy-tailed in a blue polo. I could not fucking believe it.

"Cutie!" said my sister Lisa, sipping orange juice.

I froze, forgetting to run, and yelled, "Prince Charming!" as I was hurled off the back of the treadmill and into the wall. Then I brushed off my knees and limped, defeated, over to the couch.

"Are you OK?" she asked.

"No, OWWWW," I said. "But I know that guy! That's Kristoff. I met him at an orgy in Hollywood and then he ate my booty."

"Of course he did. You are wild. Please remind me to get more gay friends!" She laughed, munching on Tostitos. "It sounds like a fucking blast."

CHAPTER TWO

MORGAN

After our California extravaganza, I returned to journalism school with a dismissive attitude. I was impatient to hit the real world and start constructing a legacy. It was no secret to me that I was born a star from the time my mom started loading VHS tapes with my dance shows at age seven. Two days after I returned to school, I asked the head of the journalism department about internships. She said those were not an option until second year.

"I wouldn't hold your breath, though," she said. "Journalism is a dying industry. There are no jobs and thus few internships."

"Then why are you taking students' money?"

"Well, not everyone goes to school for jobs," she said. "Some come simply to learn about a subject."

"Fat chance," I said, annoyed. "People are expecting some way to pay off their student loans! You took in 900 students knowing jobs are next to none? This is criminal."

"Well, I'm afraid I can't help you, Jordan." She shrugged. "But feel free to apply in first semester of year two. We'll see what is available."

"I'm not waiting that long," I said with a huff.

I decided to circumvent the process by emailing the program director of a local talk radio station in Toronto. Talk radio is a bastion of hard-nosed, mostly conservative opinions; I knew it would be a perfect home for my unrestrained sewer mouth. I was flummoxed when I received an invite to interview for an intern (see: unpaid) position four days later. My interview would be with one of the show producers atop the food chain, a man named Morgan. The night before the interview, I googled the location of the studio and found it was serendipitously across the intersection from my apartment. It was fate.

The next morning, I met Morgan in the coffee shop located in the lobby of the studio tower. I got a matcha green tea latte and paid for his medium, extra hot Americano. I spent the first five minutes of the interview delivering a steady stream of lies and overpromises. I told him I was a closet conservative who had grown up luxuriating in the opinions of men like Rush Limbaugh. I lied again two minutes later by telling him I was first in my class and had big dreams of one day hosting my own AM radio show. Then I polished it off by espousing the joys of flat tax and heavy defence spending. Morality had no place in the face of career desperation.

He nodded ceaselessly and laughed at almost every joke I wove into the conversation.

OTIS: He's flirting with you.

JORDAN: He's not. I think he's just a warm-hearted guy.

OTIS: FLA-IRT-TINGGGGGGG!

JORDAN: Are you on cocaine... again?

OTIS: Espresso, seven shots.

JORDAN: Well, you're distracting me at the very

point of my career starting. Go jerk off.

As Morgan spoke about the job duties, my mind wandered, trying to deduce whether I found him conventionally attractive. His seemingly handsome face was hidden under a thick and mangy beard, which past experience has proven can act as a devilish mirage. Sure, women use makeup sorcery to contour their faces into fuckability. But little is said about the men who use facial hair to construct faux jawlines and camouflage feeble chins. Let it be noted for the record—beards are the new contour.

Morgan's head hair was also unruly, as was the unrestrained chest hair bursting through his unbuttoned baby blue polo. On a man over six feet tall with soft blue eyes and high cheekbones, the overall result was both incredibly distracting and utterly arousing. He made Gaston from *Beauty and the Beast* look like a prepubescent boy starting hormone blockers.

Despite the litany of grand delusions that litter these pages, I couldn't figure out if he wanted me. There is a fine line between full-blown homosexuality and warm and welcoming heterosexual men who are happy to make a friend. As I studied my prospective boss, I could not for the life of me determine which side of the line Morgan stood on. Regardless of these innocuous and sophomoric thoughts, I nailed the interview and was officially offered the gig 48 hours later.

The best part of working for free was that there were no awkward salary negotiations between Morgan and me. It was implicitly understood that I was an unworthy piece of shit. Unpaid internships are of dubious legality, yet major media companies tend to disagree, citing that they pay their interns in "experience." Right. I'd be sure to let my landlord know that once my account went into inevitable overdraft.

"Oh, my cheque bounced? That's strange. I swear there is money in

the account. You guys take experience, right? No? Strange."

After it was established my self-esteem would be a low priority, I began working for Morgan as his intern slash producer. My role was largely pitching show topics to the hosts, such as standard socio-political debate topics or topical news stories. I also chased guests and took care of other miscellaneous table scraps Morgan sent my way. In the first month, I learned a shit ton about the business of talk radio. For one, it was my job to manufacture faux outrage, and we often did it by not painting the full picture of a story, like any silver lining. I researched marketing theory and what makes people addicted to shock jocks like Howard Stern. As a producer, I made mountains out of molehills daily. We didn't just lean into controversy, we fellated it.

Listeners were driven by emotions of positive and negative valence. Thus, we went to work pulling them in opposing directions as they drove to their office jobs, brimful with rage. We'd hold live debates on the air, and recycle angry audio, usually from talking heads in the far-left orthodoxy, to stir the pot again and again. Then we'd take callers and pit them against each other. We even encouraged listeners to text in to the show, despite circulating in-house marketing stats which showed a large majority of them listened while driving. It was unadulterated chaos and I was a puppet master on crack.

As for Morgan, I didn't know what to think about him. I gave up on questions about his sexuality three weeks in. Any love he had for any gender was dampened by his lust for the company he worked for. This guy was a keener through and through who had no interest in commencing a search party for my lonely prostate, which at that exact moment was more elusive than that Malaysian airliner.

My desk was across from a fellow producer (though full time

and paid) named Beth. She remains one of my best friends to this day. In fact, she's the person who largely inspired me to pen this book after telling me I was "the funniest fucking person on the planet."

Beth is the poster girl for daddy issues and I'm the poster boy. My issues tend to manifest themselves in creative ways, but I've never actually dated anyone over 38. Beth, on the other hand, has never dated anyone who isn't currently receiving old age benefits. For Christmas, she gifts most of her boyfriends a toe tag.

We were like magnets, catalyzed by the fact that we were the only two employees who had no future intentions of shooting up the place. Our colleagues were a cast of deranged characters. It was an invariable platter of personality disorders run amok.

I once had a friend who worked in a senior-level producing job on a reality show. He told me potential contestants were subjected to a standard psychological screening. If the test revealed they were devoid of crazy pants, they were disqualified from consideration. Well, it seemed that our HR department at the talk station ripped a page right out of that playbook.

Here are just a few descriptions of those on payroll:

Jeremy

Jeremy, one of the hosts, was gay (rare in the world of conservative talk radio) and in his late 40s, with a radio voice like butter. Incredibly soothing. This guy could have read *Mein Kampf* to a Synagogue audience with few complaints.

Well, it turns out it was manufactured from years of costly vocal training. I know this because of alcohol, that great equalizer. The first time I heard his real voice I laughed because I thought he was doing an impression. After three cosmos this guy went from Dan Rather to Fran Drescher.

One day he invited me to his house for what he labelled "a young gay men in media" dinner. I was the only one under 42. After dinner, I told the table I needed to leave early to go hot-tubbing with my then-boyfriend. I grabbed my bag and left the kitchen to get my coat. The men slurred and clapped in unison and demanded that I model my bathing suit for them. Well, *that* was the last dinner I was invited to at Jeremy's house.

Billy Ray

Another of the radio hosts was a man named Billy Ray, who was imported from the U.S. as a sort of Rush Limbaugh-light. He brought his entire family to Canada, along with every quality I find repulsive in Republicans. A walking contradiction, Billy Ray loathed banking regulations, yet lost his house during the subprime mortgage crisis. In his eyes, if you were poor, well, you were probably lazy, and UNPATRIOTIC.

He loved guns, trans fats, and sweatshirts from the '90s. He drove a Harley Davidson to work with an American flag affixed to the back. I surmised that in order to bring him to orgasm, you had to either criticize a member of Black Lives Matter or place an eagle on his cock tip while singing *America the Beautiful*.

He would cycle through a new producer every couple of months. Whenever Billy Ray hired a new one—usually after the last one quit in tears—Beth and I would introduce ourselves and immediately encourage them to apply for jobs on Monster.com. They almost always thought the comment was in jest.

Constance

Our receptionist was a flamboyantly gay black man named Constance. I thoroughly enjoyed him because he had no fucks to give and mastered the art of passive aggressive telephone manner.

He was probably one of the first black people Billy Ray regularly interacted with.

He wore pounds of makeup, had a better attitude than anyone in the building, and sang Whitney Houston's full anthology in the washroom while taking explosive shits.

I told him he made me feel like a natural woman and let him in on a secret as a thank you for all his compliments to date. You see, the sales department had an exceptionally lavish washroom with soft music, brand new tiles, and old movie posters. Constance seemed like a man who deserved a luxurious lifestyle. I told him about my 10:30 a.m. "sales shit" ritual, which was a secret between Beth and me. I hated those sycophantic ingrates and my daily bowel movement in their exclusive space was my way of evening the score.

Well, about a week after I told him about the sales washroom, I entered to hear him belting a few notes in there. I ran out of the washroom and pumped my fist outside the door like Tiger Woods. Two days later, one of the sales reps told a producer there was a woman singing in their men's washroom. My work was done.

Lacie

Beth's first and only encounter with HR was after a fellow producer emailed them with a formal complaint. That person was Lacie.

It was in my dealings with her that I finally started to learn what histrionic personality disorder could look like.

Every day Lacie would storm into the office with papers in her hand, a classic tactic to create the illusion of an overworked employee. (*Yeah, we're all onto you guys.*) And this huff, well, it wasn't just any huff. It was the kind a Looney Tune would practise in front of the mirror while lacing up their three-inch pumps.

"I'm here!" she would yell, storming into the producer's office.

We would all murmur "Hi" to indulge her, but Beth refused.

Day in, day out.

"I'm here, everyone!"

"Hi," I'd say, refusing to look up from my keyboard.

More radio silence from Beth.

After this continued for two months, she stormed up to HR and filed a formal complaint against Beth. The cited reason was that Beth wouldn't say hi to her and Lacie feared she didn't like her. Well, she absolutely did not. Neither did half the office, and Lacie had worked damn hard to earn that.

So off went Beth to a meeting with the HR director, our head boss Carl, and Lacie.

"Beth," the HR director started, "Lacie here says she can tell you don't like her as a person."

"Well, I don't," said Beth stoically.

"OK," said Carl. "Why don't you explain to us all why you feel this way?"

Beth looked at Lacie. "Um, sure. Do you mind if she leaves the room? It could get bad."

After the meeting, HR mandated that Beth say hi to Lacie daily, so in the following weeks it started up again.

Heels clacking. Papers flying. "HELLO, EVERYONE. I'M HERE."

"Hi," I muttered.

"Hi," said Beth.

"Oh, HELLO, BETH," Lacie would gush. "How was your weekend, sweetie?"

Lacie's brother was in jail in Florida for soliciting sex with a minor on Grindr. He'd sent the alleged minor nudes and planned to meet up with him in public one afternoon. Well, that "minor" was actually an undercover cop employed by Homeland Security. A big oopsy doopsy. He was busted in a theatrical sting and defended himself by saying he was "role playing." You know, the one where you pretend to make love to a child?

One day when I was discussing the plight of having an active profile on the nightmare that was and still is Grindr, Lacie's ears perked up.

"Jordan," she said. "You need to delete that app. It's bad. People on there are not who they say they are."

"Correct!" I replied. "I am one of those people."

"Well." She stood in front of my desk and put her hands on her hips. "I happen to know of one person who was fooled on there."

"Oh?" I said, pretending not to know the story of her brother's arrest, which had circulated through the office like Ebola. As if I could somehow have missed her accepting collect calls from her brother for the past month at her desk.

"My brother," she said. "My brother is a victim."

She then told me in detail the story of his "entrapment." I was barely listening, playing Candy Crush as she prattled on with a story less believable than the tooth fairy. I nodded and smirked, then opened Microsoft Outlook to an email from Beth, sitting seven feet from my desk with her back to me.

"He's really the victim of a conspiracy here," said Lacie.

BETH: IS SHE SERIOUS RIGHT NOW? THIS IS REALLY HAPPENING.

"Right," I replied.

"I mean it is total entrapment," said Lacie. "We've hired a couple lawyers and the mayor is going to help us out."

JORDAN: SHE IS CUCKOO FOR COCOA PUFFS.

"Why would the mayor meddle in this?" I asked.

"Well, he understands it's a gross miscarriage of justice."

"I'm not worried, Lacie. I've never had the urge to fuck a child," I deadpanned. "Even a *really* hot child. You know when they have their cute little summer tans and Lacoste polos. Absolutely adorable, but again, does nothing for me sexually. You know?"

BETH: PEE DOWN MY LEG.

Although Lacie's brother had been given a jail sentence of 20 years, he got out in much less than that for good behaviour, by which I mean he was a white man of means. What exactly constitutes "good behaviour" in that situation? His drug of choice—children—aren't known to inhabit maximum-security prisons and we know pedophilia is a preference that never goes away.

Well, never one to miss an opportunity for attention, Lacie showed us a photo of her clinking champagne glasses in the air with her brother, days after his release. She then shamelessly posted it to social media. I thought it was odd to celebrate the release of a sex predator with such zest.

Two months after that I received word she was walking around with her brother arm in arm at a networking event. She introduced him to everyone as "her brother that was in jail."

Other honourable mentions from the cast of characters:

1. Micah was a Catholic puppet and author/speaker who contributed to the morning show weekly. He constantly reassured me that he loved me, but I would be subject to fire and brimstone if I didn't repent from sinful sex.

One day I told him he needed to rethink his business plan, as his elderly Catholic audience was dropping like flies each week. Fast forward six years and he was marching in the gay pride parade. Ah, that gay disposable income. Its ever-so-shiny allure has the power to transform any man.

2. After three months of employment, Jane, the new producer on the lowest rung of the totem pole, secured a gig giving pro-bono "talks" at college broadcasting programs. Her love and devotion to a corporation that refused to give her full-time employment (or a livable wage) was nauseating.

Jane's talk was titled "How to Succeed in Radio," which was patently absurd given she was a relative nobody whose actual job duties included opening the door for show guests and foaming their cappuccinos.

3. My co-worker Amy was a sweet girl with the vocal stylings of a Lear jet. For our summer party we took a boat around the harbour, and as soon as the captain sounded the horn, I screamed out loud, "AMY, SHUT THE FUCK UP!" Obviously, it crushed.

Amy was also dating one of the station's technical producers. I shuddered imagining how deafening her carnal cries could be. Maybe it was like a lion's roar in that you could detect it from a mile away.

4. Keith, a show host, was hired because he called my boss daily and constructed two poster boards outside his window, begging for a shot. A week later, he was guest hosting for three hours a day! I think Arby's has a more stringent hiring process.

5. A month after his honeymoon, one of my co-workers, a man named Miles, drunkenly walked up to half the staff at our Christmas party and yelled, "Never get married!" Then

he proceeded to make out with a member of the sales staff, so I took photos.

These were my co-workers, five days a week, sometimes six. Totally worth the remarkable salary of $0 per annum.

Fast forward six months.

There is a staple gay bar in Toronto called Woody's. Each week, a motley crew of drunk patrons bend over for the "Best Ass Contest." You pull your underwear down, expose your ass to 300 people, and pray you don't spread the cheeks too much and reveal the eye of the storm. Some things are sacred, you know? This contest is the ultimate career killer and since I was only six months into producing radio, I figured it was the *perfect* time to implode mine.

My friend Tim browbeat me into entering. His largest claim to fame is that he invented the Facebook game *Farmville*. Do you remember that shit stain on history? If you hated nature, sunsets, fornication, accomplishments, etc., you could alternatively hole up in your parents' basement pretending you were an overzealous farmer. Then, if you hit a roadblock in the game you could pay 99 cents to skip the level, or you could simply spam your contacts with an invite. As a general rule, you should banish anyone from your life that values your friendship at less than 99 cents.

Tim was and still is filthy rich. Old money, new money, Silicon Valley money. He's not fucking around.

"I'll triple whatever you win," he said, walking me over to the ATM to prove he was good for it.

"Geez, Tim." I sipped my drink. "A guy will do anything to get a gander at my rump."

"Well, it's a great rump."

"It is, and it's time to cash in," I said. "Let's do this."

I was slurring uncontrollably by the time the drag queen made the rounds with the clipboard, looking for volunteers. I wrote my name down and waited anxiously to be called up. I tripped up the side steps, smashing my shin into the stage, and looked out into the crowd, blinded by the wattage. My head was spinning. I heard cheers and my friends hollering my name, but even squinting, I couldn't make out any of their faces. It was a sea of black. I gulped audibly.

Then I walked to the edge of the stage, spun 180, and pulled down my underwear. I pondered what sort of pride I would bring to my ancestors in this moment. Were they looking down on me pridefully from the heavens above? Maybe if I won, I would move to change our family crest to include a small artistic depiction of my anus. I'd commission an update to the shield and turn to the artist, uttering, "Yes, ummm, looks good but can you use a bit more pink for my anus pucker? Yes, put the anus right below the Pegasus at the top. Thanks."

There were three rounds of elimination and after surviving the first, four of us remained. I walked to the edge of the stage again for the same rigmarole. 180 spin. Underwear down. Shame discarded. Penis out! Yes, my dick fell out. And even though I faced away from the audience, there was a full wall-length mirror in front of us. A sombre gasp came over the joint before uproarious laughter started echoing off the walls.

The drag queen screamed into the microphone and ran to cover my dick with the clipboard. I was so drunk I didn't understand what all the fuss was about.

The drag queens debated if my dick display warranted an elimination and crowdsourced it from the audience. But like the cockroach that I am, I survived.

And then there were two. The third and final round would be a dance-off between me and a 19-year-old Brazilian.

Edge of the stage. 180 spin. Underwear down. Cover the dick. And DANCE!

I wiggled that ass like a rap video extra, recycling proprietary moves from my years watching 50 Cent videos on TRL. I dropped it low. I rose it up. I spanked my cheek. I might have even twerked before twerking went mainstream.

"WOOO, JORDAN!" yelled members of the crowd.

At one point, I laid on the stage like I was doing a push-up and started to do the worm in a wave-like motion. It. Fucking. Crushed. When the song ended, I popped back to my feet to a chant of "Ass! Ass! Ass!" I ran across the front stage high fiving makeshift teammates like I'd just secured a Heisman trophy.

"JORDAN! JORDAN! JORDAN!" Their screams echoed around the room.

I pumped my fists and whispered to the Brazilian, "Top that."

Then it was the Brazilian's turn to give it a whirl. He sauntered up to the front of the stage and started to dance. I stood back and scanned the side of the stage for Patrick and Jesus. And then I saw him. Morgan. My boss. Holding a pint of beer and smiling at me. I blinked. Oh no, he was still there. I thought I was having a post-euphoria psychosis. I mouthed at him, "Morgan?" He nodded and then walked over to the corner of the stage and motioned me to come closer so he could say something to me over the blaring rap track.

I bent down and he slurred into my ear, "If I'd seen that ass during the interview, I would have hired you way earlier."

It was like a barrage of colliding thoughts smashing into my skull. Morgan is gay. *BOOM.* Morgan is your boss. *BOOM.*

Morgan wants you. *BOOM.* Morgan just saw your ass. *BOOM.* Morgan also potentially saw your anus. At least a peek at the anus… things got pretty wild for a second up there. *BOOM.* Morgan is still staring. How will this affect my job? Will it be awkward? What now? Can I leverage this to my advantage? Will this come up during my employee review under the "takes initiative" section? *BOOM. BOOM. BOOM. BOOM.* Like the Vengaboys song.

Naturally, I won the contest. My anus had made me famous.

I took my $150 cash and ran over to Tim to collect the promised $450, then immediately ran to the bar to spend it all on drinks for my friends and fans. In the flurry of excitement, I forgot all about Morgan, my dear heart and soul. An hour later when I did a lap around the bar to find him, I realized he was gone.

Next to me, Otis teetered on a barstool and encouraged me to order another drink. ***Monday***, he told me, ***is going to be great.*** I kissed him on his filthy mouth.

But much to Otis' chagrin, Monday was business as usual in the office. Not because of me. I loved drama and unpredictable chaos. Thanks in large part to my monkey friend, I thrived in the spotlight. The laughs. Feeling loved, if only for a fleeting moment. Sharing the Morgan story would get me that, I knew. I wanted to tell everyone! But I had to respect that Morgan didn't want to. It many ways it was his story to tell. At this point, he was largely still closeted and so under unwritten gay code I decided to honour his wishes (except I told Beth of course). Talk radio tends to be a white, straight, conservative bunch and I couldn't live with myself if my blabbermouth proved detrimental to his climb up the corporate ladder. My homosexuality, on the other hand, was no secret. Though being a homosexual is considered to be a "non-visible minority," my Euro Fit clothing addiction did all the talking.

A few weeks after my famous anus became an indelible mark on Toronto Gay History, a company-wide email informed us that Morgan would be leaving in two weeks to pursue a job with a competing media company.

Shortly after he settled into his new gig he sent me a text.

MORGAN: I'm no HR expert but I'm certain that since I am no longer your boss we can socialize without worry. How about Saturday night at Nobody Writes to the Colonel?

JORDAN: Can I call you boss still?

MORGAN: If you want.

JORDAN: I want.

MORGAN: OK. 8?

JORDAN: I hope you haven't gotten the wrong idea here. I only act gay because it makes me seem more interesting.

MORGAN: lol. Well you're very good at it. See you sat.

JORDAN: C u then

An hour later:

JORDAN: I'm going for drinks with my old boss and we're gonna hook up

BEN: Omg. From the ass contest?

JORDAN: Yes

BEN: Did you remember you're dating someone?

JORDAN: Sorta. I'll deal with it.

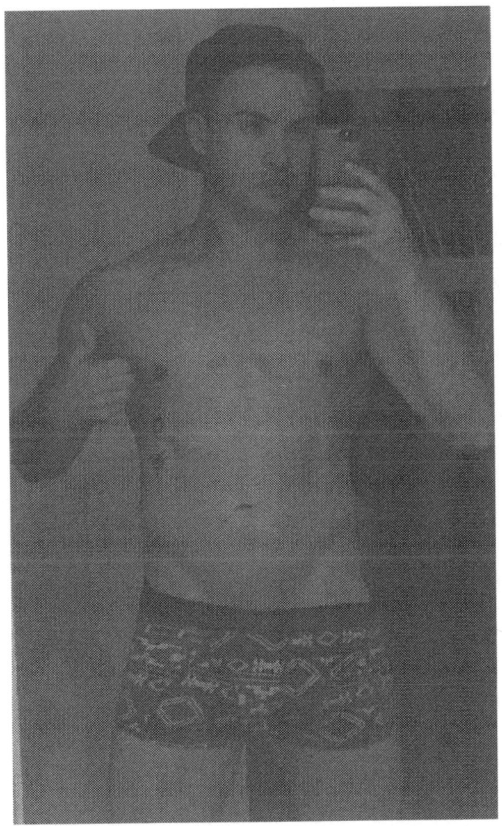

A photo preview sent to Morgan. Naturally.

Right. Jesse, the professional curler I'd been seeing for a few months. It was an unspoken understanding between us that we were on the fritz. For one, he needed a cheerleader, a man to live in his shadows and resolve himself to the fact that he would be living someone else's life into perpetuity. And that's not me. I am the guy who will support your shine, but never at the expense of my own.

To know Jesse is to understand the chip on his shoulder. He was the only member of his family to earn a post-secondary education, and it was from the worst school in the province.

His barrage of veiled comments on the regular showed it deeply bothered him. It never bothered me. I put little weight in the letters that precede someone's name. My smartest friend is actually an entrepreneur who dropped out of high school the summer before he entered grade 11. I value street smarts and intellectual curiosity. Maybe someone who can name the Mayor of Toronto, like Jesse couldn't. And when I reacted in disbelief, he told me *I* was an arrogant intellectual.

And on my end, I was aggressively stubborn, mostly when it came to supporting the sport of curling.

Curling is certainly something, isn't it? I attended two of his matches, one with my mom, and left feeling even more confused than the moment I arrived. They use a broom to sweep ice with no debris on it. It's basically housekeeping on ice. Who is paying for this nonsense?

And—Jesse aside—I don't know anyone who is into it but somehow, it's still everywhere, like the Axe Body Spray of sports.

I knew I had to end it, but Jesse beat me to the punch two days after Morgan's text. He broke up with me via text and told me he had been seeing someone else for weeks. Jesse's move was peak cowardice, but I've done it too (twice, actually). That someone else would eventually become Jesse's husband five years later. His husband is a sweet guy who has dedicated his life to all things Jesse, promoting contests, moderating fan pages, and travelling internationally. Sometimes I worry about people like that, and I wonder if it comes from a place of wishing to impose my value system on others. I wonder what happens to these sorts of people if the relationship ends. Because half of them do. And when it's over, do they go through an identity crisis when they realize decades of their youth have been dedicated almost entirely to the dreams of others?

My therapist has reminded me on multiple occasions to "stop wishing people behaved like me," but at times I just can't help myself. Sometimes I try to place myself in his husband's shoes and imagine what I'd write on Facebook as Jesse's main cheerleader.

"Jesse is sweeping frozen water and yelling at 8 tonight. Tune in, I guess."

They were a better fit.

By the time I was shaving my taint, preparing for my date with Morgan, Jesse and I were officially incommunicado. I wish I felt a tinge of sadness. I literally had to remind myself that I was due for the emotion of sadness in my life. Because I treated love with such carelessness at the time, I didn't even care about losing him. I was angry. I cared about winning and the elevation of pride over all else. I cared about getting ahead of perceived threats because they reminded me of the gay trauma of my youth.

The fact that I was devoid of an emotional response was a sobering reality so many of us encounter along the path of retrospect. It meant I had selected someone completely wrong for me as a respite from feeling alone. A distraction from myself. A way to avoid being alone and unpacking any of the dark thoughts that resided deep in my mind. After Patrick, I did that with man after man, many not included in this book. I would take anything, lowering expectations while subconsciously chipping away at my self-worth. I had to do better.

OTIS: We're falling asleep here.

Thus, I would do the mature thing and sleep with my former boss.

OTIS: Much better.

I was 10 minutes early to the bar that fateful Saturday night. I did all the things you do as a gay man when the chance of copulation is sky high. I was waxed, tongue-scraped, and shaved, with a lower colon pumped full of psyllium husk and brimful with adrenaline. Morgan, on the other hand, arrived discombobulated, shameful, and aware of the offside reality of what we were doing. Unfortunately, like many of the men I had chewed and discarded post-Patrick, he lacked the willpower to resist the intoxicating allure of my two-cheek Charlie.

OTIS: Your mission is clear: Move toward the finish line in the least amount of time possible. The drinks are a ruse.

JORDAN: Got it.

I mulled over Otis' game plan; I'd need to strike a crucial balance. Melt my inhibitions but not drink so much that I'd forget the experience.

After 15 minutes I was imperious, rapidly ordering rounds of drinks like I was Ja Rule at Art Basel. Morgan would steer us back to more neutral topics because he was a gentleman with a level of decorum. He carried himself through life with impeccable social grace, while I was impulsive, cutting through the fat to find a rush of instant gratification. I've lost years of my life to this unhealthy desire to fuel brain chemical jolts. I've passed over great men because they bored me. Sure, some were boring, but others grounded me in normalcy, which at the time felt petrifying.

Maybe Morgan had a crush on me and wanted to bring a level of intimacy? Or maybe he was the embodiment of how I envisioned most men, a non-monogamous creature of habit who needed to be discarded before he would do the same to me. Who knew? I never gave him a chance to prove himself either way.

This wasn't a natural interaction. This was a book, writing itself minute by minute as I floated above the table, powerless to stop the sideshow.

This is the life of a comedian. We are fuelled to perform by an innate insecurity. Slaves to chuckles. Like drones, we scan social situations from sunup to sundown, looking for opportunities. We run a fine-tooth comb through our lives as we look for truth. The laugh. The temporary vacation it might give us. That gift which we can then give to friends and strangers. Sometimes we find that laugh in people like Morgan, and we viciously suck them dry as a casualty in our game.

That night, I was an ego-fuelled sex maniac who wasn't above adding sexual innuendo to a banal exchange about career trajectories. I began to pepper them in slowly after I felt my dopamine levels stabilize. That wouldn't do. I'd need more hilarity to flush away any notes of human connection.

"I love television news but I'm not sure if I want to do it for my whole career."

"Did you say hole? I think you said hole. Wow, that's so forward, Morgan."

An hour passed.

"This is kinda awkward," he said.

"Of course it is," I replied. "It's a pre-show."

"Pre-show?"

I laughed at his confusion. "Are you always this coy?"

"What do you mean?"

"Did you shave your balls before you came here?"

"Um, yes," he said sheepishly. "Why?"

"Well, there we go. It's subconscious, perhaps. Psych 101. Listen, you started this whole dance by telling me my ass would have expedited my hiring. You can't just leave things like that dangling. You have to close the loop. So that's why we're here with hairless nuts. It's not complicated, dude."

"You're right." He looked toward the window. "So, you wanna leave and close the loop?"

"Well I didn't eat a pound of psyllium husk for nothing."

"What is psyllium husk?"

"Never mind," I replied. "Should we head out?"

He waved over the waiter to get the check. After we paid, we grabbed our coats and walked outside the bar. It was freezing, the kind of cold that you can feel deep in your pancreas. Gust after gust of wind smacked my cheeks and my body folded forward into a C shape in defence.

"I'm freezing my balls off," I said. "My hairless balls."

Morgan looked nervous. "What do we do now?"

"We go to my apartment and get this over with," I replied. "Isn't it obvious?"

Ten minutes later, Morgan and I stumbled into my condo in one of those sloppy movie make-out scenes, fuelled by months of bubbling sexual tension. Since Ben had introduced me to a life of alcoholism, I still possessed a level of motor control incongruous with seven ounces of top-shelf bourbon. I don't usually drink bourbon because it tends to lift mental fogs, and I much prefer operating in the comforting gear of sheer denial and avoidance, but tonight was a special occasion.

I started ripping off Morgan's shirt before he even unlaced his boots. I unlatched two buttons on his shirt then kissed his neck.

"Wait, wait, my boots!"

"Fuck your boots!" I waited for my corneas to turn fire red.

"No, I really think I should remove my boots. They're Doc Martens."

I ripped off his belt and threw it down the hallway, like a coked-out dominatrix.

"You can't break the flow, Morgan. If you break the flow, we may not recover. It's science."

"It is?" he asked, befuddled. "What part of that is science?"

I lunged forward again and kissed him intensely while simultaneously undressing him further, like I was one of David Blaine's assistants getting him out of a water torture stunt. It was remarkable and also kind of grotesque, even for me. After 45 seconds, the man who used to ask me to fetch him coffee stood shirtless in my foyer, half erect, with his pants around his Doc Martens. I took it all in and then nodded. It's true what they say, kids. Life comes at you fast.

At some point the Doc Martens were discarded and strewn across the hallway outside my bedroom, along with the rest of our clothes. Once we were nude, I threw him onto my mattress and kicked the door shut with the bottom of my right foot, like a horse. Then I crawled on top of him, and we played a most rigorous game of "Hungry Hungry Homos" for 15 minutes.

"Wait!" He interrupted me. "Your phone keeps vibrating."

"Who cares?" I said, kissing his neck.

"Well, what if it's a work emergency?"

"You would say that, you keener." But I rolled over and retrieved my phone from the nightstand.

There were 31 pending messages from the group chat with my closest friends. Either someone in the group had died or contracted an STI. I opened the thread. It seemed Jesus, my roommate, had returned home about five minutes after Morgan and me. He'd snapped photos of our clothes all over the living room, and the 31 messages were play-by-play reactions like:

JESUS: I just heard a loud smack on someone's ass

PATRICK: For sure Jordan's. He's a naughty bird. Can we talk about the fact that he's hooking up with a man who wears fruit of the loom underwear? I mean how low can he go?

BEN: Put your ear up to the door and tell us what else you hear

JESUS: I did. Giggling, gagging, and some moaning that is kinda high pitched

BEN: High pitched?

I hopped in:

JORDAN: Hola! I'm putting my phone on silent and resuming but I'd like to state for the record that the higher pitched moaning is not yours truly. I can't control the sort of bliss men experience when exploring the holy caverns of my body. You're all just jealous you don't get to sleep with your former bosses. Your lives are boring. God bless you all.

Later, Morgan stood over my bed buttoning his shirt and I lay half under the covers, grinning ear to ear and typing into my phone. Otis was on my lap, fanning me and feeding me grapes as a reward for following through on my goal.

"I'm thinking it's best if we keep this between us," he said. "It's a small industry."

"Of course." I looked up from my phone, already mid-SMS to my colleague Beth. "I'm the paragon of discretion."

"Great," he said.

BETH: Like a bird noise?

JORDAN: No, not a bird. I'd say more like a howler monkey.

BETH: Interesting

"Let me walk you out," I said to Morgan, tossing on my Jack & Jones boxers.

After Morgan left, Jesus popped his head out from his

bedroom door and with a smug ass grin said, "Soooo, who was that? Tell me everything."

"That," I said. "That is how you scratch an itch, homeboy."

"He's not even that hot."

"Come on. He's cute."

"You've done better."

"Yeah, but he's my former boss," I replied. "It's hilarious! It's worth it for the story even if I'm not that attracted to him."

Jesus raised an eyebrow. "You sure have a lot of stories."

"What's wrong with that?"

CHAPTER THREE

NATHAN

Eight months went by and I was still climbing the ranks of the talk radio biz. I'd dropped out of journalism school entirely. My official title was now float producer, which came with an hourly rate of $19. As a float producer I would help out with multiple shows on a sporadic, unpredictable schedule. Some evenings I'd assist with the 7-10 p.m. show, while other days I'd pitch in on the morning show.

The morning show shifts started at 3:30 a.m. Those weeks were the cuntiest of my life. Even a pinch of happiness felt like a distant memory. I couldn't go out socially because a) I'd have to be in bed by 9 p.m. and b) I was horrendous company. I also looked perpetually ill; my skin took on a blueish-gray hue with grim raccoon eyes. One of the FM producers, who had been in the game for 10 years, had it too, so I dubbed it "the morning show face."

They tell you it will get better, but it never does. You try to nap after the show but it messes with your mind further. Your weekends are a desperate attempt to regain stable health but they flash by in mere minutes. I cannot comprehend how anyone could hold a job like that long term. They must have just died internally years ago and not realized it. That's the only reasonable explanation I'm willing to accept. Mark my words, you could offer me $100 million for Howard Stern's job and I'd spit in your crumpet by way of response.

Eventually, I was thrown a lifeline from my morning show duties in the form of a mostly full-time job as producer of the noon-hour show. It was the only show on the lineup that was limited to 60 minutes, meaning it was largely neglected by both the sales staff and general management. $19 an hour meant I had just enough to cover my rent, score some H&M jeans, grab a gym membership, and make minor dents in my student loans.

The beauty of the noon-hour show flying under the radar was that we could pretty much get away with anything. "We" was me and the noon-hour host, Melvin Peters. At one time, Melvin was one of the most popular comics in Canada, which meant internationally he was about as famous as Melissa Joan Hart. He was bald with the sex drive of Gene Simmons. A walking health contradiction, Melvin was the kind of guy who would wax on about the benefits of coffee enemas and daily juicing while chain-smoking two cigarettes at once.

We were the perfect duo. Two rebels with a similar sense of humour and total disdain for all things authority. Melvin is strange, a tortured genius with zero work ethic. He needed his comedic brilliance because he was disgracefully lazy. He'd prep for the show in less than 30 minutes and then after (one hour I remind you), it was time for his nap. That was his day. 90 minutes of hard-earned glory. What a life that slob led.

And his mind simply couldn't rest. He'd hit the cigarettes every hour, bounce around people's cubicles like a court jester, and send company-wide emails (we're talking 300 people) complaining about the Coke machine.

When he wasn't doing that, he was sexually harassing me. No, not like that. He's as straight as they breed them. And before I continue, let me be clear on three things:

1. This was pre #metoo era and never at any time was there anything predatory about it. I thought it added a sort of inimitable flavour to my weeks.
2. I was knee deep in Stockholm syndrome.
3. I thought it was hilarious.

And it wasn't, like, grabbing my cock or anything. Ass spanks. Comments about my calves when I'd wear shorts in the summer. Questions about my sex life. In fact, it went on for a year undetected before others started to complain. Don't you love when people get offended on behalf of others? Wasn't it my call? He was a straight man. I didn't feel any of it was rooted in reality. Was I playing a role in fostering a climate by letting others know I didn't mind the chatter? It's a tough one.

One by one, the onlooker complaints piled up and before I knew it, I was being summoned to the 7th floor for an upper management meeting with Melvin. There was a zero percent chance it would be a fruitful one. Melvin thought it was horseshit, so the day before, he jammed his tongue down my throat in the parking lot in front of upper management. It was astonishingly brazen.

"Look! Look!" he'd screamed. "He is consenting."

I remember that meeting as *the* funniest one of my life. And it only lasted 10 minutes solely because of Melvin. He gave no fucks. You had to give it to him. His humour was unmistakably dismantling. Every person in that meeting was laughing two minutes in. The unforgettable highlight was when he stood up to leave and said, "Listen, none of this is going to hold up in court.

I sexually harass everyone equally around the office." Two days later he told his then-girlfriend (on a loudspeaker in front of six of us) that he couldn't wait to make her "cum like a rocket." It was my ideal work environment.

I thought he was harmless but years later I'd learn that perhaps Melvin hid a side of himself from me. He was accused of harassment by a woman he dated—nothing of the sexual variety, but some scary stuff. I never saw it coming. Melvin was ridiculous, but in my dealings with him I thought he had unwavering integrity, a quality noticeably absent in our office of mostly undiagnosed sociopaths. But Melvin wore a mask, like all of us, and I had to make peace with the uncomfortable fact that I may have known him as an artificial construct. Had he made jokes as a shiny distraction from his sinister truths? Was that what drove the unmistakable bond we had sparked on day one?

But during the time we worked together, I didn't care. I saw the flashing lights and an opening. With my creativity and Melvin's comedic timing, we started to push the limits of our dog and pony show solely for our own amusement. There was no theme to the show. Melvin was a comic with a hot mic. That was it. Unlike when I'd produced the morning show, I had little direction from management as to how Melvin's show should be executed. So, like my current podcast, sometimes I'd just go for tried and true laughs. Low-hanging fruit. Sex. Frat boy antics. Pure ID radio. We'd place prank calls and fail to identify ourselves live (illegal, by the way). We turned show callers against each other in verbal fights. One time I booked a dominatrix on the show called "Miss Kitty." On another occasion, I had a woman on to talk about how she shaved her vagina hair in the shapes of different animals. I'd book one of these ludicrous guests one after another, in awe that no one was telling me no. I felt powerful. I had a large platform and nearly 100% control. After booking a new guest, I'd immediately tell Beth the bit. Then we'd erupt in laughter and both scream in unison, "SHOOOOWSSSS ALL DOOONNEEE."

You must remember this was incredibly edgy for the time. This was before podcasts moved into the forefront. We were on an AM signal, government regulated and with an average audience age of 45-65. But because my boss was largely pre-occupied with the other flagship shows, he didn't notice. Sometimes I wondered if he was even listening to the show. In fact, it seemed we flew totally under the radar for months until the CRTC complaints started to pile up. Then, we were under a very watchful eye in the form of Carl, the radio director. Carl was relatively young, early 30s, but pulling in close to 300K a year. He had a natural knack for talk radio that he had polished in his late twenties. Even though he was smug, I had mad respect for his hustle.

Eventually, he caught onto us.

We would be in the middle of the show on a random Monday and I'd get an email with the subject line in all caps: *MY OFFICE RIGHT AFTER THE SHOW*

Then we'd walk in with our tails between our legs.

"Have you seen these?!" yelled Carl.

"Seen what?"

"CRTC complaints. They're piling up!"

Melvin started laughing. Then I started laughing.

"Guys, it's not fucking funny." Carl picked up a paper and waved it in our faces. "Look at this one!" he said with fury in his eyes. "Did you have an etiquette expert on as a guest to talk about the ins and outs of offering anal sex at a dinner party?"

What could we say? We absolutely did that. We absolutely did much worse.

"And this one," he said. "You called the Four Seasons hotel

about their bed bug problem and pretended to be the CEO."

"In our defence, he believed us," I replied.

"You forgot the part where I told the front desk staffer to say, 'Nighty Night, don't let the bed bugs bite' to each person that checked in," said Melvin. "That's the funniest part, so please don't leave it out if you're gonna yell at us right now."

Eventually, Carl would crack, and lose any sense of professionalism. Like most of us do at naughty jokes. That's the beauty of humour. It's involuntary. Sure, I made an offside joke, but you're the one who laughed. Aren't you complicit?

"I'm really the best," said Melvin as the three of us cackled, clutching our sides.

Somehow, we kept it up.

At some point, the ratings started to rise and Melvin negotiated a pay raise on my behalf, for which I would be eternally grateful. I had value. And I was somewhat happy. It was one of those times in your life when you don't realize just how content you were until it passes you by. You wish you had more gratitude in the tank at the time. Or you wish you could relive it again and do it right this time. And if you could, you wouldn't rush it. You'd savour every single laugh and never once, on a Wednesday, wish it were the weekend. When you do what you love, it almost never feels like you're working. And I loved entertaining.

I always proclaimed I got to where I am today without a mentor. But it wasn't until I was reflecting on my time at the radio station that I realized Melvin was the closest thing I had to that. He taught me comedic timing, the math of jokes, when to pull back, and when to go for it. There are times I catch myself on my own podcast sounding like Melvin in both my cadence and perspective. There are parts of many people in every comedian, but my largest part might belong to Melvin.

One weekend in October, I stumbled upon a website where you could write letters to inmates in maximum security prisons across Canada. I emailed the owner, Maria, about working in tandem with our show to promote her page. She agreed to meet me for coffee a week later. I'm pretty sure she was a homeless derelict. She rolled with a ton of unsavoury types, people like gang leaders, drug dealers, and pimps to name a few, and I racked my brain trying to figure out how we could use these connections to our advantage.

Two days later, in the shower, it came to me in a flash of undeniable brilliance. We'd have maximum security inmates call in to the show and Maria would act as the liaison. In return, we'd plug her web URL at the beginning and end of the segment. The free plug would ensure that her target demo, obese women who frequent bingo halls, could find out about the website, sign up, and write protracted love letters to the inmates.

Carl must have been high when he agreed to the segment, even though the sales rep assured us it would be impossible to find a sponsor.

A call would roll out like this:

MELVIN: We have Jason on the line. Your name is Jason and you're in jail for first-degree murder?

JASON: Yeah.

MELVIN: You do understand the irony here.

JASON: No.

MELVIN: Right. How's the food today?

JASON: So bad, it's like third world in here.

MELVIN: Oh, so like you have tandoori chicken?

JASON: ....

MELVIN: Soooo, Jason, who's the lucky man for you in there?

One day in the middle of a segment in which an inmate was literally walking our audience through every step of hotwiring a car (yet another moment that I'm sure was also illegal) my Facebook messenger started to pop off.

His name was Nathan Parker and the man was pursuing me like I was the last sign of life after a bird flu wiped humanity off the globe. I had maybe seven or eight separate messages waiting, just from the start of the noon-hour show. In short, he'd never missed an episode of Melvin's power hour. He said my producing skills were "commendable" and that he would like to take me out on a date sometime. Methinks Nathan started listening to the show as a way of courting me, but I'll never know for sure. Sort of a chicken and egg scenario.

Anyway, I rebuffed his initial advances after taking a glimpse at the way he smiled. It was all wrong. Unnatural. Like someone had asked him to imitate the most uncomfortable smile in the world. It's sort of the way Britney Spears now smiles on the red carpet, you know, like she made a doody in her thong.

So, he tried again. Day after day until he wore me down. At some point in time, the domineering attitude started to look like commendable zeal. I gave in and decided to have dinner with him on a late summer Thursday.

My former lovers tend to fall into two categories:

1. Men I could laugh with, and
2. Men I could laugh at

I'm sure you can guess which one he became.

The day of our scheduled date, he texted to confirm the reservation, which was a 15-minute walk from my house. I told him I'd walk and meet him there a few minutes before the reservation time.

Why, babe? he texted. *I can pick you up in my car.*

It's nice out, I replied. *I like to take advantage of nice summer nights by walking.*

Weird, he said. *I've never heard any man turn down a ride in the Audi.*

It was on.

He had severely underestimated both my comic arsenal and personal values when it came to love. He was flash and strained overcompensation. It was all so transparent, and Nathan's was built on such a shaky foundation of conjured self-esteem you could have knocked him over with a straw. On that day it became my civil duty to bring that man back down to planet Earth. And so, I did. For three months.

The first step in plan "Bring Nathan Back to Earth" was telling him our first date would have to occur somewhere with lobster. This was because I love lobster with all my heart, and also because I knew he would posture by paying the hefty bill.

Where do you wanna eat? he asked via Facebook chat.

I'm only eating crustaceans this summer, I replied. *So we'll have to go somewhere with premium lobster, preferably two pounds as I'm also on a very serious weightlifting regimen and need the extra protein.*

So that's just what he organized. Our first date was at an expensive seafood joint in Toronto's Queen West neighbourhood. After he browbeat me into allowing him to pick me up, I looked out my second-floor window to see him idling outside in his A4 Audi. As I got into his car, I reached back to grab the seatbelt. He abruptly stopped me with his right hand.

"No need, babe. The car passes it to you," he explained. "I'm all about luxury."

This was going to be great.

Three minutes into the car ride (and I swear to God this is true), he took a call from his "financial advisor." I knew a planned stunt when I saw one, mainly because I was throwing them daily as Melvin's producer. It was a faux phone call dressed up as mere coincidence. The setup, the orchestration, the delivery—it was all so artificial.

"Just calling to let you know everything is looking great," said the man on the phone, like he was reading lines from a cue card.

"Oh, really?" said Nathan.

"Yeah," said the voice. "You're in really good shape financially."

"Thanks, Peter." He hung up the call and put his phone away, like he'd nailed the entire stunt.

By the time we sat down at the restaurant, I was starving and immediately started to scan the menu for two words: market price. I saw that most of the regular entrees were $60-$80. What a bargain… for me.

"I have to tell you, Jordan," said Nathan. "I've never heard of someone being on a crustacean-only diet. It sounds a little expensive."

OTIS: We're in comedy heaven. Don't screw this up.

"It can be." I shrugged. "But I'm very focused on helping to even out the lobster population, one bisque at a time. The oceans have become overpopulated with lobsters. It's kind of like Mumbai."

"Really," said Nathan. "God, you're so up to speed on this kind of stuff."

"Lobsters and anthropology are my two greatest passions," I said, toasting his wine glass. "Along with love, of course."

Thirty minutes of insipid chatter followed, with a few notable highlights.

"So, what is it that you do, Nathan?" I asked at one point.

"I work in the world of financing," he said. "But we deal with a specific clientele, to help people get financing who are not usually good candidates for a loan."

I dipped my lobster claw in garlic butter. "Like, they have bad credit?"

"You could say that, yes," he said. "So, since they wouldn't normally be able to get a loan, we offer them one but at a much higher rate than you would see elsewhere. It's their only option."

"How high?"

"Around 30%. Somewhere around there."

"Gutless. You sound like a loan shark!" I shrieked in disbelief.

"A what?"

"A loan shark."

"Is that a type of shark? Like a great white?"

"They can be white, yes." I nodded. "Hey, Nathan, do you think I could order some shrimp scampi to go? This place is fantastic!"

After dinner, Nathan took me back to his place so I could get an up close and personal look at his prized Harley Davidson motorcycle, a likely sign that a micropenis is about to be shipped directly into your palm.

"I was thinking maybe we could hop on the bike and head over to the Jewish Film Festival," he suggested.

"The what?"

"A client of mine comped me some tickets for the Jewish Film Festival."

"But isn't that every film festival?"

"I guess," he said, missing the joke entirely. "Well, what do you wanna do, lobster man?"

"I wanna cruise on this bike. That would be fun," I said. "I don't know how to drive this thing, though, so I guess I'll ride on the back." I swung a leg over the back of the bike and settled into the leather seat.

"Great!" he said, rubbing his hands together. Then he pulled out a rag from his back pocket to polish up his prize before we hit the open road.

"I am very nervous," I admitted. "How fast are we going to go?"

"Not too fast," he said. "Maybe 110-120 km/hour at times."

"Holy shit."

"Babe, chill. The bike can detect your nerves."

"The what can what?"

"You gotta feel it," he said. "Lean into the experience."

"Whatever," I said, rolling my eyes. "After we get going, I'm going to need you to make some stops."

"Whatever you say, babe," he replied, igniting the engine.

"We've known each other for mere hours," I said. "I'm not your babe."

"Yes, you are," he said. "Now hold on tight and let me show you how I command this bad boy."

And off we went. Up city streets and service roads. We even hopped on the Gardiner Expressway and zoomed in and out of traffic in the passing lane. I was keenly aware that a single remarkable pothole had the potential to end my life. Every once in a while, we'd pull up to a light and I'd wonder what we looked like to the cars beside us. The only thing gayer than riding on the back of a motorcycle, firmly hugging another man, is if you decided to also insert a pink butt plug during the experience. I knew if anyone who teased me in high school saw me at those stoplights, I would have died having lost the upper hand.

Each of the addresses I had proffered were stops for my closest friends, including Ben, who upon seeing me on the back of a motorcycle with Nathan fell over into his planter, laughing.

"This is so stupid," said Ben, shaking his head.

"What's stupid?" asked Nathan.

"This." Ben gestured vaguely at all of me. "This is very stupid. I mean look at you, Jordan. The sideshow continues."

"I'm a new man," I said, planting a kiss on Nathan's cheek. "Summer lovin', had me a blast."

"He's very happy with me," said Nathan, grinning ear to ear.

Nathan never picked up on anything. Context. Irony. Absurdity. He was about as smart as an SOS pad. It was a comedic wet dream, a waterfall of material splattering into my lap. But he was also oddly sweet, even though it all felt rehearsed. What could I say, though? In one date he was treating me better than any previous suitor. During the entire time we dated, I couldn't distinguish if I was running away from his faux intimacy, running toward comedy, or a wild combination of both.

That moment, on the bike, I stopped waiting to connect with him intellectually and leaned into the high jinks that were sure to come. I waved to Ben from the back of the bike and sailed off into the night.

Weeks went by and nothing changed. Dinner after dinner. Antic after antic. On our third date we went to The Keg and he demanded "his table" even though we were the second couple in the restaurant and there were 60 open tables.

"Tell Kevin I'm here. I know Kevin," he said to the hostess.

"Would you just stop?" I shook my head, laughing.

Hanging with Nathan also had the shelf life of an avocado. You had to hand it to the man, he was well-intentioned when it came to love, he just had absolutely no clue of how to healthily express it. He always had to pay, name drop, show you off like a prized calf, or be reassured you liked him four or five times over dinner. I see it in so many gay men, the way we seek love, process love, and reject it. His method was all fluff and transaction. At times, I just wanted to shake him and say, "Buddy, you are enough. Tell yourself that. I mean absolutely not for me, but I'm sure someone else out there is looking to be brutally smothered with artificial intimacy."

But it wasn't just limited solely to his romantic exchanges. Nathan hated himself so deeply that he projected it onto just about everyone he came into contact with. He'd talk down to waitstaff, or be riddled with such crippling social anxiety that he'd say things I knew he probably didn't believe like, "Well, some of us work hard. That's why we have lots of money."

And his roommate Piers, whom I adored, got the brunt of his daily shenanigans in their two-bedroom condo that Nathan owned. (He told me three times just how much he paid for it.)

"Piers!" he would yell. "This plate has been out for two hours. I let you live in this beautiful condo and this is how you treat it."

"Sorry," said Piers. "But it's one plate. This place is always spotless."

"You don't appreciate this place, Piers," said Nathan. "You don't appreciate the hard hours I've worked to pay for this place so you can live in it."

"You talk like he's your trophy wife," I'd chime in. "He's your rent-paying tenant."

"Exactly," said Piers.

"Well, he doesn't seem to get that it's an honour living here," said Nathan. "An honour. You don't thank me enough Piers. Lots of people would kill to live in this beautiful condo."

More weeks went by. The antics seemed to amplify, possibly due to me fanning the flames. Sometimes I'd text Ben.

JORDAN: You're not gonna believe this one

BEN: Tell all. These stories are delicious.

I'm not going to try and make excuses for myself. I was an entitled menace during the months I dated Nathan. I had never possessed so much power over another human being and it brought out a very ugly side of me. I was bullied my entire youth for being gay, and I offloaded that by bossing Nathan around like a puppet on my strings. I spent years of my youth feeling neglected, so I tried to make up for lost time. Little did I realize; I was wasting even more of it.

I got away with anything. I could have keyed the man's car and convinced him it added character. It got to the point where I started entertaining myself by testing what I could get away with. I told myself it was a way of making Nathan pay penance for the way he treated others, which was at most a half truth. But it was still what I told myself daily.

By the second month, we were in an incredibly unhealthy spin cycle where he'd offend everyone in his life, and I would punish him each time as a sort of third party on neighbourhood watch.

He would call the waitstaff "plebs" one night, so I'd retaliate a week later by showing Jesus his secret iPod touch, with 27 different naked mirror selfies.

"Why is his penis wearing a helmet in that photo?" asked Jesus as he scrolled through the iPod.

"Dunno," I replied.

Sometimes Nathan would yell at Piers for what seemed like merely releasing CO2 within the sphere of the condo. Piers would retreat, dejected, to his room, and I'd crack open his door and whisper, "Don't you worry, baby, I'll make him pay." Ten minutes later Otis would chime in with an idea, like, ***Send Nathan on***

a grocery run and place dirty dishes in plain sight all around the condo.

I'm pretty sure Nathan flatlined once or twice when he returned. I felt like Gotham City's hero. The great neutralizer. As long as I was around Nathan, I could cancel out his transgressions by carrying out my own. Perfect logic, or so Otis said.

🐒 🐒 🐒

I must have been drowning in mercury poisoning from all the lobster by the time I agreed to copulate with Nathan. He invited me to an intimate soirée at his apartment via a text message.

NATHAN: Piers is gone. Come by Thursday night. I have something special planned. It's really special and unexpected.

JORDAN: Does that mean you made him homeless without his permission?

NATHAN: No, silly. He is up north.

JORDAN: OK. With you I always feel like I have to ask. You are incredibly unpredictable.

NATHAN: Thanks. When you get here just open the door, no need to knock. It will be dark. I've got a very special surprise planned. You won't see it coming. You're gonna sleep over too ☺☺☺

I was intrigued, even though it's public knowledge I am no fan of surprises. I did have to hand it to Nathan. For one, it was obvious he cared for me deeply. He was putting in more effort than any other man I had dated by a long shot. And two, well, I'd never heard date rape encapsulated in such a charming manner.

It was about 10 p.m. when my cab pulled up outside his condo, located just on the edge of Toronto's Gay Village. The building was called The Verve, a notable high-rise packed with homosexuals and the women who constantly trail behind them. It was a legendary place that Jesus and I had frequented for coke-fuelled ragers during the previous summer. I took the elevator to the 32nd floor and slowly opened the door without knocking, as directed. It was dark, with dozens of tealights positioned all over the living room and kitchen. Smooth jazz echoed soothingly off the walls. Love balloons were inflated. Champagne was poured. Normally I would find this behaviour charming but with Nathan it felt icky and contrived, like I was being romanced on *The Millionaire Matchmaker*.

I think that's what always irritated me about the situation, though I continued to participate in it. I abhor inauthenticity more than anyone. It's deep rooted. It's the foundation my dad built most of his life on. So yes, I'm extremely sensitive to it. These gestures by Nathan weren't thoughtful. They were cheesy regurgitations of reality show moments. They weren't the natural progression of a healthy relationship; they were carbon copies. They were corporate constructs of Valentine's Day we've all seen for decades. And I know you're learning that ya boy likes a lot of variety. I'm not saying it wasn't thoughtful, but I am saying I would have been very cool with a cheese pizza and a stimulating conversation.

"Hey there, radio man." Nathan was standing by the kitchen island in a purple polo, his face lit by candlelight.

"Hi. Are we playing Ouiji board tonight?"

"We could. Why? Do you wanna play Ouiji board?"

"Um, no."

"Well, that's good." He pointed to a plate of strawberries. "Because I made chocolate fondue and that will be our main activity, among other things."

"Delicious," I said, picking up a strawberry and shoving it in my mouth. Half of them seemed to be cut into hearts.

"Hey, hey." He reached out and put a hand on my arm to stop me from taking another one. "Slow down. I cut those with love and care."

I rolled my eyes and started to make out with him, my back against the kitchen island. He unbuttoned my shirt and started to kiss the side of my neck as I undid my fly.

"Turn around," he said, feeding me a chocolate-covered strawberry. "I have an idea."

"What kind of chocolate is this?" I said. "My teeth are sticking together and it hurts."

"Toblerone."

"You used Toblerone for fondue? Wow, Nathan."

"What's wrong with that? Toblerone is great," he said. "Now how about we explore what I originally wanted to use it for? To lick it out of your ass."

"Sure. Why the hell not? Feast away."

Nathan started lapping melted Toblerone from my crack like a Bernese mountain dog. Thirty seconds into the act he paused contemplatively and started staring at the grey linoleum.

"Umm, excuse me, sir," I said. "I have needs. Mush, mush."

"I can't," he said, shaking his head. "I'm sorry. I felt like I was going to dry heave. I didn't think about the visual optics of smeared brown liquid down an ass crack."

"Right," I said, pulling up my underwear. "Let's take a shower then. I think I have some nougat pieces in my rectum."

After our shower I told Nathan I'd need to head home. I will likely die alone for many reasons (read between the lines), the largest being that I can't achieve a satisfactory level of REM sleep in someone else's bed. Nathan insisted I stay and told me he'd give me one of his sleeping pills that would "100% do the trick." I was no stranger to pills with mysterious origins, so I felt the presence of an official pharmaceutical label was a definitive upgrade. I asked zero questions and took the green pill, which made me comatose within minutes.

I woke in a blurry haze the next morning. I took a quick look around and noticed the pillow was drenched in saliva. I touched my face and my lower jaw felt sort of frozen in place. I could lift my limbs but only by exerting maximum effort. I felt like Rosie O'Donnell was sitting on my chest.

Then Nathan entered the room in New Balance running gear, chipper as ever. "Someone slept well!"

"What the fuck happened to me?" I asked, squinting my eyes.

"You were sleeping so I was going to go for a run," he replied. "Are you OK?"

"No, Nathan," I said. "I'm not OK. I think I might quite possibly be a paraplegic, which is not how I saw this week unfolding. What did you give me?"

"A sleeping pill."

"This was not a sleeping pill."

"Yes, it was. I take them all the time."

"All the time?!" I asked. "Am I moving my legs?"

"Yes, Jordan. You are moving your legs."

"Ugh. Pass me the pill bottle," I replied, extending my hand. "I can't believe I trusted you for a split second. I feel like I'm waking up from general anaesthetic."

I looked at the label and typed it into my phone. It was a heavy tranquilizer of the highest recommended dose, because of course it was. If anyone needed heavy sedation, it was most certainly Nathan. He was drugging himself down from mania at a dosage reserved solely for circus elephants.

"You need to drive me home," I said. "I'm in a haze and I don't trust myself to get a cab."

"Sure thing!" he said with a wide smile. "To the Audi we go."

A week later, I told Ben if I spent another week with Nathan, I'd very likely hit a raging point that would result in a murder suicide.

"It's like dating a funhouse clown," I said. "Nothing adds up. It's very very confusing."

"I'll give you $50 if you last two more weeks," he said. "And I'll throw in a lobster."

"That's not fair," I said. "You know I'd saw off a limb for a lobster."

He smirked. "I know."

"Fine," I responded, shaking his hand. "Two more weeks."

Besides most of his personality, one of the most off-putting things about Nathan was the coterie of wildly wealthy, intolerable alcoholics who filled his social sphere. Many barely worked yet maintained a lifestyle like a Rothschild. One of the members of the group, Danny, was a real piece of work. Pushing 45, his condo was referred to as "Club D" and was a cesspool of ceaseless drug use. I was naturally drawn to him at the time because I was also dangling by an emotional thread. You know, birds of a feather.

Danny was blond, charismatic, full of quips, and always had a glass of vintage pinot noir glued to his hyaluronic acid-injected face. This was along with whatever pharmaceutical assistance seemed to be causing a pool of drool to form on the corner of his lips. He ended each sentence with "honey" like it was a punctuation mark. Three weeks after I met him, he insisted I join him at his cottage two hours north of the city.

"With Nathan?"

"Sure, honey."

"Is that a yes?" I honestly could not tell. "Wait, where are you going?"

Danny had walked away to refill his glass and never returned.

Dane Cook famously said that in every group of friends there is one person no one likes. The theory is that this person is kept around as a sort of sport so everyone can mock their life choices. It's one thing to be that person. It's quite another when you realize you are dating that person.

Why are they even friends with him? I often pondered.

Part of the reason I stuck around is that I wanted to see if I could change Nathan, to watch him transform into someone who gives you the rawest version of themselves, even just on a few rare occasions. Did Nathan even have another version?

I felt bad for him in a way. His friends weren't perfect. They were elitism and privilege personified. At least Nathan had a personality (albeit an annoying one he'd built from GQ magazines) but his friends were flavourless, dismissive, and vacant. Even I had limits when it came to being mean to Nathan—I mostly restricted myself to his ridiculous life choices, but they brutally skewered him worse than anything Otis and I could have come up with.

One of them was a vile cunt and former radio DJ. She drove an Audi TT and when I told her my goal was to one day work hard and own her car she laughed in my face and said, "Honey, dream higher and work harder." Ironically, she hadn't worked in four years. My friends weren't rich in the traditional sense, but they were overflowing with loyalty and character. It made me value them further. I had it pretty great. Nathan may have been rich, but he was destitute when it came to the real currency of life.

And who knows? Maybe there was a real connection among the members of their group, but I could never find it.

Two weeks later, Nathan and I hopped in his Audi with two of his friends to haul ass to Danny's cottage on the outskirts of Parry Sound.

Here are my diary entries from that weekend:

Day 1

We've arrived at Danny's cottage, which isn't so much a cottage but a seven-bedroom mansion beside a lake. I'm pretty sure most cottages don't have a bidet. Danny is the marriage of both old and new money. You can feel and smell the money in the air. I say this figuratively but also perhaps literally as I'm sure if I pop a couple floorboards, I'll find a few stacks of bills, which I will assume are either from money laundering or used merely for insulation.

One of the older couples attempts to solicit me for a threesome. I have to politely decline as I tell them I haven't been tested in an uncomfortable amount of time and who the hell knows with Nathan?

I can also confirm that Nathan is very likely a sociopath. One of the couples has brought a seemingly rabid dog that won't cease barking. It's annoying but manageable for all of us, except Nathan. His anger at the dog boiled to an ugly head when he shoved it from the top of a flight of stairs. It tumbled awkwardly, hitting the bottom and barking in horror. Amid the commotion, the owner slapped him across the face. Because said dog owner lacked a modicum of testosterone, his slap did not leave a lasting mark.

I told them Nathan wasn't a bad guy, just incredibly broken. Was I lying?

I begin to wonder why I am here and if I would be in such a situation if my father had hugged me tighter as a child.

Day 2

Danny insists we roast marshmallows and watch his old VHS tapes from his days as a former reality star. Instead of a bonfire, we gather around the white rug to toast marshmallows on his porcelain sticks over the fireplace. I don't want to wait so I use a BBQ lighter to toast mine as Danny & Co. chain smoke on the sofa.

The couple who insinuated I join them for a threesome are bickering nonstop and I'm predicting there may be a cage fight to the death. I think this could happen because cocaine abusers are known to be quite physically volatile.

I miss my friends.

Nathan reaches around me and holds me tight. I would beg him to just be himself tomorrow but I know deep down he doesn't know who that is. I'm dating a cyborg.

Day 3

Because I have smoked nearly six joints to myself in two days, I am noticing a serious decline in my mental function. I look for my phone for 45 minutes before finding it in the ice cube tray; it won't turn on. Nathan offers to buy me a new one. I tell him "that's too much money," but then I remember my bank account balance is $43 and realize I'll take him up on his offer before sundown.

One of the other cottage guests starts his morning with yoga on the dock. I am in serious awe at his sinewy body structure, which seems to largely defy science. I tell him about my personal fitness regimen and earnestly ask him his secret. He rolls his eyes and states, "Peanut butter." I tell him I find his secret to be quite befuddling. For one, I wasn't aware Kraft was now selling anabolic-steroid-infused peanut butter.

When we returned to Toronto, I texted Ben to let him know I had survived the two weeks and would be coming by to collect my $50 and lobster.

Fresh, not frozen, I wrote. *And at least three pounds. None of this midget lobster shit from No Frills. I want a lobster that knows his way around a buffet. A BBL. Big beautiful lobster. I deserve it and don't you dare pretend I don't.*

OK. Did you end it? He texted back.

End what?

End things with Nathan.

No, I'll do it Friday, I texted. *And don't forget the herb and garlic butter, I know how cheap you can be.*

That very Friday, I went to Boutique Bar in the village with two of my friends. After a dirty martini or four, I left around 2 a.m. to walk to Nathan's pad. Two blocks from the target destination I ran into Steve Peterson, a guy in my high school graduating class. It seems the rumour mill was correct. Steve had finally come to terms with what we'd all known since he was 16: his undeniable, indefatigable gayness.

Steve regaled me with stories about my former high school girlfriend, who was also his best friend and the reason we met. He told me after high school she skipped first-year university and moved to Africa for missionary work. This was presumably due to being emotionally scarred by a gay boyfriend who used to touch her pussy like it was a hot stove element.

"Are you blaming me for her leaving the country, Steven?" I said, laughing.

Steve laughed. "No, but I will say she seemed pretty adamant about getting a fresh start."

"Oh, so it's my fault she had a vagina?!" I exclaimed. "That thing looked like a day-old Reuben sandwich, like all vaginas."

"I remember my last girlfriend had to literally pull me by the hair to go down on her," he said.

I cackled at the mental image. "You were always sooo gay. I saw you peeking at my junk in high school."

"Probably," he said. "And look at us now, two homos in the big city."

"Welcome," I replied. "Oh shit, I totally forgot I have to go break up with someone. I gotta let you go."

"Of course you do," he said. "You're still ridiculous. It's like no time has passed at all."

"Right? Well, give me a hug, bitch," I said, reaching in and pinching his booty.

"I liked that," he said. "I liked that very much, sir."

I tailgated into the building behind a young couple and strolled into Nathan's condo like I owned the place. But I didn't. He did, remember? $315,000 with 10% down.

"Nathan's in there," said his roommate Piers, pointing to Nathan's room. He was sitting on the couch with two strangers.

"OK, but can I get high with you guys first?" I asked. "I need a little courage."

Fifteen minutes later, I walked into Nathan's room and delivered the news to him red-eyed, clammy from the weed sweats, and eating a hunk of aged parmesan that I stole from his fridge. Upon hearing the news, Nathan went silent and then told me he wasn't really surprised.

"There were signs," he told me. "Like maybe you telling me it was 'a two monther, max,' or that you wished the devil would crack my cock like a glow stick."

"Did I say that? Sorry," I said. "But I gotta write that one down. You can't let gems like that pass you by."

Three weeks after the breakup, I received an invite to attend Danny's brother's show debuting a new collection at Toronto Fashion Week. I brought my friend Penny as my date. Nathan's pseudo-socialite pals were gathered by the bar after the show, mainlining vodka cocktails and shooting me total cut eye, one by one.

"Hmm, that's weird," I said to Penny. "I thought they loved me. I was a professional at putting Nathan in his place."

Penny looked at them over my shoulder and said from the corner of her mouth, "Well, it's not looking good. They are glaring at you and whispering."

"Yes, I see that. Thank you. There's Dustin by the washroom," I said, pointing. "Let's go say hi to him. He keeps it real."

I greeted Dustin with a hug and asked him what was going on with the rest of the group.

"Nathan told them a lot of the things you said about them," he replied. "So, they're obviously not fans of yours."

"Like what?" I said, bafflement written across my face.

Dustin listed off the insults word for word and only one of them was creative enough to have originated from my arsenal. I was furious. I had defended Nathan to those very friends when no one else would, even when the comedic opportunities were in plain sight. Despite Otis' constant cajoling, I gave up external validation for him. He had all the money one could want but was still a powerless underdog. I saw that in him and tried to shield him from those very people. And it was bad enough I had to endure subpar sexual satisfaction, nougat in my anus, and hiding my face from waitstaff as Nathan borderline abused them. And now, well, now Nathan was causing economic harm to yours truly. I was a low-level producer in the entertainment business at the time, remember. Those socialites had the power to blacklist me for eternity. I had to take action.

"What are you doing?" Penny asked.

"I'm texting Nathan," I said. "This is a clear case of slander and I won't stand for it."

Instead of taking the time to apologize, Nathan wrote back with a text along the lines of, and I'm paraphrasing, "you deserve it."

I stomped my foot, and Penny and I left the venue. We waved down a cab that would take us back to the Green P, where her car was parked for the evening.

"I need a lawyer," I said in the back of the cab, my hands clenched together. "A vicious, ball-busting super lawyer to stop the flow of slander in its tracks."

"My uncle Dave is a lawyer," she said.

"Penny. Your uncle is a mid-level family lawyer and he's Portuguese," I said. "I need a Jew. Jews get it done. Open 411.ca and start looking for a Cohen or a Schwartz. A Star of David is a sign of success."

"What about your friend Lenore?" she said. "I always see her on TV. She can be kinda terrifying."

"I totally forgot!" I said. "Yes, Lenore. Lenore will do just fine."

The next morning, I told Lenore the full story and she asked me what I wanted her to do.

"I want it all to stop," I said. "So please release the hounds, Lenore. Release them good."

"That's not a valid legal strategy," she said. "I need something more concrete to go off of."

"Well, what do you suggest?"

"A cease and desist letter asking him to stop or we will seek damages," said Lenore. "And I'll courier it to his apartment same day. That should be enough."

"God, you really know how to give a girl closure in the midst of a breakup." I was impressed. "Thank you! I won't forget this."

"Anytime, boo boo! This one's on me. Take it from me. Men are trouble!" She roared with laughter and hung up the phone.

Sure enough, the next afternoon around 3 p.m. I received a carbon copy of the letter she had couriered to Nathan. I ripped along the FedEx fold line and held back tears at the sheer beauty of seeing a legal template, only slightly customized into a letter, labelling me a "well known media figure." *Fuck Disney, this is my fairy tale.*

Years have gone by since Nathan and I dated, and I've always had an internal debate over whether he was a deeply broken human being or sociopathic. And the conclusion I've come to is that he lacks any discernable empathy for the marginalized, which is ironic since he's a gay man. His Facebook is a litany of posts that read like dog whistles and shrines for gross income inequality. So I'll admit, I went hard on him on this chapter with no desire to sand the edges.

Nearly three years after we broke up, I ran into Nathan at a Pride party and he hadn't changed one iota.

"We should grab dinner and catch up," he said to me beside the outdoor barbeque.

"No thanks," I said.

"Well at least unblock me from Facebook."

"No thanks. I gotta pee." I walked to the kitchen instead.

Nathan turned to my ex-boyfriend Patrick, whom I had abandoned in my desperate flight to the kitchen, and said, "You know he's a handful. There's no doubt about that one. But if I'm being honest, he's probably one of two people that I have ever loved."

"Yeah, well, nothing quite kills that love like a cease and desist, buddy," said Patrick.

CHAPTER FOUR

BRAZIL

At the end of my freshman year in university, I was diagnosed with a chronic bowel condition called ulcerative colitis. This autoimmune disorder results in the formation of open ulcers along my lower colon, starting at exactly 13 inches north of the rectum. Before I was diagnosed, I spent the final months of freshman year battling debilitating cramps, copious amounts of blood loss (out my ass!) and scheduling eight or more bowel movements a day at 30 minutes a pop. As a silver lining, it was a facile way to shed the freshman 15 and then some.

My condition requires I endure a colonoscopy every three to four years which, in short, is basically deep-sea diving with a camera in your colon. Cyclically, I squirt a corticosteroid enema into my anus, or during a flare of symptoms, toss back eight pills a day. I am constantly being anally probed by the fingers of medical professionals, dripping in cold petroleum jelly. And not one of them has been able to provide a level of what I feel is sufficient bedside manner, like kissing the small of my back to warm me up.

During the colonoscopy they loop you up on IV drugs that

don't completely render you unconscious, like a general anaesthetic would. Through your hazy gaze, you get a joyous front-row seat to watch the footage of your insides broadcasted on the operating room television.

Usually, my dad's former best friend performed my colonoscopies but over the years he started to get a little too casual for my liking. During my last procedure he and his nurse prepared to breach my butthole while also enjoying slices of two-tier chocolate cake. I was aghast. All I ask for is a moderate level of respectability while I'm violated anally. I don't personally know Cheryl, the birthday girl, but frankly I don't think she warrants the temporary loss in professionalism.

"Umm, do they eat cake at the Mayo Clinic?" I asked, as the anaesthesiologist loaded the IV port into my forearm.

The nurse ignored me and proceeded to show off the hose that would soon spend 10 minutes in the catacombs of my digestive tract.

"It's only this size across," she said, lifting it in front of my face as I lay horizontal. "Maybe three quarters of an inch. It won't be too uncomfortable."

"I'd actually feel a lot more at home with some more girth on that thing, ya know?" I said in response. "Anywho, that's fine. That won't be a problem at all. Feel free to go up a level in hose to NBA player if you want."

After the procedure, I lay on a hospital bed with an aftercare card. The nurse came by to let me know she had called my friend Lara.

"She'll be here in 20 minutes," she said, checking my blood pressure on the monitor.

When it stabilized, she lifted me off the bed and walked me out to the waiting room. She reminded me to head straight home and rest on my couch for the next 12 hours. So, as someone with the highest respect for authority and directives I did just that. Just kidding, I went grocery shopping for Raisin Bran.

"I don't know," said Lara as she pulled out of the parking lot. "Are you sure you should be out in public?"

OTIS: Tell her to kiss your ass.

"I've had four of these colonoscopies before," I replied, unconcerned. "I'm just a little high still. It's totally fine. I'll just grab two boxes of Raisin Bran and we'll be on our merry way."

After I found the two boxes and a tub of Greek yogurt, Lara and I made our way to the express checkout lane and I placed my three items on the conveyer belt.

"$9.02," said the cashier. "Do you collect points?"

I shook my head and took out my Visa card. Then, with zero warning, I completely blacked out.

I woke up an indeterminate amount of time later to the sight of a Marxist hipster with purple hair and giant holes carved out of her ears. She was hovering mere inches from my face. *Had I died and gone to Burning Man?* She was furiously dialing 911 on her phone and shaking me side to side.

"He's had a seizure!" she yelled. "I've seen this before with my sister. It's a seizure."

A bottle of orange Vitamin Water crossed my gaze. The hipster put a straw in the top and held it up to the corner of my mouth. I took the straw between my lips and my first conscious words were, "Actually, do you have the one with Stevia? I don't want to get cellulite."

"He's talking!" she exclaimed.

"Or even just water," I said. "Water would work, guys."

The store manager called 911 and paramedics arrived within 10 minutes. They lifted me onto a stretcher and ushered me into the elevator. Lara said she would take the stairs and meet me outside to see me off before driving herself to the hospital.

I felt a warm trickle of liquid down my ass crack that started to pool at my taint. It was all too familiar. Nostalgia hit me like a truck. I was taken back to the first year of my colitis diagnosis, disposing of boxer briefs on a weekly basis like they were made of tissue paper.

"Psssst," I whispered, tapping the female paramedic on the shoulder as the elevator doors closed.

"Yes?" she replied.

"I'm not quite sure what the most opportune moment to say this is, but I may have shit my pants during all the chaos," I uttered, shamefaced.

Her face softened with kindness and pity. "That's OK, honey," she replied. "We will check it out when we get to the hospital. No need to be ashamed."

As soon as we got to the hospital—and I mean within seconds of us arriving at the triage desk—the paramedic rolled me toward a nurse and screamed, "OK, he's all yours," before scurrying out the automatic doors.

"Geez," said the nurse. "That was abrupt."

"It's because I shit my pants," I said. "It happens when I get too excited."

"Oh. What were you excited about?" she asked.

"Oh nothing, maybe Raisin Bran," I said. "I guess it also happens when I black out."

"Hmm, let's get you something for your pain," she said.

The nurse left to retrieve me some painkillers. I had almost no pain but would take any respite from existential dread, and possibly Otis, with open arms. She hung a bag and delivered it through an IV port she installed. It was around then that Lara came into the room and asked me why I was laughing.

"I am incredibly high," I told her, and then she was laughing too.

Thirty minutes later, the nurse returned to check on me. I told her it was probably time we cleaned my crack and underwear (or discarded them). She pulled back my pants and told me there was nothing there. It was a nice change in my life. I took it as a harbinger of brighter days ahead.

She looked at the IV pump and laughed. She told me every time I pushed the button to drive more morphine into my veins, the system recorded it. But I could really only get a new dose every 10 minutes. She then told me that I've already pressed it over 40 times during the hour, like a foam-mouthed, famished junkie.

Thirty more minutes went by before she returned and asked me what my pain was on a scale from 1 to 10. I told her it was a 9. She left to retrieve another bag of morphine. I whispered to Lara, "it's a two," and then burst into uncontrollable laughter. Lara joined in. I wondered if laughing would prolapse my newly sensitive anus, like a rose bloom of flowers.

Sometime after that, my mom entered the room in a panic and said, "Jordan, it's always something with you." I nodded and turned to Otis, who gave me a thumbs up.

A doctor came in the room and told me I likely had a concussion and provided me with verbal and written instructions for a couple of weeks. When I was discharged, Lara and my mom took me home to sleep. They handed me a cardboard device to pee in, as they didn't want me walking around during the night. After my mom placed it on my nightstand, I threw it across the room like a maniac, yelling, "I will not piss like a peasant!"

I woke up 14 hours later.

Because of the concussion, I was instructed by the doctor not to use technology for at least four days. I largely complied besides a small break during which I wrote a text to Ben that read, *Assburgers or Aspergers. You can only choose one.* Ben ignored it but wrote back the next day to let me know "Jizzle," the Gay Village drug dealer, had retired and written a long goodbye letter to his client base. Obviously, my friend circle, comprised largely of spiraling degenerates, were on said list. I'd never heard of a drug dealer quitting the game in such a chic manner.

I replied, *So what you're saying is I'm not getting any more morphine?*

Another side effect of having a delicate colon wall is the high incidence of chronic anal fissures in the rectum. This is no doubt exacerbated by haphazardly shoving dicks into the region on the regular. If you're unfamiliar with a fissure, picture the sharp pain of a paper cut. Now multiply said pain by 10 and place it directly in your ass. Or for the '90s kids, imagine shitting Sonic the Hedgehog.

The fissures become chronic once you have exhausted regular treatment options over the span of a couple months. So, one Wednesday afternoon, my gastroenterologist broke the news to me that surgical intervention would be required.

"Jordan, we're going to make a small incision in—"

"Wait," I interrupted, narrowing my eyes. "What the fuck is on your forehead?"

"Ashes," he said dismissively. "It's Ash Wednesday. I'm Catholic."

"You look like a Chilean miner," I said.

"A what?"

"A Chilean miner."

He stared at me vacantly. I hate dead air, so I jumped in.

"So, where on my asshole will you be cutting exactly?"

"At the top," he said. "Just a couple of small muscle fibres."

"Brutal," I said, shielding my eyes. "JUST BRUTAL."

"It will be quite uncomfortable for a while. We can carry it out with local freezing or a twilight anaesthetic, like Propofol."

"Drugs, definitely drugs," I said immediately. "I'm not staying conscious for this."

"Very well then." He closed my chart. "We'll do it next Thursday. You can finalize the details with the front desk."

When I arrived for what I deemed to be a funeral for my favourite hole—asshole version 1.0—I wore all black. I brought a gorgeous flower arrangement. I hired an 80-year-old Nonna to wear a veil and cry into a silk handkerchief in Italian, and two Irish bagpipers in kilts to stand in the middle of the lobby. They played me out as I marched into Operation Room #3, the place where its impending death would take place.

When the doctor was done, I hobbled into the lobby with a gauze pad collecting blood in my boxer briefs. Lara was there again but this time she was adamant that we follow the doctor's orders and head directly home. Do not pass GO. Do not collect another concussion. I agreed. I already had two boxes of Raisin Bran in my cupboard.

Lara linked arms with me; she led me up the elevator and right to the edge of my couch. She ordered me to stay put for eight hours until the anaesthetic had completely worn off. I nodded and turned on one of my favourite movies, *Enemy of the State*. When the movie was done, I determined there was nothing more I required in this world than fresh pancakes. So once again, I defied all orders and put on my shoes to head to the grocery store, a mere three blocks from my house.

Everyone knows the most exciting adventures happen when you're high, said Otis, bouncing on my shoulder, his tail curling lightly around my neck.

DIARY ENTRY FROM THAT DAY:

In a post anaesthetic haze, I walk three blocks to the grocery store dressed like a Russian landlord in a full tracksuit. I request a single "prepared" lobster with garlic butter from the woman at the counter. She calls a manager over to explain that they "don't do that" and I should try Red Lobster. A look of bewilderment crosses my face. I ask her if I can take the lobster home as a service animal. She declines. I ask her if she might change her mind if I use a leash to walk him home. She turns to help the next customer.

Slightly defeated, I start to buy ingredients for pancakes. It takes me 45 minutes to find six items. This is not the behaviour of an adult.

I receive a text from Ben: Where the hell are you?

JORDAN: At home watching a movie.

BEN: No, you're not. Jordan, you sent me selfies in front of a lobster tank.

I scroll back through our text history. He's right. I did.

JORDAN: I'm deep sea diving, you idiot.

BEN: You're going to get another concussion. I'm coming to your house and you better be there by the time I get there.

It feels like a blink, and I am suddenly back in my kitchen, whipping up a storm of blueberry pancakes without a care in the world. The buzzer for my apartment goes off and it's Ben, who enters my condo to the sight of me eating a stack of seven pancakes with a butter knife.

I turn to look at him, my bite of pancake halfway to my mouth. "Greetings, earthling."

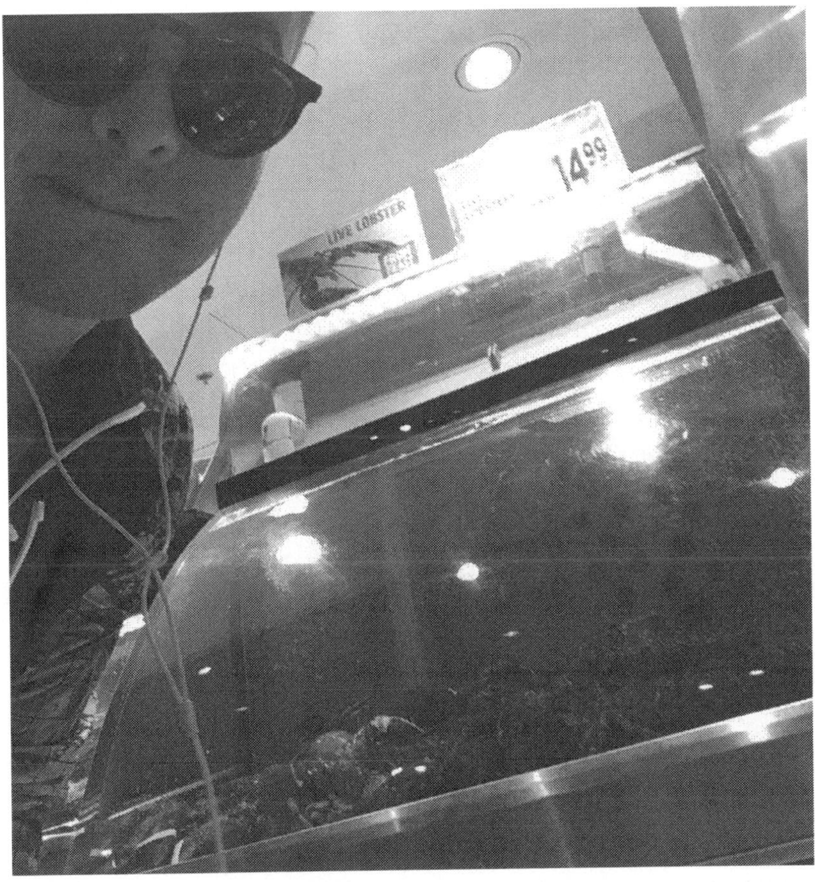

With my favourite crustaceans.

"This place is a fucking mess," he says. "You can't live like this, man."

"Ben, I bring good news from the higher land," I say from under my hood, ignoring his chastising. "You, sir, just won a FREE trip to Braaaaaaa-zillllllll."

"What?" he asks. "How?"

"I got bored, so I bought us a trip to Brazil," I say through a mouthful of pancakes. "And by free, I mean you'll have to e-Transfer me your half within 30 days."

"You are a goddamn menace." He sits down beside me "At least give me a pancake."

My stepdad once asked me how my infamous vacations with Ben go down. As succinctly as possible, I explained that we commence drinking in the airport lounge and hit a blackout sometime after we exit Canadian airspace. The vacation itself is one giant blackout, and we return to full consciousness a few hours before we're due back in Canadian customs, by which time I'm nearly always up 10 pounds and battling an undiagnosed mood disorder.

One of the most wondrous things about being gay is you gain access to the underground homosexual railroad. It's a glorious network of hairstylists, flight attendants, interior designers, and high-end retail clothing workers. A sexually gratifying, anonymous hookup may unknowingly result in you being upgraded to first class on your next trip or with a student discount applied to your next Club Monaco purchase. I like to think it is a form of surreptitious prostitution that is rarely talked about.

At the time Ben was sleeping with his neighbour, Pedro. Every Sunday like clockwork he would travel down in his white bathrobe to the 9th floor of his condo like he was getting a spa treatment. Pedro, a secret staple on the gay underground railroad, hooked us up with 20% off our economy tickets, vanity kits, and premium alcohol all the way to Rio de Janeiro. By the time we landed, Ben was basically rolling me up to customs, lifelessly draped over his suitcase.

"I'm so confused," I said, straining my eyes at the fluorescent lights. "Why is no one around here speaking English?"

Ben rolled his eyes and hailed us a cab.

"I can't believe we didn't learn a word of Portuguese," he said. "We are true morons. It's like we have perfected it to an art at this point."

"Not true—I know at least two Portuguese words," I said in protest. "A Brazilian guy in Toronto once told me he wanted to give me the *beso negro*."

"What is that?"

"I think it translates to black kiss, like licking a butthole."

"Great, well, that should be all we need to survive here, Jordan." His sarcasm was palpable.

Ben and I settled into our hotel, adjacent to the uber gay Ipanema Beach. After sobering up and pressing our shirts, we strolled two blocks toward the unofficial "tourist zone" to mow down some tapas and stiff margaritas.

"I can't understand a word of this menu," I said, visibly distressed. "Get the Google translation app out."

"We left our phones at the Airbnb, remember?" Ben frowned at the menu. "We have to. We can't take them out. All my Brazilian friends said pickpockets are ubiquitous in this town."

"OK, let's just point to something and we'll eat that," I said. "How about that?"

"That's a terrible idea," said Ben.

"You're a terrible idea," I replied.

"Well, your mom had a terrible idea decades ago."

As we bickered back and forth for several minutes, I noticed we had caught the attention of a local, one table over, adorning a deep red soccer jersey and sitting alone with a novel. He had curly, dirty-blond hair, broad shoulders, and blue eyes. He had also built up nearly every muscle group possible in a homo sapiens.

"Hola," I said, waving him over. "Do you speak English?"

He nodded.

"Are you a homosexual?"

He nodded again with a smile… a cock-loving smile.

"Great," said Ben. "We're going to need a translator. Do you want to join us?"

"OK," said the man, pulling up a chair beside me.

I mouthed "shotgun" to Ben and shot the mystery man a wink.

"I'm Jordan." I extended my hand. "And I've had all three HPV shots. This is Ben."

"Lucas," he stated. "You are Americans?"

"Canadians," Ben corrected him. "I assume you live here?"

"Yes, yes," he replied. "Five years this year."

During dinner we learned Lucas was a 24-year old refined, sugar-sweet single man working as an executive assistant for a billionaire in Rio. We both quickly realized that he was a self-assured man you could depend on through thick and thin. A man who would love you for your insides and outsides, and open his heart expecting extraordinarily little in return. No drama or games, just the purest form of romanticism.

OTIS: And who the hell has time for that?

To best ensure I would be shooting like a Bellagio fountain later that evening I decided to lock the majority of my personality deep into a vault. I'd tried this sort of tactic in the past to maximize a man's attraction and I found it often yielded the highest returns.

So… I wouldn't roast him. I would be a demure lady, desexualized and non-threatening. I'd tiptoe around his delicate male ego and chuckle at every one of his subpar jokes. I wouldn't tell him his future career plans had more holes than Swiss cheese. I was a new man, just for Lucas. Don't consider it growth. Consider it vacation street smarts.

By dessert, the plan had hatched successfully. Lucas rubbed my leg and looked deep into my eyes as I told him about donating my kidney last summer to save a young orphan boy in Tanzania. I asked him if I could wear his gold cross because I was a disciple of the Lord. I even sweetened the pot during dessert by letting him know that for Lent this year I was thinking of giving up water entirely.

"Are you sure that is safe?" he asked.

"It's in God's hands," I replied.

"You two are going to be something great," said Ben, raising his glass of wine. "I can just feel it."

I clinked Ben's glass with mine. "It's in God's hands."

An hour later, Lucas took Ben and me to a local gay bar off the beaten path, where we washed down our tapas with mojitos. It was a minuscule place with a fire capacity of less than 100. In the sea of deep tans and jet-black hair, there was only one redhead (Ben) and a blondie (Moi). The locals licked their chops and began to circle around us like a pack of famished hyenas.

"Do you feel like everyone is staring?" said Ben.

"They are staring," said Lucas. "All staring."

"I feel like Claudia Schiffer," I replied, curling up in Lucas' shoulder nook. "Do I look like her, Lucas?"

"You are more beautiful, Jordan," said Lucas.

"We're Brazil 10s!" yelled Ben. "Rio is going great already."

A group of men moved within a few feet of us and started to form a half circle, as if Ben and I were conducting a press conference at the podium. Lucas acted as translator as they posed questions. They looked at us with wonderment, like we were Martians who had descended from a faraway galaxy.

"What are they saying, Lucas?"

"Basic questions. Like where you're from and how long you're going to be here. And that last guy said he's really happy there are tourists in town because that usually means that he's about to get laid."

"He's right about that," said Ben.

"Hey, my mojito doesn't have a lime," I said, ignoring the onlookers.

Lucas kissed me on the cheek. "I'll get it."

It was indisputable. My Brazilian boyfriend was a provider. I knew one day he would fetch limes for the little *meninos* we would adopt together, once they began drinking in grade seven, like their father.

"I think I felt an egg drop," I said to Ben. "Tonight, we make love."

"You cannot go home with him," said Ben. "You don't know him and our one rule was that we would not go home with strangers. It is too dangerous. Don't be stupid for once in your life."

"I know, I'm not an idiot."

But by now, you know I am.

Nearly six hours after our plane had touched down in Rio, I broke the golden rule and stumbled shitfaced across Lucas' apartment, ripping my clothes off in the kitchen. Within minutes we started having sex in his shower as the steam escaped through a screenless, open window. I poked my head out and surveyed the full moon illuminating the distant mountains. I had arrived, bringing cross-border relations to the country of Brazil, the official ambassador for white privileged imbeciles everywhere.

I heard the Canadian national anthem start to play in my head as I saluted the night sky before me. Blackout sex, the great unifier. An expression of faux intimacy. I felt like I was melding our nations' cultural differences.

I was just emerging from a blackout moment to find we had moved to a new position, me on all fours, when it happened.

First, a small speck out of the corner of my eye. The tiniest brown object surfing a stream of water, slowly moving toward the drain.

I gasped.

Oh no, I thought. *That had BETTER be the world's smallest Glosette Raisin.*

It was not.

It was digested Moqueca tapas rearing its most ugly head. I watched it hit the drain and sit dormant, lodged in the grate. I gasped again, felt my stomach plummet, and then panicked, grabbing a shampoo bottle to smash it deep into the ether.

SMASH! SMASH! DIE, DEMON! SMASH SMASH!

Lucas slapped my ass and asked, "Hey, what are you doing, Canadian?"

"Sorry! It was a baby bug," I said, smashing it for the second time. "But I think I killed it."

Maybe it WAS a bug, I thought. My vision was blurring over and I felt the onset of the spins.

"OK," said Lucas.

"Umm, you're welcome," I replied. "That bug could have REALLY ruined the mood."

He slapped my ass again, and I gently faded into another blackout.

Eight hours later, I woke up naked in Lucas' bed to piercing sun rays bouncing around his all-white apartment. My hangover was nothing short of barbarous. I ran my eyes up and down the walls, which resembled a medical clinic. The shifting on the mattress woke Lucas, who turned over and put his arm around my chest.

"Oh no," I gasped, grabbing my throbbing skull, and then stopping to check for organ removal wounds. "This is not good, Lucas."

"Why?" asked Lucas. "This is good. We can be happy now and I'll come visit you in Canada."

"Canada?"

"Yes," he said. "You are my man."

"Lucas." I had to level with him. "I fear I released a micro turd in your shower last night during our lovemaking. Am I seriously the sort of man you want to build a future with?"

"It doesn't bother me," he replied, smiling.

"Oh, great. You noticed. Just great. Listen, I need to head back to the hotel," I said. "Ben is going to be furious with me. I don't have my phone, so you'll have to write your number on my forearm. Also, I'll need two Advil just to be able to walk. Sound good?"

After Lucas pulled up Google Maps and provided me with cursory directions on how to get back to my hotel, I left. Within ten minutes I was lost on the beach in Rio with my shoes in my hand. Realizing I might never kiss my mother again, I bought a coconut with a straw and drank it on the rocks, holding back a tsunami of tears. Fifty minutes later, I somehow made it back, a journey that I would later find out was only six minutes from Lucas' place.

I found Ben in the lounge enjoying the hotel's gorgeous continental breakfast: lukewarm milk, mangos, and cold cuts.

"Oh, that's nice." Ben smirked. "Looks like I won't need to call your family today and tell them you're being buried in a park in Rio de Janeiro."

"What's wrong with me?" I said. "Why didn't you try to stop me?"

"Have you met yourself?!" he asked, infuriated. "No one can ever stop you. I tried, but you pushed me off and yelled, 'Don't wait up!' I think you tried to wink at me but you were using both your eyes. Then you just slithered away into the night."

"Oh God. Well on the positive side, I umm, don't mean to brag here, but Lucas wants to meet my family."

Ben threw his head back laughing. "He's sweet," he said. "I'm sure you'll sabotage it like I would."

"It's not a great romance," I said. "I don't want to be tied down on vacation."

"Yes, of course." Ben was well used to my modus operandi. "Why have one great guy when we can have eight awful ones?"

"Exactly," I said. "That's what I'm saying."

I paused and poured myself a coffee and then returned to Ben's table.

"Anyway, Lucas is totally in love with me."

"Well, that's not surprising," he said with a chuckle. "Don't flatter yourself. You're a one-way ticket to permanent residency and clearly gullible as shit."

"He doesn't just love me for my citizenship," I said. "He loves me for the fake persona I've been putting on this whole time."

"Oh whatever," Ben replied. "You are an easy target around here with your stupid blond highlights."

Rio's beaches are both disordered and perilous. Usually once a week, the children from the ghetto storm the beach in a pack of about 80, charging at people and ransacking their valuables. Screams erupt and people take off in all directions, their bags in

Hiking in Rio.

hand. Then the police chase them with helicopters that hover 25 feet or so above the water. This whole madness carries on for about 15 minutes or so. It is incredibly scenic.

Amidst the sea of shabby marijuana and salty seafood vendors, I waved down a local carrying a sign for henna tattoos and a mangled white binder tucked under his armpit. Once he passed me the binder, I flipped through the pages to find a design I could sport ironically.

"I'll take the tribal," I said, pointing to the third design down on the first page.

"I want one, too!" yelled Ben. "On my upper arm."

"OK, copycat. What do you want?"

"Ummm." Ben flipped furiously through the pages. "I'll take

the shark, please. The shark emerging from the water with the fish coming out of its mouth. And sir, can you add a few extra fish for free?"

The tattoo "artist" nodded and woefully freehanded my tribal design. After he finished, he moved to Ben's, which upon completion looked nothing like a shark and more like an eel that had an apartment in the heart of Chernobyl. I started to think that like Prince, the man was "the artist formally known as the mojito guy." After we paid him in full, he asked us if we needed anything else.

"I have tours, bathing suit, and fun fun party stuff," he said with a wink.

He had piqued my interest. "Explain the last one."

"Well, whatever you need to have fun fun. Maybe the ecstasy or cocaina."

"Cocaina," said Ben.

"OK," he said. "Where I deliver?"

Ben gave him our hotel address and told him to come by just after 6 p.m. He nodded and provided us with a business card with his cell phone number circled. It was a thunderbolt. The man was an employee of the Ministry of Tourism in Brazil. Talk about international accommodations.

After our tattoos dried, we voyaged into the petrifying waves to cool down. We returned to dry off and were abruptly approached by three local Brazilians. They were some of the skinniest men I had ever laid eyes on, and I suspected together, they weighed a combined 300 pounds.

"We been watching you guys," said the first. "Very white skin on the red one."

"Yes," I said. "He has a terminal illness."

"Like AIDS?"

"Kinda," I replied. "It's not looking good."

"Weeks to live," said Ben.

"Oh, I sorry," he replied.

"That's fine," I said. "You didn't know. Where's the party tonight? We got cocaina."

"Oh we love cocaina," said the second.

"We go to top of Favelas," said the third, whose name sounded like Donatella, so I called him that. "Um, you come?"

"Yes, we come," said Ben. "We come everywhere."

"It sounds incredibly elegant," I replied.

Donatella smiled and nodded, then gave his number to Ben. Around 7 p.m., we showered and devoured a protein bar each. When the tattoo "artist" arrived with our gift, we smashed two rails while preparing for a rousing evening in the Favelas, which we imagined to be an extravagant secret society.

"Do you think they'll have a terrace?"

"Maybe," Ben replied. "I mean if it's overlooking the city it's probably some sort of fancy house party."

"Should I wear my silk boxers?" I asked, applying a coat of bronzer to my face.

"No, and wait. I'm going to text Lucas to make sure it's safe," said Ben, reaching for his phone. "We really didn't probe them for much information at all. I'll send him the address and see what he replies."

Ten minutes passed.

"Lucas wrote back," said Ben, handing me his phone. "He highly advises against it."

"What does he know?" I dismissively replied. "Let's head out."

Ben and I hailed a cab and ordered the driver, in broken Portuguese, to take us directly to the Favelas. Ben told him the address as best he could. He gave us a look like we'd ordered him to tandem parachute us into Darfur. That should have been our signal to abandon our plans with the boys from the beach, but because we both have an obsessive affinity for wild adventures at any cost, we trekked onward.

The cab ride took 15 wild, swervy minutes, and eventually stopped beside 20-30 cops holding AK-47s. It looked like a four-car crash scene. Siren lights on top of cars were rotating, hitting our faces and then flashing against a concrete wall. We looked up. There were small apartments, several stories high with little to no space between them. They were very dilapidated, and some were painted in bright pastel colours. Some had windows smashed in. The air felt tense.

The driver nodded and opened the door for us.

"Favelas?" said Ben to the driver.

He nodded again and took off without another word.

It was just Ben and me and the police. Oh, and all of their unnervingly massive guns. I was confused. Were these men private security for the luxury party at the top of the mountain? Wow. How VIP was this?

"Where the fuck are we?" said Ben in his baby blue Banana Republic shorts. "Is this a checkpoint?"

"Maybe it's private security for the party."

"It's definitely not that," he replied. "They're regular police."

"What is this place?" I paused and took in the scene again. "It looks like someone's about to put a gun in our mouths and ask us where our cartel leader is."

Ben nodded. "Hmmm. Yes. This is not good."

Then we saw Donatella and his friends. They approached

us calmly and Donatella said, "OK, you pay $5 and then get on motorbike and man will take you to top where bar is. Five minute."

"And then we just wait to die?" asked Ben.

"Donatella," I said. "This seems like an awful idea. Everyone is in SWAT gear. What are the Favelas?"

"Like a ghetto," he said. "Where poor people live."

The favelas were "cleaned up" just before the World Cup in 2014 and the 2016 Summer Olympics. Since then, the Foreign Office advice for British tourists has been quoted as follows:

"There are high levels of poverty and very high levels of violent crime in shanty-towns (favelas), which exist in all major Brazilian cities. All favelas are unpredictably dangerous areas, and remain high risk given the level of violence within them and the severe strain on police resources."

Not exactly a fancy soirée.

"And what's at the top?" Ben asked Donatella.

"A bar," he replied. He walked forward, his two friends following behind him, and stopped at a line of motorcycles in a row. Each had a Brazilian man at the helm waiting for a passenger. He paid the first driver $5 and hopped on the back of the first bike in the line.

He turned back to us. "Very very beautiful view, boys. You will like. OK, now we go."

"These are the days of our lives," I said to Ben, rubbing the top of his back.

Donatella entwined his hands around the driver's waist and just before they headed up the mountain, he yelled back to us, "You hear guns, you stay calm!"

Then he was gone.

I watched his two friends do the same, zooming up the hill and around the bend.

"Did he just say if you hear guns, stay calm?" asked Ben.

"He absolutely said that," I replied.

I hopped on the back of the bike and the driver, without saying a word, started to ascend the mountain at breakneck speed. From base to peak, it was a five-minute, wild, meandering journey. Small boomboxes blasted Portuguese rap tracks as we whizzed by. Families of six were eating dinner on makeshift porches, each of their suspicious gazes following mine. A few pit bulls, restrained on chains, lunged at the bikes. I looked in the side mirror and saw the headlights of two other bikes, tailing close behind.

When we pulled down a small alley and arrived at the bar, I was shaking. We paid our cover and walked around the back to the patio. It was a long drop after the back fence, maybe hundreds of feet down to sea level. A shift in tectonic plates could have shaken the whole bar right off the edge. I heard gang music playing in the distance. Three guys sat on their motorcycles and stared at us with ominous gazes from the parking lot. I swear they never blinked.

It was as scary as the bottom of the hill but in a different way. We couldn't actually see the guns but I could feel them. Illegally procured for sure. There were red Christmas lights strung across the open wood ceiling planks which made up the roof. It almost looked like a Tiki Bar. That's all I can remember.

But I could never forget the view, which was nothing short of stupendous. You could see Ipanema Beach and thousands of city lights reflected in the ocean. Hundreds of palm trees surrounded the top of the mountains and the bar. There was a cool ocean salty breeze that moved through my Goldwell-bleached highlights.

We danced for hours with Donatella & Co. Like nearly every South American resident I've met, they had a natural sway in the hips. They twirled us around, pouring shots in our mouths, each jockeying for a position to copulate with us. When we tried to speak, they'd cover our mouths, fulfilling the wishes of most of my ex-boyfriends.

"Shhhh. If they know you not from here, then danger," said Donatella. "Quiet."

This cautionary comment might have been something I would have treated with a level of solemnity if my travel companion did not look like an understudy for Casper the Friendly Ghost. We were totally fucked. Easy targets. People thought we were millionaires. Donatella and his friends kept asking us how many servants we had. I didn't even have a car. I'd rob me in a second. In my head, I started a five-minute countdown to shank-fest.

Then the bar started to fill with a crowd that looked like they were on a day trip from a maximum-security state penitentiary. I danced in the corner with the boys and Ben, trying not to make eye contact. More stared. One winked.

My heart rate nearly doubled.

Ben looked at me. "This is one of our worst ideas and you know there are tons to pick from."

I felt my primary anxiety response kick in. Lower back sweat. I dabbed it with my pink Ralph Lauren polo.

Twenty minutes later, a fist fight broke out. Our reaction, analogous to 14-year-old-school girls, sent more eyes on us. We were defenceless tourist bait and we weren't welcome here. It was palpable.

We were trapped on a mountain with three skinny ectomorphs who couldn't possibly defend us. Plus, we lacked cell service and even the most basic homemade knife.

I wondered if these were my final hours and a wave of

distress washed over me. I couldn't die. I had accomplished so little. I promised Patrick I'd find love again and I wasn't even close.

I hadn't been to Italy, or eaten escargot in bed.

I hadn't contracted an STI that no one had even heard of yet, and then sat down with Diane Sawyer to talk about being patient zero.

And I hadn't adopted a homosexual dog, one that I planned to rescue after he was bullied by the other dogs for betraying gender norms and painting his nails.

Ben and I started mainlining drinks to fight the looming trepidation, but he was beating me two to one. Fifteen minutes later he told me he had a secret. I prayed it was a plan to get out of the bar.

Then he said, "Soooooooooo I found out that Donatella's friends are a couple, an open couple, and they are so in love it's absolutely disgusting. I found them at the bar and guess what, they are so grossly in love, they made up their own love language."

"Ben, that's Portuguese."

"Shut up!" he yelled, and slapped me across the face.

"Stop drawing attention to us, homo!" I yelled, and slapped him back.

More eyes on us. I swear they were moving closer.

"Are we going to die here, Ben?" I exclaimed. "How do we even escape? We barely have any money left, no cell service, there don't seem to be any cabs, and I'm not doing that 30-minute walk down the mountain at 2 a.m. You think these three skeletons are going to defend our honour? They couldn't even beat a chicken in a fist fight."

"Listen to meeee," said Ben, with slitted eyes. "We're like catsssss. We have 12 lives."

One of the onlookers coughed, then winked.

"Cats have nine lives," I replied.

"I said nine," said Ben.

"You're useless," I replied. "A total waste of cells in a moment like this."

"I am not," said Ben. "Let's go make friends."

"Do not make friends," I said, nervously scanning the room. "We are royally fucked, you know that?"

Ben sat on a picnic bench beside me.

"This is my fault," I said. "Fuck." My right leg started to shake and I started to pull on my right eyebrow hairs one by one, a symptom of a disorder I have called Trichotillomania.

"You're doingggg it againnn," slurred Ben. "Your eyebrows. You told me to tell you when you're doing it."

"Shut up!" I yelled. "It's warranted."

OTIS: Hey drama queen. One friend wouldn't hurt.

JORDAN: Dude, would you shut up for three seconds? I'm trying to strategize.

I went to put my hand over his tiny monkey mouth but ended up covering his whole face. ***God, I feel like a PARENT with you two idiots,*** I told him.

I looked toward the bar and the onlookers. There were even more of them now. The air felt tense; the stars looked dimmed. I gulped.

And then I saw him, walking toward me with his cheery smile and bursting biceps, his baby blue polo and gargantuan thighs.

"LUCAS!" I screamed.

Ben reached out his arms. "WE'RE SAVEEEEDD!"

I ran as fast as I could into Lucas' embrace.

"My puta," he said, kissing my forehead.

How many more signs did I need? He was my one and only. Uninvited, he had scaled a mountain through dice rolling and first-degree murder plots to save me. He sensed my radiating pain and swooped in in response. In Toronto, I couldn't even get a man to make a dinner reservation.

It was all I had ever wanted. Unconditional love so powerful it could bring a tear to my eye and warmth to my heart. It was transcendent. *You better get ready sir,* I thought. *Tonight, I have ANOTHER micro turd with your name all over it.*

"Oh Lucas!" I cried. "You saved us."

"Not yet," he replied, kissing my forehead again. "We should leave after some Samba. OK?"

"OK," I said, nodding.

So we did just that and then scurried out of the bar, leaving our three new friends to fend for themselves.

"Carry me down the mountain," I whispered to Lucas.

"What?"

"I want to be carried down the mountain by you, my white knight, while you feed me acai berries," I whispered.

"Shh, don't make noise," he said. "We still are in danger."

"We can never be in danger with love by our side," I said, putting my arm around his waist.

In the days that followed, Lucas was both my life partner and our tour guide. He told me Canadians were generally cold and detached but he knew I was different. Was I? I thought I was still acting. All the Brazilian men we met were nothing like stereotypical Canadians. They were insanely fit and operated like five-alarm fires, scorching us with hot love.

Periodically Lucas would stop and ask me, with full sincerity, if Christmas would be a good time to meet my mother. Ben and I would laugh, and Lucas wouldn't, and then it would happen again eight hours later. It's a real ego mind-fuck when you don't know if a man can separate his love for you from his love for a potential green card.

One night he took us to the nightclub, where we all smashed rails in a bathroom stall while two guys banged one stall over. Guys blew air in our face to signal a makeout with us, which we did, to the tune of three men each. Lucas didn't care. He was happy just to have a small part of me. It was freeing. At 7.a.m. we left the club to blinding sunlight and took a cab back to Lucas' apartment. I suggested we make a pit stop to run in the waves and we did, in our boxers, until a wave engulfed us and rendered Ben's iPhone kaput.

"Santa Maria!" he screamed.

"Our clothes have lots of sand," said Lucas, once we arrived back at shore. "We shower at my place now!"

"Don't yell at us," said Ben. "It's bad enough I lost my phone and now I don't need an angry voice in my ear."

Lucas grinned and screamed, "Inside, bitch!"

"Lukey, I love it when you get nasty." I kissed him on the lips.

"And I love you too," he replied.

"Oh, ummm." I was caught off guard. "I love me too?"

Then the three of us went back to Lucas' place and showered naked, playful ass slaps and all.

"Where was the *bug*?" asked Ben.

"Oh, it landed right there." I pointed to the grate.

"He killed it," said Lucas.

I nodded. "Like a real man."

"You're a disgusting animal," said Ben.

"Oh, well, SORRY for digesting foods."

Then we all nestled into bed together and Lucas turned on a gay Brazilian movie with subtitles. I caught my reflection in the side mirror; I looked deathly ill, with a skin tone that resembled a roti.

"I'm going to fall asleep," I said to Ben and Lucas, then turned on my side.

"Aren't you going to watch to the end, puta?" asked Lucas.

"It's fine," I said. "Every gay movie ends the same way. Ass licking, family turmoil and then one of them dies of AIDS."

Lucas kissed me on the forehead. "This is true."

I fell asleep that night with Lucas spooning me and Ben conked out on the far side of the bed.

I thought about how Lucas was the kind of man I could really get to know better, to understand deeper and to build a connection with that I would remember for a lifetime. I vowed to stay monogamous until my flight to Sao Paulo 39 hours later. After that, all bets would be off.

Old habits die hard.

And everyone knows dying alone is the new relationship.

CHAPTER FIVE

COLOMBIA

After Rio, Ben and I returned to Toronto with a completely warped sense of self. Weeks in Brazil had bred delusions of grandeur that seemed to proliferate each day of travel. The incoming crash down to Earth would be undeniably devastating.

Let's go to Woody's this weekend, I texted Ben, two days after our return to the city. *I still feel that spell over us. My pheromones are the boldest they've ever been.*

Well, I do feel more confident, he replied. *But perhaps that's just lingering from the past week.*

Only one way to find out, I texted back.

OK let's try.

It was a total letdown.

Just like we speculated, Brazil had only temporarily altered our overall sex appeal. Our looks, which were an invaluable commodity less than a week ago, now felt like mere penny stocks. It was all a cruel mirage, a short tease into the fairy tale life of a Dolce & Gabbana supermodel.

"Why is no one hitting on us?" asked Ben, as we congregated near the back bar. "It feels odd."

"I was thinking the same thing." I felt almost disturbed. "We're coming down hard off an unending avalanche of external validation. We need to go back to South America before our egos crumble to specks of dust."

He nodded.

I mentally consulted my social calendar. "March?"

"Too far away," he replied. "What are you doing in three weeks?"

"You're not serious, Ben." I stared at him. "It's an entirely different continent."

"Well then, what's a cheap, easy trip we can do in a weekend?" he asked. "Vegas? What about Vegas?"

"Absolutely not."

I hate Vegas. It's a shit stain of wretched excess. The casinos are piled high with morbidly obese Americans, many of whom are from states I never plan on visiting. Vegas is the embodiment of nearly all the things I loathe about modern American culture: high-fructose slushies, quasi-pimp bouncers, gluttonous buffet brunches, neon tube dresses, and the little Cirque du Soleil performers who I kept finding in the bottom of my jean pockets.

And the dry desert heat is diabolical. Sure, maybe it is tolerable for a couple days, but around day three, every orifice in your body starts to dry up. By day four, you should expect to receive a text from your now chapped and disintegrating asshole that reads, *Yo man, we gotta get the hell outta here.*

Vegas was completely out of the question.

"Ben, I'm not going to Vegas." My tone was firm. "We're probably considered even less hot there. Toronto is the most diverse city in the world. We should be able to find some men of South American origin around these parts, no?"

Two weeks later, Ben called me.

"We're going to Colombia."

"Colombia?! Are we working for the cartel now?"

"No. That's the old Colombia. The new Colombia has cocaine, yes—and it's $5 a gram by the way—but also great food, stunning weather, $1 beers and lots of great sightseeing."

Fourteen minutes later I called Ben back.

"OK, *The New York Times* says it's grand! Let's go."

"I'm so excited."

"And I'm so sick of being a Canadian eight. It's downright demoralizing."

Several months later, we touched down in Bogota, an incredibly accommodating, unexpectedly safe city, set 8600 ft. above sea level. The mountains were picturesque, towering above a city which oozed that unmistakable South American hospitality from every corner. Hugging, touching, double cheek kissing, the whole nine yards. It's nice—and consensual about 80% of the time. People stay off their phones for the most part and connect on a deeper wavelength. It feels like all they need is a good, vintage red wine and three-hour conversation. They even look into your eyes more deeply when you talk.

Because of the dramatic altitude changes in Bogota, it is recommended that you don't drink in the city on day one. Ben and I circumvented that rule by arriving shitfaced and washing it down with cocaine that we procured a mere hour after checking into our hotel. But this wasn't your ex-boyfriend's watered-down cocaine in Toronto—you know, one part cocaine, 10 parts hydrofluoric acid. This was the holy grail… with no warning.

I know this to be objectively true because we decided to try a minuscule line before dinner and then didn't speak for the next 40 minutes as we concentrated on not dying. We devoured our entire meal in total silence, like an 80-year-old Eastern European couple.

Four nights later, we went to a nightclub called Theatron. The entrance fee was $20 USD, which was for both cover and *unlimited alcohol all night.* Upon entry, you're handed a plastic cup. Whenever you desire another drink, you walk up to the bartender and extend it forward, like you're in *Oliver Twist.* "*Please sir, may I vomit another?*"

At some point, everyone is utterly blitzed and loses their cups. I realized it was probably for the best when someone vomited on my shoes, like in *The Exorcist,* at 4 a.m. Gagging, I turned to my bestie and said, "Let's go man, the vomit was tonight's Theatron swan song."

Ben reluctantly agreed, but as we made our way out of the club, he stopped in his tracks and slurred, "I just spotted my sooooulmate."

"No, you did not." I had no patience for Ben's sudden foray into romance. "Every man within these walls thinks they are our soulmates. It's like you told me in Brazil. We are walking targets. Drunken fools who will do anything for cheap external validation. I mean, I would totally target us. Wouldn't you?!"

He ignored me completely "I'll be riiiight back," he slurred, stumbling away.

Ben chatted with his "soulmate," who was named Mateo, for the better part of 45 minutes. I entertained myself by shimmying up to his best friend and dancing with his arms draped over my shoulders. It was a lot of fun. That is, until he twirled me around and shoved his hand down my ass crack.

"NO... ME... GUSTA!" I screamed, shoving his body four feet.

People think I'm kidding when I say testosterone is a poison. But I'm not kidding at all.

I grabbed Ben, who was situated by the back bar, looking like he was completely high on Mateo's perspiration, and dragged him toward the exit. Mateo and the rapist followed us outside the club and casually asked us, in a tone usually reserved for questions about the weather, if we would like to engage in a foursome.

"It's a no from me," I said. "Besides, we leave for Cartagena at 6 a.m."

Ben shot me a look, but capitulated and followed me into the cab, glued to his phone the entire ride back to the hotel.

That "glue" proved to be imperishable, as Ben was still obsessively texting Mateo the next morning at the airport. He barely looked up from his phone from the time we passed security to the second the plane accelerated off the tarmac. I was worried. Ben and I were like a Venn diagram, different in our personalities but overlapping in our snark and in our secret quest for love, disguised as high jinks. I knew the lengths he would go to be loved, and they were even further than my own.

"Why do you keep texting him?" I asked. "You're never going to see him again."

"You never know," he said.

Cartagena is a beautiful city, located off a major port on the coast of Colombia. The old city (the most notable area) is encircled by a colossal wall. The streets are uncharacteristically narrow and home to some of the best cuisine that has ever touched my palate. And all for no more than about $60 for a five-course meal.

If you go, visit Carmen for the tasting menu. Tell them Jordan Power sent you. They will have no idea who you're talking about, but it will be our fun little game.

After Ben and I checked into our hotel around sunset, he hopped in the shower. I didn't waste a second, perusing the Grindr prospects within the vicinity of our fourth-floor suite. I hadn't even made it to the sixth line of the grid when I heard the trademark Grindr sound: *DAH-DUM.* I opened the message.

His name was Hugo, a citizen of Colombia with roots a two-hour plane ride to the south. He was on vacation with 15 of his family members, sleeping in adjacent hotel rooms on the penthouse floor.

When Ben left the washroom after his shower, he had a towel around his waist and a white comb moving through his red hair. I told him I had made plans for us. We'd be heading straight up to the roof for a quick drink and an itty-bitty smooch with my new boy, Hugo.

"That was what, seven minutes?" he asked. "You're an absolute maniac."

"Yeah, but I'm your maniac." I raised my eyebrows seductively.

Hugo was easy to spot, one of only eight people at the pool, and the only fuckable one. I grabbed two piña coladas and walked over to his lounger.

"Is that for me?" asked Ben, walking beside me.

"No, it's for Hugo," I replied. "Get your own."

Hugo spoke fairly fluent English and caught on to almost all of our Canadian idioms and attempts at sarcasm. This was my nightmare. My personality, while unveiled entirely, is an anti-aphrodisiac. Men want to be entertained but most hate being roasted and, as you've probably learned by now, I can't help myself. It

Our hotel rooftop pool. Coming for you, Hugo.

wouldn't last. He'd be soft within an hour. Sadly, I had no choice but to revert to the Jordan of my Lucas days to get what I wanted. I'd become a milquetoast, respectful, saccharine suitor, who would not overshare his sexual past or dispose of men like tissues.

OTIS: In short... a demon from hell.

"You're like no one I've ever met," Hugo said, as we waded down the steps into the pool.

"Oh no, you noticed?" I rubbed his shoulder. "That's not good. Geez, I must be even more of a nightmare than I originally thought."

"Huh?"
"Nothing."

Cartagena, as a tiny walled city, isn't exactly what you would call a major party town.

Our friend Lorenzo in Toronto had insisted we meet up with his friend Pablo, who managed a seafood restaurant within the walls. He had a giving soul, oozing with alcoholic tendencies. He took us on a mini-tour in and around the city for two days, eating tapas, sampling cocktails, and watching the sunset. He also talked me out of bringing several stray dogs home with me on the plane.

"I would be a great father. You know I'd be a great father," I said, as we all started into a mid-day blackout. "Pablooooooo, tell me I'd make a good father. I need to hear you say it, big boy."

"OK," said Pablo. "Yes, OK, you will."

I started to pet two of the dogs at once. "Daddy's going to get you out of here, boys," I assured them. "Daddy is taking you both home."

"Oh, for Christ's sake, Jordan!" yelled Ben. "I can see the ticks jumping from here."

"Leave them alone." I scratched my new canine children behind their ears. "It gives them character."

Around sundown, Ben told Pablo and me that we had one more box to check before leaving the city two days later. He pulled a small piece of paper from his left pocket with a single phrase scribbled on hotel stationary.

"We need boner spray," said Ben, waving the paper in our faces. "Lorenzo said we absolutely have to try the boner spray."

"Excuse me?" I replied. "What is boner spray?"

"Boner spray is a spray you put on your tongue and then soon thereafter you get a boner. It's just as it sounds," said Ben.

"I have never heard of this thing you say," slurred Pablo, his arm around my shoulder.

"Well, I hadn't heard of it either, Pablo," said Ben. "So that is why we have to try it!"

"Is it Viagra?"

"I don't know," he replied. "Do I look like a fucking doctor?"

"What you look like, sir, is an imbecile with no information at all," I said. "Do we need a prescription for this magical boner spray?"

"No," said Ben. "Lorenzo said you just ask the pharmacist and it's usually right on the counter."

"Well then, Pablo, you're up!" We sent him to the pharmacy across the road with a wad of cash in his hand.

After he left, I turned to Ben, "So after the three of us take this boner spray in the hotel room, what exactly are we supposed to do?"

"I don't know," said Ben. "I didn't really think that far ahead."

Pablo found the spray and danced back across the road, waving it in the air. We took a 30-minute walk across the shoreline as a full moon emerged through the sparse clouds, leaving a warm glow on our cheeks. We passed the boner spray back and forth, spraying it onto our tongues two times each, like the package recommended. It tasted like what I imagine ammonia tastes like.

Ben and Pablo were holding hands, which was all the

foreboding I required to know that at some point I would inevitably be left in solitude with my boner while they hooked up. That would not do. I texted Hugo and asked him to join us on our balcony in room 402.

He wrote back, *Great, and I will bring marijuana. OK?*

Hugo arrived 20 minutes later and pulled up a chair as we drank vodka tonics overlooking the vacant beach. Ben asked him to open his mouth and sprayed twice on his tongue, without telling him what it was.

"What is that?" asked Hugo.

"Boner spray," said Ben. "You'll thank me later."

"Anyone feeling anything?" I asked the group, poking my crotch.

"I think I'm feeling a half chub," said Ben.

"Same," I said. "About one-fifth erect. Pablo?"

"No boner," he replied. "I want boner."

Hugo began to talk at length about his personal branding company, started two years prior. He pulled up the designs on his phone, which were printed across hoodies, T-shirts, tanks, and beach towels. Each option was more hideous than the next. They looked like Ed Hardy knockoffs created with substandard ink machines. They were tacky AF. As he spoke, Ben, Pablo, and I passed a joint. After we killed it, we immediately started to roll another.

"Can we translate these for you?" I said, with bloodshot eyes. "This one just says 'the party is to party,' which doesn't make sense at all."

"It's slang," said Hugo.

"OK, but I've never heard anyone say this."

"I like it," said Pablo.

"Guys, where's the boner spray?" Ben searched under his

chair. "I'm ready to see what this city has to offer."

"We've already done the max dose," I replied. "Just wait a bit more."

"I do more," said Pablo. "I do now."

Then he sprayed it twice more onto his tongue and did the same to Ben.

"Jesus Christ," I said.

Then I paused and opened my mouth to receive a double spray. "OK, well, I guess if I must."

I held the boner spray up to Otis.

OTIS: Bitch I'm only 8 pounds.

JORDAN: Right.

"Hugo, you're up."

"I did two," he said. "Again?"

"Yes, again," I replied.

"He's gonna stroke," said Ben.

"Stroke?" said Hugo.

"It's slang, like your shirts. It means you're gonna have a great time." I pried his mouth open and gave him a double spray.

"This boner spray sucks," said Ben, 10 minutes later.

"Yes, sucks," said Pablo.

"Just give it a minute," I replied. "It tastes rancid, which leads me to believe it works. Otherwise, why would they make it taste like this?"

"Well, it better," said Ben. "I had high hopes."

Twenty minutes after that, Pablo stood up. "Whoaaaaaaaa." His boner was at full mast, brutally restrained under his jean shorts. "HA-HAAAAAAAAAAAAA!"

"It's like, almost painful!" yelled Ben, pulling his raging boner back and letting it violently smack into Pablo's calf. *SMACK. SMACK. SMACK*

"OW!" I grabbed my crotch. "Guys, I feel like mine is about to blow off the balcony and land on the beach." I winced. "I feel like I did too much."

It throbbed like a toe I'd just stubbed on a wall. It was the most engorged my penis had ever been in my life. I felt like a rockstar but I'd need looser shorts.

"THIS is kinda awkward." Ben stood up to head into the hotel room, erection still bursting at the seams. "Um, anyone need a refill?"

"I'll come with you," I said. "I need new shorts."

We returned with four triple drinks. I grabbed my phone, linked it to my Bluetooth travel speaker, and launched a Spotify playlist called "Girls Night Out." We all danced and grinded on each other like it was grade 11 prom, and at some point Hugo and I disappeared to the shower. Things were starting to get hazy and streaky.

"Should I ask to play? All of us to play?" he asked, as I hopped in the shower in my birthday suit.

"No, no," I said, shaking my head. "It's not that kinda party, Hugo."

"OK," he said, following me into the shower and grabbing the back of my head to make out.

"Can you turn down the heat?" I said, stopping him. "It's too much. The pressure, you know? I feel like my head is gonna blow off."

"OK." He adjusted the dial. "Better?"

"Yeah," I replied.

After we finished, which is a delicate way of saying, "sprayed semen all over the shower walls," we towelled off and Hugo pranced around the room admiring the size of his still insanely engorged penis. I ran mine under cold water to shrink it back down, all to no avail.

KNOCK! KNOCK! KNOCK!

Ben was at the washroom door. "We got a situation," he said, swigging from the tumbler in his hand.

"Excuse me, sir!" Hugo ran right past Ben, stopping to helicopter his penis in the middle of the room. He dropped the towel and started to increase the helicopter speed.

"Oh, my God." I sat, covering my eyes.

He swung it over and over, then he reversed direction.

"LOOK… AT… MY… PIJAAAAAAAAA!" he sang, totally shitfaced. "PI-JA… PI-JA"

"Oh, my God," I repeated, laughing.

"For the love of God. Put that away, Hugo!" yelled Ben. "Jordan, we have a situation."

"What's going on?"

"Well I'm glad you asked," said Ben. "While you two lovebirds were off lathering each other up, Pablo started to puke. First all over the balcony and then all over a pillow."

"Oh no," I replied. "I'm sorry. I would have helped you clean it up. I thought you guys were hooking up out here."

"No," he said. "No, we did not. I got a dry, 10-second hand job and then undigested calamari down my leg. Also, I saw olives in it."

"Where is he now?"

"I put him on the balcony with a towel over his head in an indefinite time out."

"How do you open this?" said Hugo, fiddling with the balcony sliding door. "I want to show Pablo my pija!"

"Would you just let him be, you idiot?" Ben groaned. "Stay inside."

"Hola, Pablo!" yelled Hugo.

He pulled his cock back and then flicked it forward like a catapult. It hit the glass and left a streak, like a handprint. Then he did it again. And again. *WHACK… WHACK.* It's a sight I can never unsee.

"Hugo, put that away!" I started to laugh uncontrollably, clenching my obliques. "HAAAAAAA… I'M SORRY, BEN… HAAAAAAAAAA."

"Oh, my God," said Ben, pacing in circles. "Oh, my God."

"I'm sorry," I said. "HAHAHA. Seriously, I'm sorry. HAHAHA."

Then Ben's face started to go beet red and he looked me right in the eyes.

"Jordan." He paused. "I don't think you understand the gravity of the situation. There is vomit everywhere. I smoked so much weed I can't even feel my face. Pablo's shirt fell off the balcony and hotel security came by the room while you two were in the shower due to noise complaints. And everyone is just RUNNING AROUND HERE WITH BONERS LIKE IT'S ALL GONNA BE OK!"

I continued laughing so hard I fell over the bed. My towel, which was secured around my waist loosened. It slid down my left side, exposing one of my ass cheeks.

"WELL, I'M GLAD YOU THINK IT'S FUCKING FUNNY." Ben was not amused. "BUT I KNOW FOR A FACT WHEN PEOPLE ARE JUST RUNNING AROUND WITH BONERS THAT MORE BAD THINGS ARE GONNA HAPPEN. OH MY GOD. I'M SO HIGH."

I suppressed another round of laughs. "It will be fine," I said, putting my hands on his shoulders. "I know how to calm this maniac down. I'll get right to it after I put my dick in the ice bucket for a minute."

I gave Hugo two melatonin and told him they were boner pills so we could "go at it again later." He took them both and passed out 20 minutes later. We carried Pablo to Ben's bed, *Weekend at Bernie's* style, and soon after, Ben and I tried to join them in the land of sleep. At 4.a.m., I woke up and angrily poked at Hugo to disrupt his slumber.

"Yeah, hi," I said.

He groggily opened his eyes to a slit.

"Listen, I'm about to tell you something that is going to change your life. You have a condition called sleep apnea. Write it down on the hotel pad."

Hugo rolled over and grabbed the pad as I handed him a pencil. I took them both from him and wrote on it in all caps—SLEEP APNEA—then folded it in half and placed it in his pocket.

"I suggest you have it treated immediately, as it could kill you, sir. Now please see yourself out."

The next morning, I woke up to the sound of Ben in the washroom. After he exited, I said, "Jesus Christ, that was the longest piss I've ever heard in my entire life."

Sheepish, he replied, "That wasn't a piss."

"Well it's not a South American vacation until one of us is shitting liquids every six hours." I replied. "That's for sure."

"I know. We need digestive enzymes," he said. "I think it's the meat."

"It's not just the meat, Ben." I shook my head. "It's the salty veggies, beer, wine, cocaine, and lest we forget... boner spray."

"Get showered," he replied, ignoring me. "Remember my ex, Marco? Well, he's an hour away, so we're going to meet up."

"I didn't agree to this."

"And I didn't agree to cleaning up vomit last night," he

replied. "So you're most definitely coming, especially since he casually sprung on me that he would be bringing his ex-boyfriend, with whom he is on vacation."

"The fucking nerve," I said. "What did you reply?"

"I just wrote back, *ohh that's nice,*" he said. "What else could I say? *I admire the way you move through life without an ounce of tact, sir?*"

"Well, I'm sure you sporadically sharting yourself all day will show him exactly what he's been missing."

"It's fine," he replied. "I don't even care about him anymore. I'm already in love with someone else."

"Oh, you're in love with Pablo?" I rolled my eyes.

"No, I'm totally falling for Mateo," he said. Right. Mateo. Friend of the rapist. Ben's "soul mate." I suppressed the urge to roll my eyes again.

"He lives in Bogota," I said. "What's wrong with you? Let him go. Find a guy within driving distance of your apartment."

Five months later, Mateo came to Canada.

Ben was relatively reticent in the months leading up to Mateo's arrival. He sporadically mentioned they'd been chatting daily via SMS and video. But I never thought it was to the extent that he was seriously considering shipping the man to Canada like a pair of orthotic sandals.

In the years since, people have asked me for my reaction to Ben importing a relative stranger as his boyfriend. The answer is, I'm not surprised. Ben gives endlessly and sometimes men see that quality and suck him dry. He and his partner think they have chemistry. But what they usually are is the coupling of a giver and a taker, connecting like north and south magnets.

But what is chemistry in the traditional sense? Sure, there are intangibles that maybe we'll never understand, but what else is going on? I'll let you in on my $250-an-hour therapy session takeaways: Sometimes, what you think is chemistry can actually be the worst characteristics of your absent father staring you square in the face at a BBQ. Sometimes "chemistry" is just unresolved childhood trauma, dressed up in skinny jeans and a flattering tee. Sometimes it's the desire for a mere thrill with someone you feel is out of your league. A high. A rush. A quick jaunt. Chemistry is like a drug, except cocaine doesn't cum in your eye by accident.

For me, chemistry often meant seeing a guy as entertainment and thinking we had a deep connection. I wonder though, what drew most of them to me? Sure, I was kinda fuckable, a ton of fun to be around, and always up for spontaneous adventure. But I was also stubborn, aloof, impatient, and incapable of more than a surface connection. Was I their bad mom or dad, a second shot at making things right in their mind?

(Psychology is kinda incestual, no?)

When Ben gives too much to men in his life, sometimes there is nothing left for the rest of us. We drift apart as friends, though we eventually find our way back to each other. It's been that way for years. He drifted again this year, so far away that I can't write this book and pretend we'll ever be the same. He's such a beautiful soul at his core but today, he's damn near unrecognizable. Processing the loss of the person I used to speak to every day has left me traumatized on what feels like an irreparable level. When the one person you think would never leave does, can you ever really fully trust anyone?

How do you stop yourself from being reminded of others that left, as well? Like my best friend Penny of nine years, who was gone the second she met a homophobic man. Or my dad, who made leaving look damn effortless. Sure, I kinda expected that one. He had his foot out the door from the time I was a teenager. But it didn't make it any easier.

Rationally, I know all these people are mutually exclusive. But these undeniable patterns ache deep in my stomach. There was once a time when I could barely make eye contact with people for fear of any sort of connection sparking.

My mind tells me not to blame myself, but my scarred heart keeps whispering that I'm unlovable. That I'm not worthy of someone who will always stay.

And it's hard to be around this quality in Ben. It feels contagious at times. My therapist says it shows the potential that still lives in me when it comes to men. Maybe that's on me. Maybe I should get over it. Or maybe I don't want to slide back into lowered expectations anymore. I lost a lot of years. I wish I had them back. If Ben wanted to lose even more, well, that was his choice.

I know they say we accept the love we think we deserve. We do. And I did during this decade. But what about the reverse of that? In growing, we learn what we don't deserve. We learn that because we get burned over and over until a non-negotiable is created. No more! Not another second! We put our foot down for good and find invaluable self-respect. Some never make it there because they haven't had enough. Not yet. Some never find the love they deserve.

It hurts to watch the Groundhog Day of Ben's relationships, largely because it means losing the person I love during the process. We see his disasters coming. I wish he did, too. But the litany of hearing, "I'm fine," and, "Nothing's wrong," like a mantra, is all too familiar with him, until suddenly, *BAM*! He drops hard, brushes himself off, and does it all over again. Mateo was just the most extreme on the continuum of Ben's former lovers.

Don't get me wrong, we all wanted the best for our friend when it came to Mateo. But could this really work? If it didn't, well, we also selfishly wanted a front row seat to the uninhibited extravaganza that was unfolding. And by "we," I mean Otis and me. I wish I could say I was an entirely unwilling participant.

Sometimes the greatest wakeup call a person needs is someone to divebomb into their life and blow it to smithereens so they can rebuild it, brick by brick. Yes, I really did want Ben's relationship to succeed. I wanted to see him happy. But I hoped if it did fail spectacularly that he would change. That he would flush the last of his need to save men who couldn't be saved. He's always had this drive to save men so they would need him. Why did that quality bother me so much?

When Mateo arrived, he had no job or plans to enroll in an educational program while in Canada. This didn't faze Ben one iota. On day one, he imprinted himself on Ben's couch and stayed there for close to three months, floating on a magical undercurrent of homosexual yearning.

During those months, under Mateo's direction, Ben was forced to shave his armpits down to nothing. A shrine was erected in his bedroom with an oversized candle of Mary and two rosaries. To further fend off sinister spirits, Mateo placed three bowls of water around Ben's apartment with half of a lime in them. One was in the corner of the kitchen, another on a table in the living room, and the last was directly under the bed. Predictably, the limes would start to brown after a few days, which Mateo claimed was proof of evil spirits lurking within the walls. The brownest bowl was in the kitchen, where the spirits must have spent the majority of their time eating what I consider to be the devil incarnate—carbohydrates.

The bowl under the bed, protected from sunlight, took at least a week to brown. Mateo had an explanation. He concluded their lovemaking was producing more wholesome spirits, which fended off negative energy. Ben said it was just mould.

In public, Mateo's jealousy knew no bounds. Occasionally Ben would run into a platonic friend, and after greeting them with a hug, Mateo would start kicking up dirt.

"Who was that?!" he'd scream.

Ben would smile placatingly. "An old friend, Matt."

"Did you fuck him?"

"No, I did not fuck him," Ben replied. "And I resent the question."

But Mateo was never convinced. "Yes, you did. I saw it in your face. You fucked him."

The camera cuts to me devouring popcorn in the corner with Otis. I had to watch. I'd tried everything and Ben had largely shut me out.

"Whatever," Ben would say, pulling him closer.

"Whatever?! Whatever. How could you say 'whatever' when I'm talking about our love?" he'd reply, storming out of the bar.

JORDAN: Hey Otis, go get some butter on this.

The spin cycle continued, weekend after weekend, blow up after blow up, like Mateo was a gay, male, chemically imbalanced version of Sofía Vergara. You had to applaud his consistency.

Sometimes, if Ben and Mateo didn't have sex for three days, he'd break into his phone to peruse his chat and Facebook messaging history for clues. The play by play was gripping. I felt like I was knee deep in a telenovela.

And because Mateo was a chef in Colombia, he would spend all his free time whipping up a storm of meals built on a foundation of oil-laden rice and potatoes.

"What's going on with your body?" I said to Ben one day

after our beach volleyball match. He was usually an active guy, but he had lost a lot of muscle tone (and what looked like testosterone). He was filling out in his love handles area and moving into A-cup territory right before my eyes. I swear his nipples winked at me through his white T-shirt.

"My body?"

"You look like Caitlyn Jenner," I replied.

"Oh no. It's the Colombia carbs!" he yelled, aghast. "I told Mateo to cool it and now I'm transitioning and I didn't even realize it. Fucking great. Which Caitlyn Jenner do I look like? The final Caitlyn Jenner?"

"No," I said. "I doubt it would ever get to that point without a doctor involved. Like, do you remember when Bruce started to change without any sort of public announcement, and he was like, pumping gas in a vintage T-shirt with itty bitty titties poking through?"

"Yeah," he said, looking miserable.

"That's basically like you right now," I brutally replied. "It's a weird mid stage where you could either lean in and go full bodacious beauty or pull back and stop taking the hormone injections. You know?"

"This is not comforting."

"Well, would you rather I lie to you?" I asked with a shrug.

Close to the four-month mark, Mateo abruptly left the country to "fix some issues with his visa." Once home in Colombia, he called Ben to tell him he wouldn't be returning to Canada until Ben flew to meet his family, preferably within two weeks. Ben, with little resistance, booked a trip immediately. Some of the most bewitching love stories in history were built on cross-nation ultimatums, after all.

Once in Colombia, Ben attempted to ingratiate himself with

Mateo's family, who spoke not a word of English. He went to church with them on Christmas Eve and even sat in the front row while everyone cried, muttering unintelligible Spanish. Later, Ben blew out the family's Jesus candle, which usually stayed lit 24 hours a day to ward off spirits. He thought he was being practical, mitigating against fire risk, but that's not how Mateo's family took it. They thought he'd invited evil spirits directly into their home and doused him with holy water while reciting verses from the Bible.

After Ben returned to Toronto with Mateo in tow, I started to intervene.

"He needs a plan," I said. "He can't just sit on your couch all day and then go in the kitchen sautéing the building blocks of your titties. Can't he get a job?"

"He tried," said Ben. "He can't find anything, even though he has like eight years' experience as a chef."

I hatched a plan and called an ex named David, who runs a chain of Italian eateries stationed around the downtown core.

He was not happy to hear from me when I called. "Yeah? What do you want?"

I scratched my head, trying to remember the way I burned said bridge to the ground. I needed a creative way to bring up Mateo without sounding like an a-hole. I told him I had a dream about him, in which he was oiled up, cooking in my kitchen in nothing but a silk apron.

"Then you made me pasta carbonara and looked deep into my eyes," I said. "And I realized that I probably shouldn't have ghosted you."

"You are so full of shit," he said. "I'm kinda busy so what do you actually want, Jordan?"

I told him the story of Mateo, explained that it was a

desperate situation and that I was doing my best friend a favour. I told him poor, wandering Colombian boys should get a chance at love in the greatest country on Earth. He paused, huffed, then agreed to hire him on a trial basis.

When Mateo heard the good news, he started prancing around Ben's apartment asking him to lead a prayer "to the Great One above."

"The Lord didn't get you a job, Mateo," said Ben. "Jordan did, and you should really call him to thank him because I did not think anyone he dated still spoke to him. If you wanna see a real miracle it's that one of his exes answered his calls."

"The Lord has a plan," said Mateo. "The Lord always has a plan."

"What plan?"

"Well," said Mateo, sitting Ben down on the couch. "The Lord had a role in making sure Jordan and David did not work out. Now I have this job and we have our life. We can't understand the ways of the Great One."

Listen, I am firmly non-religious and if there are deities that have been overseeing any of my romantic relationships, they have mostly certainly been asleep at the wheel. Maybe Carrie Underwood knew a different God but if at any point Jesus had accidentally "taken the wheel" in my romantic life he likely also suffered a pulmonary embolism and sent said car off an overpass.

Mateo's wild antics carried on unabated in the weeks that followed. One day, when Ben and I were getting matching taint waxes for an article I was writing, Mateo called his phone, incensed. He had broken into Ben's Facebook account and read a backlog of messages between him and two other men. The slew of dirty messages was from long before Mateo and Ben had even met. Over the partition, I heard Ben calmly repeating, "Would you please calm down? Would you please calm down? Please!"

The very next week, Mateo exploded again, telling Ben it was obvious to him and his entire social circle that he was totally in love with me because he once saw us kiss on the lips, something we do daily.

I'd reached my limit. I dragged Otis by his tail out of an underground rooster fighting ring he'd recently joined.

JORDAN: Wipe the coke off your face. Operation Buh-bye Mateo starts now. Start spitballin'.

OTIS: Let's knock him out, put him in a crate and ship him back to Colombia, return to sender.

JORDAN: I already ran that idea by Ben and he said it was a little aggressive.

OTIS: We don't need his consent. This is wartime. It's time to start drafting new rules.

JORDAN: Well, Mateo won't go willingly. That I know for sure. We need to think smarter.

We scoured the Internet for a credible supplier of chloroform. I decided to buy Mateo a bottle of "cologne," as a gesture of goodwill. I would then build a fort on Ben's balcony and wait for the moment he spritzed himself into a light coma. I had learned from Saturday morning cartoons that the best way to transport a body was by rolling it into a rug. I had three Persians among my cell phone contacts, but much to my chagrin, none had an extra rug handy. Luckily, it wasn't necessary. Three days later, close to the five-month mark, Mateo hailed a cab to the airport for a 4 p.m. flight back to Bogota. It was over for good.

I took a cab to Ben's house and plunked myself on the sofa with two bottles of pinot noir. His phone vibrated ceaselessly on the coffee table for an hour.

BZZZZ... BZZZ...

"Just turn it off," I said. "He needs to go. You gave it the old college try and then some."

"It's not even him."

BZZZZ… BZZZ…

"Who is it?" I replied.

"It's his hombres in Toronto," Ben said, sipping his wine. "They have been texting me nonstop asking me if I'm going to run to the gate at the airport to stop him."

I scoffed and reached for the bottle to top off our glasses. "You can't even get to the gate anymore."

"I know," he said. "I don't even know how the three of them got my number. I guess Mateo gave it to them."

BZZZZ… BZZZ…

"Give me that fucking thing," I said, tossing his phone over my shoulder.

"Someone needs to tell these Colombians that life isn't a Rachel McAdams movie."

CHAPTER SIX

ANUS

It was 7:12 a.m. on Groundhog Day. I hadn't even tamed my morning boner yet when my phone vibrated off the bed and onto the ground. Pretty notable, considering it started its journey inside my anus.

Kidding.

I had three successive Facebook messages from a high school classmate named Peter Fiorino. I hadn't spoken to him in about 14 years and would have been thrilled for that streak to continue. I was sure it had to be a most pressing matter.

PETER: Hey Jordan.

PETER: I can't believe we're reconnecting like this but I have something to share with you.

PETER: I can't even remember the last time we chatted.

I rolled over in disgust.

JORDAN: I can. I can remember it quite vividly, Peter. You were chasing me into the men's locker room while yelling "pillow biter."

PETER: HA! Wow. Water under the bridge eh?

JORDAN: No. I'm a shell of a man.

PETER: Oh. Listen I wanted to send you a personal invite to a stag and doe/jack and jill party I'm having.

JORDAN: A what?

PETER: It's sort of like a fundraising thing for my wedding next year.

JORDAN: I'm invited to your wedding? Why?

PETER: Hmm well not exactly. You're invited to the stag and doe.

JORDAN: So I'm not invited to the wedding?

PETER: No

JORDAN: I'm fundraising for a party that I'm not even invited to?

PETER: Sorta

JORDAN: WTF? What exactly happens at this party?

PETER: It's fun. Sort of like light carnival games. Tickets are $25 and there is a bar fully stocked. Plus you can meet my fiancée.

JORDAN: Hmmm… Open bar?

PETER: No. Cash bar. It's a fundraiser.

JORDAN: So I get to play Pin the Tail on the Donkey while reliving high school trauma? And whom do I make the cheque out to?

I must have missed the moment it became socially acceptable to invite relative strangers to fundraise for your life choices. I asked Peter if he had any other life goals I should be aware of so I could start budgeting accordingly. Maybe I could set aside a small portion of my paycheque for a rainy-day fund in his name. Maybe we could all play ping pong to buy him a new washer and dryer.

And apparently these farces are more commonplace than I realized. My friend Stacey told me her sister made $11,000 off her stag and doe, which I guess has also now become a profit-making endeavour.

"So, do you then return people's money?" I asked her over brunch one day.

"No," she said. "I guess it's for their new life?"

"Oh, that's nice," I replied. "Who buys knick-knacks for this sad single man?"

I never did make it to Peter's party. Most of my graduating class had physically peaked at age 12, like the Olsen twins, so I didn't see the point. (Not me, of course. I am still borderline perfection.) Their lives had descended into sonogram photos, pumpkin patches, and exploding pants buttons. My life had taken a different course, filled with nudes, chronic bloating, and exploding anal fissures. I had put off my now second anal fissure surgery (yes, second—see chapter four) for as long as I could muster due to concerns about lost elasticity and incontinence.

What sort of man would I become without my signature butthole?

Would I recognize the man in the mirror staring back at me?

Was this what Michael Jackson was alluding to?

One day my asshole decided to swell completely overnight and make the choice for me, with zero consultation. I went straight to the ER as per my doctor's orders and turned on the theatrics to increase my priority level after hearing it was a five-hour-plus wait.

I'm often reminded of my disdain for the general population when I am forced to spend prolonged amounts of time around them. I really don't like to leave my house unless it's to exercise, have drinks with friends, or do business. The beauty of living in a major metropolitan city is that you can order anything you want from your phone, sleep a ton, and limit interpersonal interactions. If I had a spirit animal it would probably be a koala, especially due to the fact that more than 70% of them have chlamydia.

After two and a half hours in the ER waiting room, I was shown to a bed and told to change into a gown. I'm not sure who can actually fit in a hospital gown. It seems they needed to come up with a universal size so they just erred on the side of hippopotamus. I put on the gown, took a look in the mirror, and laughed. Moments like this are humbling and important in life. You see, it's very tough for someone like me to stay grounded with such a nice ass.

The medical resident came in 10 minutes later and asked what the issue was.

"I have a fissure. I'm a patient of Dr. Stephens and he told me to come to the ER if things got bad," I said. "It's swollen shut and my farts sound like a flute."

"OK," he said, jotting down notes. "Thanks for that animated description."

"You're welcome."

"Can I take a look?" he asked.

I rolled onto my side to get the first of multiple finger bangings over the coming days. It was excruciating; he could barely get one finger in.

"We'll need to take a few photos for Dr. Stephens," he said. "I'm going to grab a colleague."

He returned with two more medical students. It was at this moment I would learn I was in the city's largest teaching hospital, and my anus was today's pop quiz. Sure, I could have refused exams by medical students, but then I wouldn't have been able to live with myself knowing future buttholes could be in jeopardy. It's called integrity and I'm chock full of it.

"If you could just bend over the table and spread your cheeks, we're going to take a few photos," said the first resident, his voice shaking with nerves.

I bent over and stared straight ahead at the brown wall as I heard the iPhone camera click over and over. I sighed deeply in my diaphragm and longed for simpler times.

OTIS: This is great. You're going to be famous, my

friend. Don't forget to smile.

"Call me a filthy slut while you take the photos," I said. "It will produce a more fruitful result."

"Hmmm," he said. "I'm wondering if you could spread your cheeks a bit wider."

"Oh, God," I responded. "The fall of a gay icon."

I pulled my cheeks apart with all my might as the three of them assessed lighting and angles. After the third camera click, I let out a very audible fart.

"Oopsy, but did that fart help with the visuals?" I said. "Did it open up the area?"

The residents struggled to maintain a level of decorum.

"Do you need a white balance?" Sweat trickled down my brow. "I took a photography course once!"

"No, much better," he said, taking more photos.

"OK, aaand I think you're good." I stood and retied my gown. "Dr. Stephens doesn't need the Annie Leibovitz treatment on my brown town. He knows my chart."

"Right," he said, handing me his iPhone. "So if you could just consent to these…"

I swiped right to view nine photos of my anus in various expression stages. I could see jubilation anus, gaping anus, and very antagonized anus.

"Hmmm," I said, still staring at the screen. "Not my best work, Doc. Any chance we could slap a filter on it?"

He smiled apologetically. "We cannot alter the image or it could compromise the photo."

"I know, it's just that photo is a lot to take in under fluorescent lights," I said. "I prefer soft lounge lighting. Also, real talk, man to man, should I be bleaching?"

"Bleaching?"

"My anus," I replied. "I hear about this all the time but I think it's just an urban legend."

"I'm going to go send the photos now, Jordan," he said, visibly annoyed. Then he left, closing the curtain.

Three minutes later, the curtain shifted again.

"How's your day?" asked the unsuspecting nurse who had been sent to check on me.

"Pretty good," I said. "I slept in and we just did an artistic photo shoot of my butthole."

"Oh." She looked at the floor. "Can I get you anything?"

"Drugs!" I said cheerfully.

"OK, do you need them?"

"Need is subjective—let's just say I would enjoy some," I whispered. "I mean, I'm sure I need them, too."

"Well, what's your pain out of 10?"

"Oh, at least a 7," I said, without even attempting to conceal my countenance. *I had played this game many times before.*

"OK." She winked. "I'll get you some hydromorphone. It's like morphine but without the nausea."

"Only the best for my anus."

Within minutes, I began to circle Saturn. I sent a text to the guy I was dating that said, *So I've been doing some thinking about my situation: If you were really a true liberal like you claim to be, any hole should be OK with you. Do you feel me?*

He wrote back, *What the fuck are you talking about?*

I followed up with a selfie of my bloodshot eyes and hospital-couture gown, and wrote, *How you like me now, Daddy?*

Jesus, he said. *You look bat shit. Are you in the hospital? Do you need me to come by after work?*

No! I said. *I look hideous and it's probably time we have an honest conversation about you dating an able-bodied man. I'm letting you go.*

But I don't want to go, he replied.

It's fine, I wrote. *It's better this way.*

I put down my phone and fell asleep. Dr. Stephens pulled back the curtain around 8 p.m. and I popped back into consciousness, albeit also in a drug-induced panic.

"This shit's ridiccccculous," I said.

"Why are you on Dilaudid?" Dr. Stephens frowned. "That's really not necessary in this situation."

"I got game," I said. "So, what's the plan?"

"We put you on the surgical list but you're considered low priority so your surgery won't be tonight. My best bet is tomorrow, pending no high-priority calls. You can't leave, so you'll have to stay overnight. Your friends or family can fetch your stuff," he said. "We don't have a bed for you in the ward tonight, so you'll have to sleep here in the ER. I'll come check in before surgery tomorrow."

"Thanks and I love you," I said, with an exaggerated wink.

"Oh, God," he said with a chuckle. "See you tomorrow. No food or drink, please."

When I told the night nurse I would be sleeping in the ER that night, she laughed and informed me, "No one sleeps in the ER, but I would love to watch you try."

Turns out, she was right. Every time I dozed off, the speaker above my head would sound, jolting me out of bed. I woke up this way about 75 times during the night, like some sort of Guantanamo torture exercise testing how fast I would emotionally crumble. My room also doubled as a supply closet, so hospital staff came in and out every 15 minutes.

"Umm, do you mind?" I said to each of them. "This is my bedroom!"

At 5:02 a.m., I stared at the wall, hungry, high, and agitated.

There comes a time in every hospital stay when the thought must enter patients' minds that they would rather just be dead instead. Believe me, it is all I thought about. Around noon, I was moved upstairs to the surgical ward. I couldn't bear the thought of another sleepless night without food and water so I gave my Visa card to the head nurse and paid for a semi-private room. At least I would get some credit card points from this ordeal.

I always pay by credit card when I can, and you should too, unless you're a degenerate who can't manage money. Everyone should accept credit cards. Drug dealers should take credit cards. Hookers should take credit cards. You could put a Square reader inside their butthole for swipe. Maybe tap your Visa on their penis heads, if you're not over your daily limit, of course.

I dozed on and off over the next six hours. A group of medical residents came in and asked me the same 10 questions. They each took a shot at finger blasting me. When the third one stepped up to the plate, I threw my hands in the air and screamed, "Enough with the butthole fingering! I am not your gay guinea pig." She immediately apologized and scurried off.

Otis, high on his own morphine drip next to me, told me to call Ben.

JORDAN: How the hell did you get your own drip?

OTIS: I threatened the nurse with HIV.

JORDAN: What did she say?

OTIS: Not much. My family's reputation precedes me.

Around 9 p.m., with no surgery time assigned, Ben came and offered me a sandwich and a sip from his Powerade bottle of vodka.

"I can't have any food or drink for eight hours before," I said. "That includes alcohol, you idiot."

"Seriously? This place is a joke. Do you mind if I drink?" he asked. "I have a date in an hour."

"It's fine." I paged the nurse. "I've graduated from alcohol to IV narcotics, anyway."

"Good for you. Do you think they have a bar on the grounds?" Ben looked around, as though he might spot a server. "I'm craving red wine."

"Are hospitals licensed?"

"Probably not," he said. "But maybe there is a bar."

"Do you have some time to masturbate before your date?" I asked.

"No, why?"

"I always masturbate right before a date," I said.

"Why?"

"You have to go in with a clear mind about the whole situation without the irrationality that horniness tends to bring," I explained. "If the mental clarity I experience post-orgasm lasted all day, I'd be Elon Musk by now."

"Well, you certainly don't have that glow at the moment," he said. "I'm actually craving merlot. Should I go to the wine store and come back?"

I paged the nurse again to ask her if there was a bar on the hospital grounds. She laughed and told us we "had issues" as she walked away, shaking her head. Apparently, there are no stupid questions, just the ones Ben and I continuously ask.

Since noon I'd been on a steady stream of Dilaudid, which I'm told has a chemical composition similar to heroin. I hadn't had any food or water since 8 p.m. the night before, which means I was extra cracked out. I woke up at 7 a.m. the next day to the nurse changing my IV.

"Do we have any updates about my surgery?" I asked. "I

can't eat or drink and the only visitors I get are here to stick their finger in my butt. And for the record I do *not* appreciate their calluses."

"They don't tell me anything, hon," she said, handing me a tray of food.

"I just said I can't eat." I pushed the tray away. "And you've brought me food three times already." I was using the term "food" quite loosely, given I had never seen multi-coloured potatoes served inside cold cut ham before.

I fell back asleep five minutes later. At noon, another nurse came in with lunch and explained she had no idea when my surgery would be. When I complained about the lack of communication on all fronts, she nodded and shoved more pseudo-heroin into my veins to shut me up.

Strung out on opiates in my hospital room.

Two more days went by, during which I crushed entire series of Netflix shows and perused Grindr with a bio that read, "Broken anus seeks broken heart." Then one morning, my mom, a physician, came by with all my stuff. No food, drink, or answers were one thing, but I would not be subject to the dehumanizing experience of being deprived of my alpha hydroxy acid moisturizer for one minute more.

"You don't look well, honey," she said. "When is the surgery?"

"Who knows." I was cutting my toenails, entirely nonchalant by this point. "No one tells me anything. Go on without me."

"Oh my God," she said, looking at my IV pump. "You're on Dilaudid? Why? Get off that stuff."

"It's all I have," I explained. "Please don't take it away from meeeeee."

"Where is your doctor?"

"I asked them to call him and they said he's moving this weekend," I said. "Mom, do you remember my hamster Rex, who was autistic? I've been thinking about him a lot lately."

"He's moving?!" She looked furious. "I'm going to get some answers. This is bullshit."

Apparently having an angry doctor as my personal advocate carried some weight, because she returned with news shortly thereafter. My surgery was planned for the next night, meaning I would get to eat one more meal before I went back to fasting.

"But do I look thin?" I asked my mom. "I'm eating like 200 calories a day."

"Yes," she said. "Yes, you look awful."

After my mom left, my new roommate was rolled into the room. He was an elderly man with his young daughter in tow, who got him settled and left. As part of his treatment he required eye drops every hour to stave off infection. Because he refused to administer his own drops, he set an alarm for every hour on the hour and paged the nurse accordingly. This meant I woke up every hour on the hour as well. This is one of the lovely perks of Canada's health-care system: paying $290 a night for semi-private rooms that are only a 50% guarantee you will be undisturbed. Around hour four, the nurse tried to show him how to place the eye drops in his own eyes. This is something he had seemingly glossed over in the past eight decades of his life.

"I'm trying to empower you, sir," she said, showing him how eye drops work.

"It's not my job, lady!" he yelled. "Drop 'em!"

Though I have been known to be quite the contrarian, I feel it is a reasonable position that if you refuse to put in your own eye drops, you should probably die. This is what white privilege looks like. You think pre-teens in sub-Saharan Africa outsource the administration of their eye drops?

The next night I was rolled into the OR for my surgery, naked under my gown. They hooked up my IV and strapped my arms down while the heart monitor beeped expeditiously.

"How are you going to get at the hole?" I asked the surgical staff.

"Oh, when you are asleep, we will hoist your legs in the air," the nurse said. "Have you ever seen a woman in stirrups?"

"No," I replied. "Does the general population often see women in stirrups?"

I turned to the rest of the surgery crew.

"How excited is everyone to see my entire situation under these bright lights?" I asked.

No one replied. Otis looked disappointed. His face was the last thing I saw before the anaesthesia took me out.

I woke up in my hospital room wearing temporary underwear,

which resembled cheesecloth. My eyes felt dry and cloudy, and I could hear my new roommate complaining to the nurse that he woke up from a blackout fall (and surgery) and no one had come by. I could make out his conversation from the other side of the curtain but could barely lift my limbs to wave.

"I feel like they just cut me up and then no one came by or told me anything," he said. "Like what happened to me?"

"I'm not sure. I'll go find out," said the nurse.

I ripped back the curtain and pulled off my oxygen mask. He was a hot piece littered with sleeve tattoos. If he ignored my advances, I would chalk it up to the circumstances.

"This place is a joke, buddy," I said. "What happened to you?"

"I can't remember much," he said. "I fell hanging Christmas lights and then woke up here with a giant cast on my arm. Do you think I have a concussion?"

"Maybe," I slurred. "I mean, good thing you're not surrounded by a team of medical professionals."

"Right," he said. "Dude, you look real fucked…"

"I have a regular face but this isn't it. This is a new face I'm trying out. Spoiler, I'm a junkie now."

OTIS: I'm sensing a vibe.

JORDAN: No! I think he's straight.

OTIS: Everyone's a little gay.

I continued, "I didn't have a drug problem before I came here but I'm about ready to start selling off assets to keep this lifestyle going, which is not a good sign. Take a good look at your future, chico. Do you want some?"

"How?"

"I dunno," I said. "Come over here. I'll jam it in your veins and then we can cuddle."

"Cuddle?"

"For warmth," I said. "No homo but also homo."

"I'm good," he said. "Thanks, though."

Two hours later I got the news that I was being discharged.

I went home and slept 13 hours in my apartment, and woke up to the sounds of my mom cleaning. She was incredibly distraught, which was an irrational reaction to years of baseboard scum. Something more sinister had to be on the menu.

"Jordan, your sister was stabbed by a drug addict during her shift in the emergency room last night," she said, while dusting my TV stand. My sister Lisa is a nurse.

My mom continued, "The patient had a needle in her sock and the cops failed to properly pat her down."

"This family is on its last legs!" I said. "Is she OK?"

"The woman tested positive for Hepatitis C. The doctors aren't sure what else she could have been exposed to, so they have her on medication to prevent possible HIV transmission. It's called PEP and it's very hard on the body," she said. "I'm heading back home in a couple of hours but perhaps you could send her a message."

I popped two morphine tabs and sent her a text.

JORDAN: Heard the news. How are you doing?

LISA: I'm fine, just nauseous. They wanted me to pay for the medication, which is like $2,000.

JORDAN: They asked for your credit card right after you'd been stabbed with a needle?

LISA: Pretty much.

JORDAN: Well, well, the bookies foresaw the wrong odds for which one of us would get HIV first, didn't they?

LISA: HAHAHAHAHAHA

LISA: I gotta go. Me and Steve are watching the game.

JORDAN: Which game? You know gay guys don't know which game everyone is watching.

LISA: Raptors! Sorry for stealing your AIDS thunder. XO

Two days into my recovery, I wasn't getting any better. I was waist deep in the trenches of depression. My days consisted of waking up in cold sweats, taking morphine, taking sitz baths, holding back tears, bleeding into a menstrual pad, and going back to sleep.

I knew it would be stupid of me not to survey the damage from the surgery but I'd lie if I said I wasn't horror-struck. Unable to get a clear look at the wound with my hand mirror, I knew the living room would provide excellent natural light given it was 1 p.m. and sunny. I was so weak that I crawled, half-drenched and shaking, directly from the bathtub. A pool of water trailed across the kitchen floor behind my naked frame. When I caught a reflection of myself in the hallway mirror, I looked deathly. I pulled myself up onto the couch, hoisted my legs in the air and opened my iPhone camera, eager to experiment with the features of iOS 10.2.

It turns out taking macro shots of your anus is a subtle art with a surprisingly steep learning curve. I experimented with different physical setups but settled for one in which I would spread eagle and use the fingers on my left hand to pry apart my anus. It was easily my lowest point. Suddenly, a cloud formation of Steve Jobs appeared above my head. I leaned into the drug-induced psychosis.

"Steve!" I yelled. "Thank God you're here. Where is the

anus feature? Should I go internal?"

"Reverse the camera, my boy!" he responded. "We built that for this very purpose!"

"Thanks, Daddy." The cloud dissolved.

I took several shots with the camera reversed and another with the regular camera in flash mode, which really just produced blurry shots of my inner thigh. Steve was right. The reference screen was a godsend.

In my panic, I hadn't really grasped who the target audience was for my photos. Given the uncertainty, I crawled back to the bathtub and shaved two strips of anus hair. I patted it dry and crawled back to the couch. Even in the most dire circumstances, I was ruled by the death grip of vanity. Once I was able to isolate the clearest photo, I surmised that the wound was riddled with infection. Based on watching seven seasons of *Grey's Anatomy*, I concluded I had less than 12 hours to live. Right then was when I thought it would be perfectly appropriate to text my doctor the photo. Oh, not my surgeon—my mom. It was the monkey's idea... for the record.

I captioned it, *ALERT: NOT A PHOTO OF A CALAMARI RING.*

She called me five minutes later. "You need to go to the ER now. The wound is completely infected. Who can take you? Ben? Lara?"

"I'm fine to go myself. I know that place inside and out."

"Are you sure?"

"Yeppers."

"Please be careful and call me when you're admitted," she said.

OTIS: I think you need a second opinion.

JORDAN: Opinion or reaction? You're becoming so

transparent.

OTIS: Both would be nice.

JORDAN: Do you ever rest?

OTIS: Bitch, I haven't slept since 2010.

I texted Ben the photo and wrote, *It's infected. I'm going back to the ER. Fuck me. P.S. I hate to keep bringing this up but should I bleach?*

BEN: Ew, for fuck's sake. I am in a fucking meeting! Is that dental floss?

JORDAN: No, it's the stitches, you moron. It's the human body. Deal with it.

BEN: How many people have you sent this to?

A moment later, another text appeared.

BEN: And yes, you should bleach but that's low priority at this point.

Through cold sweats, I packed my knapsack with the essentials. In an effort to wean myself off of tablet morphine, which was clearly diminishing my judgment, I took a double dose of marijuana edibles, which I promptly forgot about until the moment my Uber hit a traffic jam. I suddenly had no clue where I was heading or whose car I was in. It was scary, but not as scary as when you look at your app and notice your Uber driver is known for "great conversation."

"Whose car is this?!" I yelled to the driver.

"My car?" he said. "I'm Umer."

"Where are we going?!"

"To the hospital, sir."

"Well this is convenient, I thought I was being taken hostage. Phew." I shoved three mints into my mouth. "And I'm taking a bottle of water, so deal with it, Umer! I've been through a lot."

"That's what they're there for, man." He shrugged. "Five stars, please."

By the time I got to the hospital, the pain was a faded memory because my ever-present reality was high as fuck. The triage nurse ushered me in to take my vitals. My resting pulse came in at a whopping 134 beats per minute. She asked me if I was OK and I told her I was just nervous. I don't think she bought it as she watched my eyes dart rapidly left to right. My trichotillomania was also in overdrive, so I'm sure watching me pull out my own eyebrows didn't help my case. She sat me on a bench to wait for the surgical resident. I couldn't sit still so I just started pacing in circles, sweat dripping down my brow. I reached back to make sure the menstrual pad was still doing its job of collecting blood. It was gone! *Poor Umer, I thought.*

I walked to the washroom, balled up some toilet paper, and shoved it in my crack before returning to the bench to wait. *Could this ordeal get any worse?*

Yes, it could.

A short time later, paramedics wheeled in a stretcher with the body of a stranger on top and parked it near me. The deceased was, in essence, a skeleton, clocking in under 90 pounds with a thigh gap on point, and looking straight up at the ceiling. The medics hadn't even placed a blanket over his face to offer him a shred of dignity. I tried to look straight ahead but the presence of the body sent my buzz into overdrive. I stood up and moved to the end of the bench, three feet away, as the paramedics walked into the triage nurse's office.

"He's VSA but he's a DNR so we'll leave him here to process," said one of the paramedics. Thanks to the medical professionals in my life, I knew VSA meant "vital signs absent," and DNR meant "do not resuscitate," so there was no doubt in my mind that I was sitting next to a dead body. Just stellar.

"That's fine, just move him up a few feet," the nurse

instructed, pointing.

The paramedics placed the stretcher closer to where I was sitting, and walked back into the triage nurse's office to assist her with the paperwork, leaving me alone with the body.

The longer I tried to not look, the more my eyes darted back to it. I could have moved down the hall but the body seemed to have a gravitational force, piquing my curiosity. My eyes darted back and forth from the wall to the body. Then I just went into full-blown panic mode.

"SOMEONE GET THIS BODY AWAY FROM ME RIGHT NOW OR I'M GONNA START CRYING OR PUKING OR ALL OF THE ABOVE. CODE DEAD! CODE DEAD!"

The paramedics came running. "Sir, are you OK?"

"What is wrong with you? This is someone's child, not an exhibit for public display!" I yelled. "I am way too high for this shit, people!"

The triage nurse paged the medical resident and told him I was "being difficult" and "not her problem." The resident ushered me into a side room. He spoke to me as a nurse (who looked approximately 14 years old) took my blood for the lab. She jabbed at my vein twice, failed, and then on the third time snapped the contraption in half. Blood shot down my forearm and onto my pants.

I turned to the resident. "Excuse you. Who's paying for this? These are Lulu."

When the child nurse left, I levelled with the medical resident.

"Here," I said, handing him my iPhone. "There are enough asshole photos in there to fill a coffee table book. I'm way too high for an examination of any sort. Blood is flying everywhere and I just saw my first dead body."

"When you're done, please call my mom—I cannot consent in this state of mind. I'll probably be dead soon. It's time to stop playing games here. I've put up a valiant effort but we're going to need to pull the plug."

"What plug?" he said, scrolling through the photos on my phone.

"You know that saying on *Grey's Anatomy.* Don't pretend you don't," I said. "Euthanasia or pillow suffocation. Whatever will pass by management. I just don't see myself making it out of this."

"Jordan, I think you're just a little high on marijuana," he said. "We can drain the infection and clean it. It's just a 15-minute procedure. I'm going to give your mom a call. I assume her number is in your contacts?"

I nodded as he handed me back my iPhone. Ten minutes later he returned.

"Wow," he said. "She's a firecracker. I can see where you get it from. So apparently you already spoke to her 20 minutes ago in the ER waiting room?"

"I don't recall that."

"Yeah," he said. "She figured. She said you sounded completely nuts. I'm going to go find us a room and we can start in about 30 minutes. Please just take some deep breaths."

Two nurses returned and wheeled me into a small operating room, where they attached monitors to my chest. The resident and another doctor introduced themselves and left to suit up in scrubs. They returned with the anaesthesiologist, who asked me what sort of drugs I was on. I told her morphine and a lot of marijuana, but that I didn't know the dosage of the gummies, because honestly, who does? She asked me if I smoked the gummies and then she shined a light in both my eyes.

"People smoke gummies?" I asked. "I can't keep up with these millennials."

"I don't know what people are up to," she said. "Listen, I never thought I'd see a champagne flute in a grown man's anus but here I am."

"I have a champagne flute in my anus?!" I said in horror. "Oh my God, how am I so fucked up that I didn't notice? It's not even New Year's Eve."

"Not you." She shook her head. "Someone I examined last year."

She murmured some instructions to the nurse and then told her she was going to need a lot more Propofol. The team flipped me over, exposing my ass to everyone in the room. This increased the week's tally of those who had seen my pucker to nearly two dozen people, including my immediate family and best friend.

I looked up at the anaesthesiologist in both a fit of exhaustion and pure desperation.

"You're pretty," I said. "I feel like I have no dignity left. Can I cry?"

"Oh, hon," she said. "You have lots of dignity."

As she said that I heard a familiar sound from behind me.

"What are they doing?" I said.

"They are duct taping your cheeks apart in order to get better access to the anus," she said.

"Exactly," I said.

CHAPTER SEVEN

ACID

I am a 33-year-old man who orders Taylor Swift merchandise on the regular and I wish I could say I hold an ounce of shame about it. I even sign up for text alerts so I can track the packages like you would a NORAD Santa. One of those packages was en route to my apartment late in the summer of '17, a T-shirt from her Red tour a couple years earlier.

My apartment, two blocks from Toronto's Liberty Village, had a concierge service that would sign and receive packages on our behalf. There was a lag of two to three hours between the time the package would arrive and the email notification alerting us to come retrieve it. On such a cardinal package, a lag just wouldn't do. Like any stereotypical millennial, I love me some instant gratification. So, once I received the text from FedEx that the package had arrived, I was down to the lobby within three minutes.

When I got to the desk, a blond man in his mid-30s was standing behind the counter, a new hire I'd yet to interact with. He had an exceptional twinkle in his eye, which is a flagrant sign of either:

A life without permanent, parentally inflicted trauma;

Or, gayness.

"Hi, I'm Jordan," I remarked as I approached the desk. "I have a package from FedEx. It just arrived so you probably haven't logged it but it's here, trust me. I can see you signed for it already, Dustin."

"Geez, how do you know my name?" he asked. "They haven't even printed me a name tag."

"It's on the FedEx site."

"You're certainly on top of things."

"Some things. Where is Lorin?"

Lorin was my 23-year-old Indian security guard, whom I adored. Our friendship sparked the day she asked me "why I exclusively had guests after 1 a.m."

"I have a famous anus," I told her, winking. "It's a long story."

After that day we became inseparable.

She was an incredible hang and cook. Lorin baked the most incredible biryani. I'd devour the entire container in 90 seconds, blissfully ignoring the fact that I have a chronic illness resulting in open sores lining my colon. It barely mattered. Going down it was delectable. Going out was a different story. The biryani often temporarily detached my scorching asshole from my body. I think it fell out the bottom of my Nike shorts once, and a janitor found it in the parking garage.

To return the favour of her scrumptious eats, I'd buy her sex toys, like nipple clamps, handcuffs, or even a 9-inch dildo with a clitoris stimulator. She told me the dildo was like "seeing a god," which I presumed was a step up from the Domino's Pizza guy she was regularly fornicating with.

"Lorin's not here today," said Dustin. "But I'm here." He smiled at me.

"That sucks. Can I have the package?" I said. "It's on the floor behind you. It probably says Taylor Nation. That's her management company. I'm a Swiftie."

"Aren't you a little old to be into Taylor Swift?"

"Aren't you a little old to be wearing Converse?" I retorted. "Her metaphors move me. You'll never understand."

He picked up the package behind the desk and lifted it onto the counter.

"That's a big one," he said, chuckling. "A huge package for ya, man."

Then he winked.

"Right," I said, confused. "Where do I sign?"

"You think you can handle a big package?" He raised a single eyebrow.

"Uhh, sure," I said, tucking the box under my arm. "Have a nice day, Dustin."

I walked back to my condo, shut the door, and laid the package on my island. *Was he hitting on me with that hack joke? I guess that Japanese charcoal mask I did the other night is paying dividends.*

Two days later, Jesus stopped at my condo before we were due to meet Ben at Hanlan's Point Beach, located on the Toronto Islands.

"Did you bring the cooler?" I asked.

"I did, and also your concierge is an escort. Did you know that?"

"He is?!" I gasped. "The thought definitely crossed my mind but then I saw him yesterday in street clothes and he was dressed like underachievement, so I thought, well, maybe not. Stereotypes come from somewhere you know?"

"He's on rentmen.com for $245 an hour," said Jesus.

"He is?!"

Jesus grinned. "Oh yeah."

"You know, that's gay culture for ya: going on an escort site and seeing half your Tinder matches."

I zipped up my cooler bag and flung my backpack over my shoulder. Then I slathered my face in sunscreen and marched out the door with Jesus. Ben was already on the island and had set up shop on a towel just beside the flag pole. He had his SPF 4000 in hand, a valiant effort to stave off whatever sort of sun-related rash he would no doubt get. Usually said rashes wouldn't even have a page on Web MD. He's that pale. We laid down our towels and took in the scenery.

For those of you who have never been to Hanlan's Point, it is Toronto's clothing-optional beach, predominantly occupied by gay men and the pancake-nippled women who adore them. Entering the bushes behind the beach to urinate is like a Choose Your Own Adventure book. Make a right and you've contracted poison ivy. Make a left and you might run into someone being spit-roasted. Sometimes on the far end of the beach you'll see grown ass men violently masturbating in the open air, failing to understand that clothing-optional doesn't equate to disrespectful indecency. It's like a wild zoo without electric fences. There. Now you can't say you weren't warned.

As the afternoon rolled in, the boys suntanned and I went for a solo walk down the beach with my earbuds in, trying to find the Freezie Girl. The Freezie Girl and Hanlan's Point go hand in hand. She is her own heritage moment. Freezie Girl makes her own alcohol-based freezies, with flavours like basil lime vodka, and traverses the beach selling them for $10 a pop. With a flower in her hair and her sunbaked funbags waving in the wind, she's always easy to spot. I have the deepest respect for both her unwavering hustle and glaring avoidance of tax liability. That day Freezie Girl was nowhere to be found, so I popped in my earbuds and listened to "Clean" by Taylor Swift as I walked down the shoreline.

Earbuds are a fantastic reminder to others around me that I am a distrusting misanthrope, uninterested in trite conversations. Sunglasses also amplify this message. I'd actually prefer to have noise-cancelling headphones surgically affixed to my ears, but I have yet to find a board-certified doctor who would consider it.

After about an hour, I arrived back at the towels, where the boys were sucking on freezies.

I was aghast. "You found her?"

"Yeah," replied Jesus. "She was right behind you."

"Can't miss those fat titties. How was the walk?" asked Ben.

"Fine, a lot of genitals I did not need to see," I said. "Also, I bought us acid from a girl with a giant bush."

"Acid?" said Jesus. "Like LSD?"

"That's what she said." I handed him the tabs. "She looked to be having an incredible time."

"You bought acid from a stranger?" asked Ben in disbelief.

"They're all strangers, boo boo," I said. "Describe to me one of the people who cooked the 20-plus MDMA pills you've consumed in your life. "

"He's got a point," said Jesus. "But I'm not doing acid. Last time I did acid I thought they shut off all the music in the club but they absolutely did not. And then I had to poop a lot. It felt like eternity."

"Well it's 3 p.m. and it lasts 12 hours," I said. "So none of us are doing acid today, but you better believe I will harass you every day until the hallucinations commence."

"You don't need to," said Ben. "I'm totally in."

The very next weekend, Ben joined me last minute for a

housewarming party I was invited to for my friend Corbin. Ben was actually on a first date that had started at 7 p.m., but he quickly learned he was on a road to nowhere. After they finished dinner, he decided to bring the guy along as entertainment. At 10 p.m. I received a text that read, *Yo Yo. I'm downstairs in your lobby with my thug boyfriend. Get ready. It's something.*

I met Ben in the lobby and burst out laughing when I saw his date, a 25-year-old Brazilian man named Renan, dressed like a '90s rapper and throwing gang signs in the air.

"Hi, I'm Jordan," I said, motioning to shake his hand. "But I'm sure you know that already."

"Yeee brah," he said, shaking my hand in some sort of anxiety-inducing formation. "Dis place is some fancy shit."

"Can you please stop with the hand gestures?" I said. "This is King West."

"Don't talk to my boyfriend like that," said Ben.

Once we got to the party, Ben poured his "boyfriend" a drink but Renan waved him off, explaining that he didn't drink because when he did, he "always started bar fights." It was a sentence he delivered with the most solemn cadence, and of course, it immediately caught Otis' attention.

OTIS: Pour it down his throat.

"You say that like we don't want to see you start a bar fight," I said, rolling my eyes. "Grow up."

"Come on, Renan," said Ben, raising the cup to his lips. "We're on a date. And if you can drink water it means you can also drink vodka. It's science."

"OK, fine," said Renan, gulping down half the glass and

audibly uttering, "Ahhhhhhhhh."

"Now, I'm going to piss," said Renan, kissing Ben on the cheek and walking toward the other room.

I turned to Ben. "This might get violent quickly. He seems somewhat unevolved."

"Well, I'm getting something out of this night!" yelled Ben. "And if it's a fist to my face, well then, it's a fist to my goddamn face. That would be more entertainment than our dinner, that's for sure. Ninety minutes of a snooze fest."

I cringed. "That bad?"

"I've had more engaging conversations with telemarketers." He sighed. "But at least he has a great cock."

"When did you see his cock?!" I said. "Like, in the cab?"

"No, I previewed at dinner," said Ben. "A light prod during the apps. Nothing too major. I'm not an animal."

"Yes, you are. Oh, he's coming back." I pointed at Renan.

"That was fast," said Ben.

"I couldn't find it," said Renan.

"Shocking," I replied.

"Lots of gays up in here." Renan shook his head. "You know I ain't into the gay agenda."

"What is the gay agenda?" said Ben.

"All up your face, flexing, flaunting," he said. "You know."

"Please Renan, the gay agenda is just shit-talking and rosé," I retorted. "Now go pee on the lawn like a mature adult."

An hour later, we left Corbin's house to go to my ex Rahul's mansion for an after party. Renan was right. He could not handle his alcohol at all. It transformed him into a demon from hell. He was slurring and violently gesticulating as we shoved him into a cab at the bottom of Corbin's driveway.

Once we arrived to Rahul's, Ben took him upstairs to cool

down and I ordered Chinese food for seven people. Then when the delivery man arrived and asked for payment, I hid in the basement. It was my way of showing Rahul what he was missing from our failed relationship—my trademark deception.

After Rahul paid, I thanked him and snatched the bag out of his hand.

"I knew that was you," he said.

"Who else would it be?" I replied, kissing him on the cheek. "This house is incredible. You should be really proud of yourself."

"Thank you."

"I could have had a nice life here as your wife if I wasn't such a maladjusted, noncommittal deviant," I said. "Ah well, life in the big city. You want some chow mein?"

Then I heard a thunderous crash from upstairs.

"Uhhh. You might wanna investigate that," I said, placing my hand on Rahul's shoulder.

It turns out Renan was upstairs starting fist fights with Rahul's roommates and at one point punched a hole in his bedroom wall. I was sitting at the kitchen table, mowing down on an egg roll, when Renan came barrelling down the stairs. Ben and Rahul were restraining him. I thought I should bear some responsibility for what had transpired but instead of speaking up, I calmly picked up my Chinese food and moved to another room. For one, I had to protect my $7,000 second nose from incoming hazards.

Then Renan entered the living room and started to vigorously punch himself right in the chest, yelling, "I'm not gay bro. I'm not gay. I don't want to be gay."

All of us stopped to witness the display. It was incredibly conflicting because it was both heartbreaking and the most intoxicating live show I'd seen in ages. I'd seen internalized homophobia manifest in so many ways, but never like this. Why couldn't Renan just mask those feelings with drugs and alcohol like the rest of us? Why did he also have to get violent in the process? I wanted to help. I wanted to hug him. To show him how I'd overcome some of my own self-hatred.

JORDAN: I feel like I should hop in.

OTIS: What you SHOULD do is pass me a sparerib.

I fed General Tso's chicken to the dog while Renan cooled off and Ben swept up remnants of drywall. Ben profusely apologized to Rahul for the display and took Renan home to crash at his place. The next morning, Ben woke up and started fellating Renan. His lover encouraged it for several minutes, with appreciable moaning, and then suddenly snapped, throwing Ben across the room. "What the fuck, bro?" he yelled. "I'm not gay, bro."

"OK," said Ben. "The funhouse is now over. Please leave and let's avoid that awkward thing where we pretend we *might* see each other again. Bye-eee."

A year passed, and Ben and I were itching to try the acid tabs still sitting in my nightstand. We penciled in a Saturday afternoon back at Hanlan's Point. Jesus' only advice re: LSD was to set up camp away from others to avoid overstimulation. We laid down our towels and coolers on the left side of the beach, where the more reserved (see: heterosexuals) tend to camp out.

We clinked our acid tabs like beer bottles, then placed them under our tongues, letting them dissolve for the better part of 20 minutes. Then we laid back, luxuriating in the afternoon rays of a cloudless, breezeless day.

An hour went by and neither of us were feeling anything.

"She said 45 minutes," I mumbled to Ben. "Did we get scammed by Busch Gardens?"

"Well, it appears so and you are to blame," he said.

"Why me?"

"You bought cardboard from a stranger and I got all excited. Incredibly anticlimactic. And you know I'm counting Weight Watchers points. I'm sure acid is at least a point."

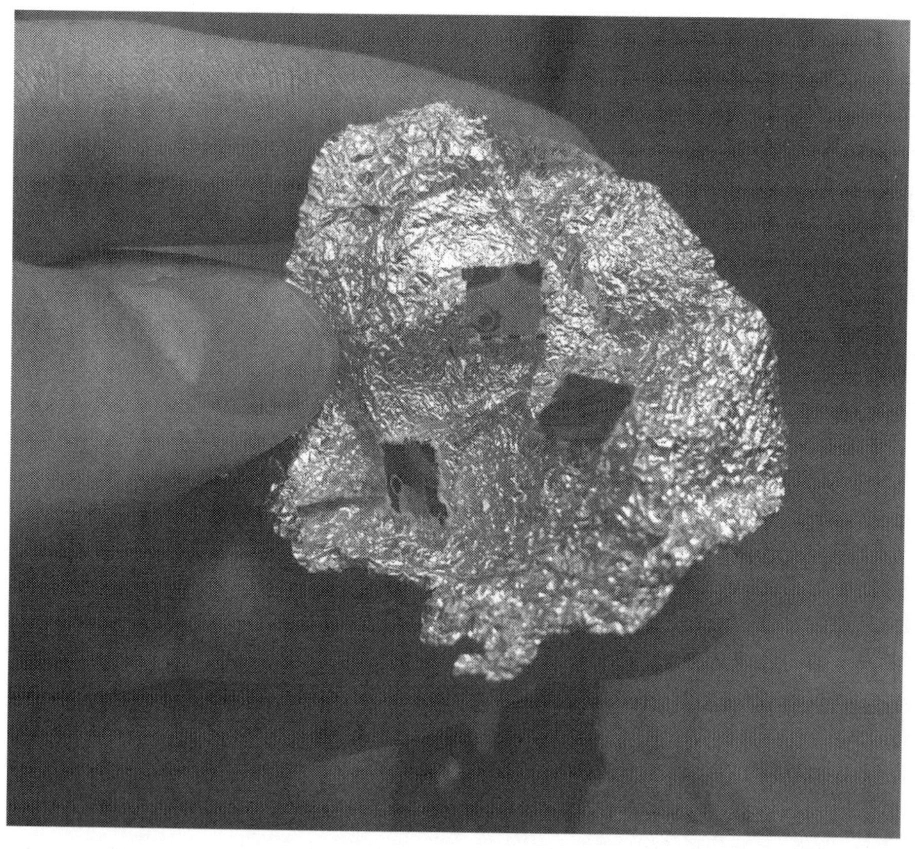

My purchase.

When the two-hour mark hit, we both resolved ourselves to the fact that today would be psychedelic-less. We gave up hope and went swimming for 10 minutes. When we arrived back at our towels, I scrolled through my Instagram feed and Ben handed me a Coke Zero. I reached down to pop the tab, only to witness said can start to melt into my palm. I let out a bloodcurdling scream and threw it in the sand, watching it land four feet in front of me. After it landed, it seemed to dissolve into the beach.

"Ben!" I stuttered. "Something is happening, Ben!"

Ben was in full fetal position, rocking side to side and laughing manically. "I knowww," he said through his giggles. "I've been trying to stay quiet here, waiting for you to catch up. I've been in this for at least five minutes."

"Houston—" I looked at Ben and nodded. "—We have landed."

When I say we laughed for five minutes straight, I promise you I am making this declaration without a shred of exaggeration. We were frantically clutching our sides, trying to breathe through frenzied gasps. A very solicitous woman even came over to our towel and asked us if we were OK.

"Better than I've ever been, lady." I clutched my stomach muscles, which felt like they were about to rip in half. "Get on our level!"

"DO ITTTT," said Ben. "You want an acid tab?"

She shook her head and retreated.

"Let's go swimming!" I yelled. "You wouldn't happen to have water wings in that cooler, would you, Benny? I don't know if I can swim like this."

"Weren't you a lifeguard?"

"Yes, but that was before acid." I chuckled. "Now I'm a fucking giraffe!"

I stood up and blinked three times in an effort to reset my mind against the landscape that sprawled before me. My mind had begun to perceive every object as having its own heartbeat. Sun rays split into hundreds of distinct beams of every colour in the rainbow.

The trees were my first auditory hallucination, softly whispering, "Ssssssssillllyyy boy," into my ear as a breeze rattled their leaves.

The familiar beach, where I had enjoyed a decade of summers, looked brand new. I was a tourist seeing every nuance I had previously glossed over. I felt guilty about every piece of the world I had ever taken for granted. I was a mere speck of homo in an expansive universe. It was both inordinate and bewitching. Childlike curiosity filled my bones as I felt the weight of the world dissolve with each exhale.

Unfortunately, I also seemed to have the intellectual capacity of a child.

People have regaled me with stories of the introspection they gained when trying LSD. My thoughts were sophomoric and akin to the entrails of a mongoose, not a far cry from those within the pages of this book.

I couldn't type, so I started to record audio memos in my phone, which, at the time, I thought were gold.

Here they are:

"How come I always take a penny and never leave one?"

"How am I supposed to study for my HIV test next week?"

"I don't think I've ever NOT drank on antibiotics."

I waded into the lake, where I saw an unending rush of technicolour shapes, shifting by the second. I was watching the cartoon version of my life play out before my eyes. When I finally dove into the water, fractal patterns lined the floor of the lake and bogarted all my attention. I couldn't conceptualize how long I'd been under but eventually my base biological functions took the helm and I came up to the surface. Ben was standing beside me, looking off into the clouds.

"I am in awe," he said, slicking back his hair and inhaling deeply. "Do you feel like you're on another planet?"

"It's like I know I'm here but I don't completely recognize this place, if that makes sense," I replied. "I also felt like I was swimming in an amniotic sac.

OTIS: You should text your mom and say, 'I think I remember your uterus.'

I nodded and told Ben the idea.

"You should." Ben nodded sagely. "But tell her you're on acid or she's gonna call a neurologist."

I looked out into the distance, squinting without my shades at the intensifying rays of the sun. Boats were anchored in the distance and rap music emanated from their speakers. I started to twerk violently while Ben shook his head in disapproval.

"Look! Someone is swimming toward us," yelled Ben. "A visitor from another galaxy. We must greet them. Pull yourself together."

The man was dipping his head under the water and sporadically coming up for air, like the calculated approach common to an alligator. Slowly up then even slower back under. When he was about eight feet from us, I burst out laughing.

"Ben! Ben! Holy shit. I thought that was Renan."

Then the man spoke. "It is Renan. Hola, you stupid cunts."

It was a stimulus we were unable to process. For one, we assumed Renan would be dead by now, a sucker punch to the head after he instigated one too many fist fights. Two, he had arrived in what seemed like seconds, right into our acid trip, like a gay Loch Ness Monster. We started up again.

"AHHAHAHAHAHAHAHAHAHAHAHAHAHAHHAHA-HAHAHAHAH." –Jordan

"AHAHAHAHHAHAAHHAHHAHAHAHAHAHAHA-HAHHAHAHA." –Ben

"What da fuck is wrong with you, bro?" said Renan. "You bitches tripping balls fo real?"

"Help! Someone!" screamed Ben. "I am not OK. Alert the authorities."

"Yo, yo, yo, Renan!" I babbled. "We haven't seen you since the near murder-suicide."

He pointed at Ben's face. "Yeah, da fuck is his name again?"

"Ben!" I shrieked with laughter. "I can see how you forgot, considering you never left your blackout."

"AHHAHAHAHAHAHAHAHAHAHAHAHAHAHHAHA-HAHAHAHAH." –Jordan

"AHAHAHAHHAHAAHHAHHAHAHAHAHAHAHA-HAHHAHAHA." –Ben

Then I dove under the water without warning. It was a total necessity. I needed to reset the overload of stimuli cracking my brain in half.

I could hear Ben screaming above the water, "THIS IS NOT HAPPENING. HELLO? WHERE IS JORDAN? OH MY GOD, HE DISAPPEARED."

Just as I broke the surface for air, I saw Ben scream, "NO ME GUSTA!" at Renan before diving under the water.

He came back up just as a woman appeared and stood right beside Renan. She was wearing a pink trucker hat, no bathing suit top, and had black eye makeup running down both of her cheeks.

"Dis my ex-wife," he said, wrapping his arm around the

woman.

"You have an ex-wife?" I could feel the laughter bubbling up again. "Is this a hallucination? Ben, make it go away. Make them disappear. I'm begging you."

"No, you do it," said Ben, splashing me with water.

"No, you do it," I said, splashing him back.

Then:

"AHHAHAHAHAHAHAHAHAHAHAHAHAHAHHAHA-HAHAHAHAH." –Jordan

"AHAHAHAHHAHAAHHAHHAHAHAHAHAHAHA-HAHHAHAHA." –Ben

"Fuck yeah, it's true," said the woman, chuckling. "We were married for two years, then I found out he's gay. I used to wonder why he always wanted anal, ya know?"

"OK, yep. That's it. I'm outta here," I said, and began frantically swimming in an entirely different direction.

It took me at least 15 minutes to find my way back to shore but when I got there, I couldn't find Ben. I walked up and down the beach for 20 minutes and finally found him dancing around a fire and keg with Renan, Otis, and eight other Brazilians. I would later find out it was Renan's cousins and sisters who rented a boat to party on over the long weekend.

"Hola, Jordan!" screamed Ben. "Come here and say HOLA TO MI FAMILIA!"

Renan's family cheered and pumped their fists to techno music while Ben refilled his red cup from a keg. Then he yelled, "I blew Renan. Mi Familia. Mi Familia!"

In thick accents, four of the family members and Otis chanted back, "HE BLEW RENAN! HE BLEW RENAN!"

This is the sort of stimulation I would be unable to process even sober. I hightailed it back to the towels like it was a CIA safe house and looked up at the clouds, which started to morph into centaur-like shapes. I tried to breathe deep in my diaphragm to achieve a semblance of stability. The sun was starting to set below the water line.

Suddenly, a charming man appeared over me. I popped off my ear buds and immediately jumped to my feet.

"Hey cutie," he said. "Are you alright?"

"Felix?" I blinked in disbelief.

Felix was a brief romantic tryst that lasted just over a month, about seven months PA (pre-acid), which was my new reference point for time. On our first date, he casually told me the granular details of his colourless hookup with Ben, four years prior. He had a fetching smile and a beguiling wiener.

"Fuck, you scared the piss out of me," I said.

"The piss?" he replied, laughing. "Oh boy."

"Oh my God. I'm British now. I hope it's just temporary. When did you get here?"

"Like an hour ago," he said. "Are you alright, man?"

"The Acid Gods are testing me today, Felix," I said, my hands over my eyes.

"Acid?" he said. "Wild. You're always up to crazy stuff."

"Yes, I am not husband material," I replied, secretly hoping he would challenge me.

Instead he nodded and motioned to the two men standing behind him.

"Jordan. These are my co-workers," he said. "Devin and Cole."

"Are you here for Electric Island, Jordan?" one asked.

Electric Island is an EDM music festival that takes place several times a year at Hanlan's Point. I went one year and I was probably one of the most sober people there… and I was on

MDMA.

"You know my name?" I asked. "How do you know my name?"

"Uh, he just said it."

"Right. Right." I nodded. "No, I'm just here for the acid. I didn't know it was Electric Island. I hate crowds, actually."

"Yeah same," he said. "I think it starts in an hour. It's about to get wacky around here. Most people are camping out on the beach overnight."

"People camp out on this beach?"

"Oh yeah," he replied. "All the time, man. Looks like they're already ramping up."

He pointed to a roaring firepit 40 feet away. As the last sliver of sun ducked below the horizon, I saw five guys dancing by the pit with Bud Lights in their hands, two of them with white shell necklaces. It seemed to be some sort of flaccid-dicked Amazonian rain dance.

The flames pulsated, and spitting embers sparked hallucinations around the rocks. An ember would hit the rock but instead of staying there, I saw it drip down, like a trail of water. The rocks grew and shrunk to the beat of my heart. It was beautiful until it wasn't.

"Oh no!" I screamed. "I need backup. Excuse me for a second."

I took off, running full steam down the beach. I stopped when I made it to Ben, who was now playing horseshoes with Renan's family, missing the mark by 10 feet.

"This game is not acid friendly," said Ben to one of Renan's cousins, who nodded in agreement.

"Ben!" I yelled, gasping for air. "You can't leave me right now! Felix just showed up and there is a naked fire dance going on. And, um. And, um. I'm pretty sure I'm going to get sacrificed. I know it doesn't make sense, but just trust me here."

"Felix? What the fuck is Felix doing here?" He handed his horseshoe to Renan. "I'll come with you, but you owe me because I fucking love horseshoes. It's probably my favourite thing. Well, second, right behind acid."

We took off running together down the beach and finally arrived back at home base, where Felix and his co-workers were now completely naked, comfortably bare-assed on my Ralph Lauren towel.

"Why are you guys naked?"

"Well, he dared me," said Felix. "Plus, it's a nude beach. Why wouldn't you be naked on a nude beach?"

"I can give you a lot of reasons," said Ben.

"Well, I like getting naked. I'm a nudist. Remember those photos I sent you from my cottage, Jordan?" said Felix.

"I tried to forget them," I replied. "Something about your leg on the birch tree. Very Christopher Columbus."

"Well, this is familiar," said Ben, talking directly to Felix's penis. "Hello, old friend. How ya been?"

I tapped Ben on the shoulder and whispered in his ear. "The other guy has a hot body and I want to look at his dick but I don't want him to catch me."

"Let me save you the trouble," whispered Ben. "I looked directly at it and it was a gherkin. A real cocktail wiener of a time. Don't bother. "

"I think we need to take the water taxi back to the mainland," I said. "I'm starting to have a bad trip."

OTIS: Now?!

JORDAN: Yes, now!

"Was it the cocktail wiener talk?" he said. "I'm sorry Jordan, but it's true. The truth is uncomfortable."

"No," I replied. "But let's go."

We discarded our trash and packed our knapsacks as the naked fire dancers started to multiply both in numbers and hallucinations.

"You forgot your towel," Felix said as we walked slowly toward the exit.

"I know, but I can't look at it. The colours are too overwhelming, so just leave it," I replied.

At this point, it was an hour or so after sundown. We strolled along the cement path, lit by city lamps, to the water taxi loading area. The beams from the lamps continued to split and sear deep into the recesses of my corneas. We donned sunglasses and clutched each other, terror-stricken, like we were about to roam through a field of land mines. After a couple of minutes, a young girl, who couldn't have been more than four, sped past us on a tricycle with her parents following behind.

"AHH!" screamed Ben. "It's a midget!"

"That's not a midget," I said. "That was a child."

"Are you sure?"

"Yes, I'm pretty sure," I replied. "And can you stop jumping without warning? I'm dangling by a goddamn thread here."

"Well, if it was a child, those parents should be reported. Children should not be doing LSD," he declared. "I might not know many things today but *that* I definitely know for sure."

"Not everyone on this island is on LSD, Ben."

"Oh, you're right," he said. "I've officially lost it. Listen, I'm having soooo much fun, don't get me wrong, but like, when does it end?"

I looked down at my phone but it was indecipherable.

"Siri!" I yelled. "What time is it?!"

"9:59," she smugly replied. Siri is smug. Don't act like you haven't thought it.

"So, we have about four more hours of this," I said.

When we boarded the water taxi, Ben and I sat chuckling in the back. It felt like everyone was staring at us.

"I'll guess we'll have to ride it out," Ben said. "Four more hours isn't so bad."

After we disembarked from the water taxi, we walked five minutes to The Westin Harbour Castle, where a line of taxis usually congregates. The building and city lights sent out luminous trails that streaked every time I moved my head. The beams crashed into each other and retreated like shooting stars. Car horn after car horn echoed and bounced through my eardrums like a Pong ball. PLING. PLONG.

When we finally hailed a taxi, the driver tried to spark up a basic conversation with us. His efforts were futile. He would quickly learn his passengers were operating like oxygen-deprived baboons.

"Sorry sir," I said, after two minutes. "It's not us! It's the acid talking."

"Goddammit." Ben pulled his iPhone toward his face then away, trying to gain a level of visual clarity. "I have a Tinder date this week with a guy I've been texting with for maybe two weeks and he has been texting me the whole day and I haven't responded once. He probably thinks I'm a total fuck boy."

"Just be honest with him," I replied.

"OK." He nodded and typed slowly into his phone. "OK, I got it."

"What did you write?"

"I said sorry about all that today but I'm on an acid trip," he said. "Is that good?"

"UM, NO!" I stared at him in horror. "That's a little too honest. He's going to think you're a derelict."

"Oh no!" sobbed Ben. "I've made a widdle boo boo."

"AHHAHAHAHAHAHAHAHAHAHAHAHAHHAHA-HAHAHAHAH." –Jordan

"AHAHAHAHHAHAAHHAHHAHAHAHAHAHAHA-HAHHAHAHA." –Ben

"Well, that's probably done," he said, powering off his phone and tossing it into his knapsack.

When we arrived back at Ben's house, I knew it was time for me to spill the confession I had been too embarrassed to admit in the cab.

"Ben," I said. "I have to poop and I can't hold it in any longer. I'm absolutely terrified. I know it's the acid because, well, I've been pooping fine for three decades. I'm overwhelmed, almost with emotion, at the idea of warm excrement exiting my body. I don't think I can do it, man."

"Jordan, I feel the same," he said. "I've been saving it all for when the acid finally wears off. I don't have the guts to do it."

"I would LOVE to ALSO do that but we both know poop lives on its own timeline," I said. "So I'm going to need that eye mask in your freezer to level myself out and I will also require the door to be open so I can sense your support nearby. Do you copy?"

"I'll be right here, my love," he said. "I'll be right here lying on the hardwood floor, remembering what my old life was like, and ordering us Uber Eats."

I made my way to the toilet and stared ahead at the bathroom wallpaper, miniscule blue diamonds that metamorphized into circles that then became ovals. The bathmat between my feet was transfixing, drawing my attention to its waving, blurry threads. It was like I could see energy everywhere. And my eyes were like two fish-eyed lenses.

"BENNN," I yelled. "IT'S COMING!"

"IT'S COMINGGGGG," he repeated.

"IT'S TOTALLLLLY HERE. BEN! IT'S HERE."

Otis leapt from my shoulder and climbed the shower curtain, hanging sideways and screaming with me. ***AAHHHHHHHHHHHH!***

Don't mind me. Just tripping on acid and wearing Ben's clothes.

To them both, I shouted, "I FEEL AN EMOTIONAL PURGE COMING. I DON'T WANT TO LET GO."

"LET IT GO," Ben replied, bursting into a Disney song. "LET IT GOOOO."

After my bowels ceased movement, I joined Ben on the hardwood floor. We lay on our backs, staring at the popcorn ceiling with matching iced eye masks.

"I think I almost cried during that," I admitted. "The human body is stupendous. Stupendous, I tell you!"

Ben chuckled. "Listen, we need adult supervision. It's very clear we are not well. I'm not going to make it to the end."

"Call Jesus. He's a seasoned drug user."

"OK." Ben scrolled through his phone. "Oh, and I ordered us food but I couldn't read the words on my phone so we have either a single spring roll coming or maybe food for 12. Or maybe Renan. I'm making no guarantees."

"HEY SIRI!" he yelled. "CALL JESUS, STAT."

"Calling Jesus," she said, smug as ever.

Jesus didn't answer so we left him a voicemail. He texted us back six minutes later: *Hey I'm at dinner but the good news is it just ends. It's not gradual. Like 100 to 0 in seconds. So that's something you can look forward to.*

"That's promising," said Ben, after reading the reply out loud. "An hour to go."

"An hour?"

"Just about."

"Hmm." I considered this for a moment. "Hey Ben?"

"Yes?"

"Have you ever been intimate with a ghost?"

"Probably," he confirmed. "At some point I'm sure I have. You?"

"I think a few," I said. "And it was kinda nice."

"Mine too. I think most ghosts get a bad reputation, you know?"

"Yeah for sure," I said. "You wanna watch TV?"

Ben turned on the Food Network, one of those cooking shows where they give you a lemon, an egg, three hip bones, and a butt plug, and then ask you to whip up a creative dessert. I put the face mask over my eyes and took deep breaths.

Minutes later, the acid trip came to a halt in the midst of a blink, just like Jesus told us it would. I stood up, stretched my arms over my head and grabbed my backpack like nothing had happened during the last 12 hours.

"OK then," I declared. "See you later?"

"Later, homo," he replied.

CHAPTER EIGHT

DENNIS

I've never understood people who make grand proclamations that they have no regrets in life. I don't believe any of these people. Usually when they state this I like to chime in with lines like, "Can I give you a few, Jessica? How about we start with your husband, Colin?"

I have thousands of regrets, three from just last night.

One such regret occurred while lying in bed, engaging in pillow talk with a medical anal suppository. It is prescribed by my doctor to treat my colitis on an "as needed" basis. Ten minutes before the clock struck midnight, I uttered, "It's just us tonight, buddy," then took a deep breath and felt it dissolve in my anus. He said nothing, as most glycerine-based corticosteroids tend to do, but it doesn't mean I wasn't hurt or that I regretted starting the conversation.

Sure, I'm an oddity but I took it as an important sign. I was all alone. My prescription medication, like most men I've dated, reinforced the prevalence of emotional distance in our society. I thought back through my long history of men, an all-star lineup of callous types that only got worse with time.

I immediately thought of Dennis, a shining star among the pool of these emotionally distant clowns. Dennis is just one of many life regrets on an ever-shifting continuum. Some of these regrets seem less severe over time, while others, like Dennis, stick deep inside me like a wad of gum.

He was a 33-year-old blithering, closeted, bisexual alcoholic whom I met in the fall of 2015. He was an idiot but he was *my* special idiot.

Here are the cards he held:

1. An average sense of humour
2. A car
3. An undergraduate degree
4. An abnormally high sex drive
5. The most beautiful penis I've ever seen

Now you're probably thinking to yourself, *Jordan, I take my dick assessments very seriously. In fact, I consider it to be an art form. Plus of course, one has to address the extreme subjectivity going on here. Who are you, Jordan, to make such grand claims?* Well, I will say that I may in fact be an authority on this matter solely because I'm operating with a colossal sample size. Are you?

The day I met Dennis was the same day I inflated a children's pool on my apartment balcony and filled it with pool noodles. I had created a Facebook event inviting over 20 people for a "Caribbean Themed Pool Party" without clarifying what type of pool I had access to. And it worked. In highly dense metropolitan jungles, pools give you massive clout. Around 2 p.m., several people entered my condo, perplexed at the site of Ben and me drinking margaritas to the sounds of Bob Marley and other staple reggae tracks. Few people stayed longer than 10 minutes, including one of my exes, who entered the condo, rolled his eyes, and said, "See, this kind of shit is why we're not together."

Here's a photo if you think I'm a filthy liar:

The "pool party" concluded around 4 p.m. When everyone left, I drunkenly used a sump pump to drain the water into my shower. It took twice the amount of time estimated by the man who rented me said pump (see: crippling gay handicap). Then, I passed out cold in my damp swim trunks on top of my down comforter for about four hours. When I awoke at 8 p.m. I had a text from Ben that said, *How many Weight Watchers points is ass?*

A wave of immense gratitude washed over me. What more could I ask for in this life than a best friend who understood the universe's most pressing questions?

I stripped off my clothes and crawled deeper under my silk sheets, spread my toes, and propped up my back with two pillows. This is my favourite position for both masturbatory activity and perusing dating apps, or sometimes on a long weekend, a combo of the two. I opened my Grindr inbox:

Message 1 - A blond man in his later 30s named Cody. He was a "life coach."

OTIS: Oh, that sounds recession proof.

Message 2 - A publicist, a profession I briefly dabbled in. It's a weird one if you think about it. I mean, who grows up with dreams of making other people famous?

He first sent a headshot, then a torso shot, and 28 minutes later, a photo of him naked. In the picture, he was on all fours with a perfect line of sight to his gaping asshole. I wondered who took that photo, or if he was savvy enough to couple a tripod with a delay timer. Maybe a friend participated in the process? I figured if I asked Ben to take on such a role, he would have me institutionalized.

Message 3 - A "Pokémon Go Enthusiast" named Kevin. Remember that summer when everyone, but mostly incels, went buck wild traversing the city with their smartphones, collecting cartoons? (Straight women who may be reading this: Please remember, no man spending his weekends setting up clashes with virtual creatures will lick your genitals to orgasm. It's science.)

It's also cultural appropriation. The game was started by the gays, who have been running around major metropolitan cities for years with their phones, playing a sexual version of Pokémon. Except our prizes are actually tangible—instead of a collection of mythological cartoons, we simply collect strains of HPV. Gotta catch 'em all, kids.

Message 4 - A 73-year-old man offering me a "generous lifestyle" as a houseboy. I stopped and considered it. I'd filed maybe four tax returns already and was totally knackered from the 9 to 5 life. Surely this couldn't continue for another 40 years.

Maybe I could live like one of those "kept" women on *The Real Housewives*. I'd wake up at 10 a.m., go to Pilates, have lunch with the girls (just chardonnay and opioids so I could stay thin and trophy-like) and then take a three-hour afternoon nap. Then, after I was refreshed, I'd wake up, splash some cold water on the old mug and get to work pleasuring him. My life would be one of elegance and putting the "job" back in blowjob.

But I had to think, what would a 73-year-old dick look like? I pictured it gray and plagued with hyperpigmentation, like in the movie E.T. when they find him lying by the river rocks.

Would a dick like that operate the same? It's a dick from an entirely different generation. Phones and audio players were different then. Would I have to start it up with a crank or awkwardly spark a pilot light? I'm not handy at all.

And then, to top it all off, I'd probably have to talk dirty to him in Latin. Right? "Lorem Ipsum Homo Analingum" or something of that sort.

I deleted the chat box.

Seven years of Grindr usage had brought me to the conclusion that the gay world was brimful with sexual maniacs, derelicts, and mismatch after mismatch. This day would be no exception.

And what had happened to courtship, like our forefathers used to do? It has been depressingly depleted to unsolicited nudes and one-word salutations like, "suck?" or, "down?" If Nicholas Sparks knew how gay men looked for romance, he would shake his head and shove a gun right in his mouth.

There was a single message remaining in my inbox, no photo, with a bio that read, "very discreet, bi-curious, love to party, not sure what I'm doing on here... or in life." Ah, the human equivalent of table scraps.

OTIS: Jackpot!

We started to chat, and then chatted some more. His name was Dennis, and he was aggressive, wildly inebriated, and seemingly hilarious, a retired former frat boy with Peter Pan syndrome to boot. I had been missing a man whose banter could rival my own since Patrick had left the picture.

I'm a little lost right now, he typed.

Send your location, I wrote back.

I don't know how, he said. *Gonna take a pic.*

He sent me a photo of the CN Tower, easily Toronto's most notable landmark, utilized in postcards, souvenirs, mugs, and even one of Drake's album covers. He was *that* lost.

You're a fuckin mess, I wrote back. *You're beside the CN Tower. Pretty much the number one most important building in the city. I'm fairly close to there actually.*

Great! he wrote. *I'm coming over. Send me your address.* ☺☺

Easy peezy.

In hindsight, it's amazing I emerged from my twenties without being sliced and diced by Luka Magnotta. Inviting strangers to my apartment never felt like a perilous choice. Everyone was doing it. It was my cruise control. Only now do I start to examine how distorted my "normal" was back then. Social cues and feedback from my gay male friends led me to believe there existed no cause for concern. But there was lots to be concerned about. It was terrifying what I would do to connect with a man. Occasionally I'd share these stories among my heterosexual female friends and be met with looks of incredulity. I guess these high jinks don't seem as crazy when you live in the middle of the cyclone.

At 10 p.m., Dennis buzzed my cell phone for entry. I smirked and said out loud, "Well, this should be a fun," a blatant sign that you have prioritized entertainment over meaningful human interactions. Upon his arrival, it quickly became clear we were in different states of cognition. I barely had a buzz, while on the opposing end of the spectrum he was barely managing "th" letter combinations.

Dennis was banker douche incarnate. He was dressed in a Hugo Boss fitted suit and a white collared shirt with lipstick stains on the left side and beer stains on the right. His tie had been loosened around his neck and had a clip on it in the shape of a dollar sign. His eyes were puffy and bloodshot but beautifully blue, the kind you could easily point out in a lineup. I will forever be a sucker for dark hair and ice blue eyes (in case you're reading this and looking to spend your life with me after the "bug" Brazil story).

"Hi," he slurred. "Can I come in?"

"I'm debating," I said, tapping my foot just long enough for Otis to flick the angel off my right shoulder and high five the devil on my left. "OK, sure. Come in."

Dennis was ruggedly handsome, I noticed as he plopped down on the couch. I poured him a glass of merlot and locked eyes with him for three seconds. Then I felt something in the air. The intoxicating allure of the bad boy. Unresolved childhood trauma. The entrance to the black hole of unadulterated chaos.

"Your eyes are pretty insane," I said, filling up my own glass of wine.

"Thanks dude," he said, aggressively gripping my right thigh. "You are fucking gorgeous."

"I do alright." I pointed to his shirt. "Who is on your collar?"

"Some bitch."

"Don't talk about women like that. I'm a militant feminist."

"OK. Some special lady."

"Hmmm." I took a sip of my wine. "And where is she now?"

"Good question," he said. "I think that's done after tonight."

"I'm guessing you're not a relationship guy?"

"You would be correct," he said. "How can you tell?"

"Well. You're emotionally unavailable. It's very obvious. You also seem to have a very short attention span and a live fast, die hard mentality."

He nodded.

"Plus, there's the crippling hold of alcoholism I'm picking up from you. That adds to it. And of course, the self-hatred that accompanies life in the closet. It all adds up to unhealthy, transient relationships," I said. "I mean, I'm just guessing."

"Do you always psychoanalyze people when you meet them?"

"Yes," I said. "Always."

"OK, well, for now," he said, placing his wine on the coffee table and leaning toward me, "let's make out."

And make out we did, to Kings of Leon for the better part of a half hour. We fit like a puzzle from the second our lips touched. It was seamless. No awkward adjustments or pauses. No stiff lips or sloppy tongues. Just a coupling of rising serotonin and dopamine, tango dancing in our minds. At one point during the session I stopped, pushed him away from me, and said, "Wait, is that a transatlantic pipeline in your pants or are you just happy to see me?"

"It's both," he said, smirking as he ran his hand down my ass crack, where a small pool of sweat had formed.

"Mmmmmm," I moaned.

"Fuck," he said. "You are soooo wet."

"What do you mean?" I said, confused.

"You're turned on," he said. "I love it."

"Have you been with a lot of men sexually?" I asked. "That's not how that works."

"I guess," he said. "Well, I dig it anyway. The wetter the better."

"Well then, you should see me after a jog," I said, ripping off his shirt and dragging him to the bedroom. "I am a disgusting little piggy."

One of the moments I enjoy most, before I usually ruin a man's life, is ripping off each other's clothes. The fumbling of buttons, ripping off a belt like you're starting a lawn mower, the internal struggle of whether to say "fuck it" and leave your socks on…

It's the spice of life. The magnum opus before the bigger magnum opus. The pulsating anticipation, the rise of adrenaline, the pause on the starting line before the gun is triggered. *BOOM!*

We hit the carpet, each wrestling to pin the other in the pitch black of my room. I ungripped my left hand and smashed it into the floor plate of my lamp to turn it on. Then, as the bulb hit 50 watts, I gasped at the majestic sight that appeared before me. There it lay, engorged across his stomach, a sexual organ with the potential to procure a Nobel Peace Prize.

It was eight inches, uniformly pink, with clean lines, flawless angles, and a velvety smooth coating from base to tip. It was the kind of penis UFOs would enter the Earth's orbit for.

"I feel like I want to cry," I said, holding it in my palm, feeling like it had its own heartbeat.

"Huh?"

"Dennis, I've been touched by the penis of an angel," I said. "Just give me a moment of silence here."

"Dude," he said. "It's not that big."

"It's not the biggest, sure," I replied. "But one does not evaluate a penis on a singular factor. There are many elements to evaluate, and this is a timeless masterpiece. The *Mona Lisa*, *The Last Supper* and now, THIS."

"Wow," he said, laughing. "You are a fucking ridiculous person, Jordan."

"Is that bad?" I said, lying on my carpet and staring at the ceiling. "I just say everything that's in my mind. It's fun for me."

"No, no," he said, turning his head to face mine. "It's not bad at all. It's refreshing. You're not afraid to be judged. That's kinda rare."

"Oh, I'm afraid," I corrected him. "I think we're all afraid. Maybe I'm just better at making peace with it."

"OK well, this isn't sexual talk at all anymore. You're getting a little deep."

"Sorry."

"No, it's kinda nice," he said, beaming at me.

"Yeah," I said. "This is weirdly nice."

We stayed up until 4 a.m., hysterically laughing at my overreaction, his Grindr escapades, my summer jobs, his co-workers. It just spilled out of us, the way it does when you crush. The way you take in every speck of their laugh. The way your eyes stick together like hot toffee. Or the way you have to remind yourself that you just met this person, even though the immediate comfort feels like something that should have taken years of work.

"Spoon me," I said as I plugged my phone into the wall. "It's 4 a.m. and I haven't slept with a cool guy in my bed for a very long time."

"Oh, I'm a cool guy?" he said. "That's good to know."

"I know cool," I replied. "Trust me."

In the morning, the sun's rays snuck through a dislodged window curtain, lighting Dennis' cock. It was asleep, just like him, but still as perfect. That penis served as the final confirmation of my undeniable homosexuality. His penis had to be protected from the elements, like a prized antique car you'd secure in a garage, maybe slathered in Turtle Wax. The rest of him was obviously dented and rusting fast, but I overlooked it, naturally.

Dennis and I were a thing for nearly the entire fall. At first, we kidded ourselves that it was entirely sexual, with meetups on Fridays or Saturdays just past 2 a.m. Then weekends became weekdays and one of us would note it was sneakily becoming kind of romantic. Both of us, total commitment-phobes, would run in opposite directions until the magnets in our hearts did their work and we'd find our way back to each other.

Just typing this, I realize part of me still misses him. We understood each other because we were two emotionally stunted misfits. We were both exceptionally guarded, potentially beyond repair. We craved love and intimacy while fearing it more than anything else. Dennis was an amalgamation of all the worst qualities of my father, dressed up in the costume of the perfect boyfriend.

It was push-pull, high to low, side to side. We pursued what we felt to be instinctual and natural, strong human connection, but always refused to stay too long. The closer we made it to any sort of "finish line," the more agonizing the journey back to our status quo of emotional distance became. Dennis and I were a torturous, toxic existence that enveloped me like I was paralyzed in the core of a tornado.

And of course, his internalized homophobia reared its ugly

head, ravaging his soul to the point where he'd drink himself into near comas. When he was sober, he was boyfriend material. When he was drunk, he was an incoherent, sociopathic monster until his buzz faded and he'd come back to me with open arms. It was four months of being entrenched in a savage love affair with both Dr. Jekyll and Mr. Hyde.

Once, he called me just after 3 a.m. after we decided to take some time apart, near convulsing amidst a flood of tears.

"I fucking like you so much man," he said, sobbing into the phone. "But then I stop and, like, I can't. Every part of me wants to. Why do you like me, anyway? You could go and get with any guy in Toronto. You have a lot going for you."

"I definitely could not get any guy," I said. "But I'm not getting it. If you like me, what's stopping you? I'll do this."

"I want a wife and I want a family and I'm bad for you. You know I'm bad for you. And you're bad for me because you consume my mind all day. No one makes me laugh like you, and you know I make you laugh the most," he said, still sobbing. "Admit it, Jordan."

"You do." I felt moisture seep into the corners of my eyes. "We're the real deal. But is it real if it's not? Is it real if it's a secret? I mean, come on, man. This is absolute torture. You're in or you're out."

"Can I come up? I'm outside your place," he said. "I just want to sleep with you tonight. I don't want to think about this."

"I don't know."

"Come on," he said. "Please. Just buzz me up."

We lay on my bed on our sides, saying nearly nothing to each other, breathing in and out, tracing the outlines of each other's eyes. In that moment, we were the closest we'd ever been but still standing miles apart. We were like two animals in a zoo, needing to bond more than anything but forced to paw at a piece of separation glass.

"You want me as you want me," I said. "Then you go back into denial."

"I know."

"I've done the closeted thing. It's a road to nowhere."

"I know."

"This is a relationship with a 900-square-foot fence."

He looked at me, exasperated with living life as a chameleon. Then he kissed me, more passionately than he ever had before. It was the only way he could communicate to me that he understood my position. That he understood why I was constantly eyeing stage left.

Emotional baggage can loom over your life (sometimes forever) like a tropical storm. So many of us date as temporary vacations from ourselves. We leave just to feel a quick lift. But you always have to come home to yourself. And your reality, without work, will remain unchanged. Real love isn't a fleeting moment, it sustains. Real love isn't an escape filled with high highs and low lows, it's a constant stream of security. Anything else you accept is a waste of your time. Trust me. The faster you stop running from yourself, the faster you'll find what you need out of life.

Being a gay man means taking a seemingly endless journey to deprogram yourself from the messages of your youth. If you want to emotionally mature, you need to trace these messages back to their source. And when you do, you'll realize they come from people who could never think for themselves. Why should anyone trust the opinions of these people? They should be dismissed as nothing but mindless regurgitations. So, dismiss them and stop letting bystanders interfere with your life.

These messages lingered in my twenties, and I chased men

that confirmed them. After Patrick, I accepted men who didn't deserve me, one after another like crashing dominos. I panned for gold in patches of horse shit. I glommed onto flashes of oxytocin to prove the world wrong. That's all these men were, cheap drugs of escapism to distract myself from my rotting heart. My time with Dennis was when I finally started to realize it.

That very night at 4:30 a.m., Dennis woke up and went to the washroom, naked, to pee. In the haze of sleep, I heard him rummaging around looking for the doorknob, followed by a long piss stream. Then, a minute later, I heard my roommate Jesus' bloodcurdling scream. "AHHHHHHHHHHHHHHHH-AHHHHHHHHHHH!"

Dennis had come out of the washroom and turned left instead of right. Then he'd quietly slithered into bed with Jesus.

I imagined the experience from Jesus' point of view. You're in a second wave of REM sleep, senses dulled, unaware that a mumbling predator is moving leisurely across your carpet. You feel a wave of hot Hennessy breath hit your neck, then an arm on your chest. Before you have time to make sense of your new reality, a silky penis starts to graze your ass cheeks. Then—"AHHHHHHHHHHHHHHHHH-AHHHHHHHHHHH!"

When Dennis returned to my room I nonchalantly turned over and asked, "Did you just crawl into bed naked with Jesus?"

"Yes."

"Accidentally?" I had to entertain the fact that anything was possible with him.

"Yes."

"OK then," I said. "Good night."

Goodnight to you too Otis, I whispered. Otis blew me a kiss.

The next morning, Dennis and I had feral sex and he left

around noon. Two days later, I was working on a digital marketing presentation with my usually reserved business partner. A year earlier, we'd started a now fairly successful SEO and content company. Halfway through the presentation, he put his pen down, furrowed his brow, and said, "Dude, why the hell do you keep wincing and grabbing your cock? You've done it like 20 times."

"I don't know," I replied. "My dick feels weird. Like a burning sensation."

He smirked. "It's finally happening," he said. "Your whorish ways have caught up to you."

"What do you mean?"

"You have an STI," he said. "I'm surprised it took this long."

I was in total denial. "No, I don't!"

"You keep leaving to pee every 15 minutes," he said. "It's at least a UTI."

"Fuck," I said. "OK, I'll be right back. I'm going to go examine it."

Five minutes later I returned to the conference room.

"GODDAMNIT!" I shrieked, the second I walked through the door. "WE'VE GOT A SITUATION."

"What did you see?"

"Either I came in my pants or I have an STI," I said. "And I don't think I came—you're not my type."

It had already been an uncomfortable amount of time since I'd been tested for an STI.

My rule is usually that you should visit a clinic immediately if:

1. Entirely new diseases have come out since the last time you've been tested;
2. You look down after sex and think to yourself, *Hmm, is that cum or discharge?*

I told my business partner I'd be back in an hour and took a cab to a walk-in-clinic near Union Station. I had been there twice in the past, once for a staph infection in my nose and another for a routine STI screening years prior. As I approached the clinic door, I was hit with a picturesque flashback from the last screening:

DOCTOR: Well, your test results came back negative. And frankly, after reading your answers to the questionnaire, I'm a little surprised.

JORDAN: God, how boring am I? I must have something, maybe a hot new strain that's trending right now. Have you done a Windows update on the computer lately? Try it again.

DOCTOR: I'm a little concerned about your attitude. You don't seem to be taking this seriously.

JORDAN: I'm a little concerned about your Crocs. You don't seem to be taking fashion seriously.

DOCTOR: How many times in the past year have you had unprotected sex?

JORDAN: What is that? Do you mean using my emotions?

DOCTOR: With a condom.

JORDAN: What's that?

DOCTOR: What?

JORDAN: I'm kidding. I use condoms. Can no one take a joke anymore?

DOCTOR: OK, and how many times have you had unprotected sex?

JORDAN: Maybe two.

DOCTOR: Toys in the mouth? Toys in the bum?

JORDAN: Of course.

DOCTOR: Do you swallow fluids?

JORDAN: No, I'm a vegan.

DOCTOR: Hmmm.

He scribbled something in his notepad.

*JORDAN: *smirks* then *smirks again**

Long pause.

JORDAN: Anything else?

DOCTOR: No, you can go.

JORDAN: See you soon.

DOCTOR: I'm sure.

With that glorious exchange in mind, I pulled open the clinic door and marched right up to the receptionist to give her the lowdown. She took my health card, swiped it, and then handed me a plastic cup to pee in. I filled it halfway and gasped at what was living within my urine. It looked like baby Sea Monkeys. Wincing, I placed it on a tray marked "URINE SAMPLES" in the makeshift lab and returned to the waiting room to be called for my inevitable verbal lashing.

Thirty minutes later, a nurse led me into Examination Room #2. She took down all my info and said the doctor would be in shortly. I prayed it would be a different doctor than last time. There was no time for smugness right now. The only thing I would accept was something that would immediately eliminate the burning sensation in my urethra.

Then the door opened and a young Indian woman walked in.

"Hi, I'm Doctor Aggarwal," she said, as she sat down. "I saw your notes from the nurse. I think you either have gonorrhea or chlamydia, but we won't know until the test results come back in a few days."

"OK," I said, staring at the floor.

"I'm going to treat you for both and test you for everything, but first I think it's important to discuss safe sex practices," she continued. "So, I'm going to ask you a few standard questions."

"Let me stop you right there," I interjected. "I'm not an idiot. I know who this is from and I used a condom so I'm sort of confused about what exactly happened."

"Did you use the condom during oral?"

"Excuse me?! THAT is NOT a thing."

"It's a thing. You should always be performing oral sex with condoms."

"Are you trolling?"

"Trolling?"

"Like kidding or joking with me to try and get a response?"

"No. I'm not kidding. I tell patients all the time."

"Listen, I get that you have to say that," I said. "But let's be real, no one is really going to do that. Most people would rather get an infection. What you just told me is probably the best tip I've ever heard for dying alone in my life. I should know many of those tips. I used most of them in my twenties."

"Well, if you don't," she said. "You may be back here soon with this again so I would say you should consider it. And in the meantime, no sexual relations for seven days, and you'll have to let your partner know immediately."

"Oh, I'm already texting him," I said, glancing up at her from my phone. "And I'm using a lot of fire emojis and eggplants."

She grimaced.

"And if he doesn't respond appropriately, I'm going to be using a lot of gun emojis as well," I said.

She looked at her notes. "I'll print you a script and the nurse will give you an injection on the way out. Please schedule a follow up appointment and we'll call you with your results in a few days."

When Dennis failed to reply to my slew of texts, I called him twice and got his voicemail. I tried him a third time and he answered.

"Dude!" he said. "I'm in a meeting. Chill."

"Oh, this will only take a second. Anything you'd like to share with me?"

"What do you mean?"

"Come on. How many people are you sleeping with?"

"What? Why?"

"Because I have an STI and my cock is currently in the catacombs of hell."

"Well I didn't give it to you. My cock is fine."

"Because you're asymptomatic. Apparently, half of people are," I said. "I've learned a lot today."

"What do you want me to do, Jordan?"

"An apology would be nice."

"Well, I didn't know. But sorry. OK?"

"It's fine, just go to the clinic," I sternly replied. "You can go to mine. They were quick. It's the one across from the SkyDome."

"Yeah I know where that is," he said. "I'll go tomorrow."

"Today," I corrected him. "You will go today and YOU WILL STOP SPREADING YOUR DEMON JUICES AROUND THIS AREA CODE. DO YOU HEAR ME?"

Two days later, the clinic's name flashed on my caller ID.

"Hello, Mr. Power?" said the woman on the other end of the phone.

"Talk to me."

"Mr. Power, I regret to inform you that you tested positive."

"What?!?!" I feared the worst.

"For chlamydia."

"Oh, whew," I said relieved. "That's a walk in the park."

"A what?"

"It's like an easy fix. You need to work on your telephone manner." Then I hung up the phone.

I texted Dennis the update and he replied with, *Yeah, I know.*

A week later, with a refurbished cock, I agreed to meet Dennis for a dinner at a restaurant called Marben on Wellington Street. My masochism knew no bounds. If a burning bacterium in my urethra couldn't kill a toxic relationship, then what would?

When I arrived, he was already two sheets to the wind, but ordered us a bottle of merlot and two porterhouse steaks. After we paid the bill, we crossed the street to Portland Variety to sample some vintage bourbons.

"Wanna come see my office?" I said to him, half leaning over the glass bar.

"Where is your office?"

"Across the street," I said. "It will be quick and no one is there."

"OK, sure."

Ten minutes later:

"So this is the small boardroom, and this is the copy centre, and this," I said, pointing to my ass cheeks, "this is where dreams are made."

"Oh God. We can't keep sleeping together," said Dennis, shaking his head. "We have to start phasing this out. We are absolutely terrible for each other and you've made it pretty clear you're not giving me more."

"Actually, that was you who indicated that. But sleeping together is still FUN, no?" I said devilishly.

"It's certainly fun, yes," he said. "There is no denying that."

I unzipped his fly and kissed his neck.

"You owe me for breaking my clean streak," I replied.

He playfully shoved me off.

"What the hell?" I asked.

"Oh, so you'll let me in your ass, Jordan, but you won't let me in your heart?"

"Well, when you put it like that..."

"I'm serious, man," he said. "You always toy with everyone's emotions."

"I'm going to take umbrage with your use of 'everyone'," I replied. "I don't toy with everyone's emotions."

"Well, me, for one," he said. "You toy with my emotions. We're off and we're on and then we don't speak and then it starts again, month after month."

"There is no future here, man," I said. "I'm sorry to break it to you but you have a ton of work to do on yourself and your desire to get closer to someone. Or how about telling a single person that you're a bisexual man? I'd say that would be part of the basic foundation of a fruitful romantic relationship."

"Well, if I told someone?" he said. "Then what?"

"Like who?" I replied, annoyed. "Who would you actually tell?"

"Well, I told the doctor at the clinic."

"Oh, a person bound by confidentiality?" I rolled my eyes. "How brave."

"Well it's a start."

"It's a start, man," I said. "Don't think I don't support that, but you can't come out for me. I don't want that burden on me. Maybe a couple years down the line when you have your shit together, we can be boyfriends out in the open. I want something more real. So until that day comes, if it ever does, I've got to keep you in this box of casual."

"Ugh," he said, dejected. "Now I feel like shit."

"You know what I do when I'm feeling down?" I replied. "I make sweet love in an office building."

So we did.

The next morning, we packed his car and drove up north on

a previously planned skiing trip to Blue Mountain. It was early January and unbearably frigid. We lasted six runs, then bailed to drink pitchers of Molson Canadian in the lodge. Around 4 p.m., we loaded his trunk with our wet ski gear and hightailed it back to the city.

"I need snacks," he said, veering off an exit into a service station. "And Coke Zero. Do you want anything?"

"No, I'm good."

After Dennis walked into the service station, I fumbled through his middle console looking for a piece of gum. On top of the gum was a white envelope for Erythromycin, with dosing instructions written in pen: *4x daily for 7 days*. I counted the pills. There were 20.

When Dennis returned to the car, I was holding the envelope in my hand, exasperated.

"You've gotta be kidding me right now," I said.

He looked dumbfounded. "What?"

"How many pills did you take?"

"I don't know," he said. "Why?"

"Well then, why don't we count them together as a family, shall we?" I said. "28 total with 20 remaining, meaning you took 8. You took 8 pills out of 28."

"So?" he said. "I took it for a couple days. I was busy."

"YOU WERE TOO BUSY TO INGEST A PILL?!" I said. "WE HAD SEX YESTERDAY."

"Well, I told you I didn't want to," he said, shrugging.

"BECAUSE OF THE CHLAMYDIA?!" I threw the envelope at his head.

"What the fuck, man?" he said. "Chill. No, I meant in terms of feelings getting messy between us."

The envelope fell under his gas pedal.

"Oh, my God," I said. "This is not seriously happening. Why didn't they just give you a single dose? I'm sure they would have given you a single dose if you shared with them THAT YOU SUFFERED FROM CRIPPLING BRAIN DAMAGE!"

"I took enough," he said. "It's fine. You're so dramatic."

"This is like special sexual education," I said, throwing my hands in the air. "It's truly unbelievable. What kind of grown man forgets to take all the medication required to cure him from an STI?"

"It's fine," he said.

It wasn't fine. On Monday morning, I went back to the same clinic with the same doctor and the same symptoms. When I told her the entire story, she looked at me in horror, like you would look at a five-alarm fire that had just roasted a family of four.

"Jordan," she said, sighing. "I don't know if this is my place but if you can't trust a person with the most basic of things like respecting your health, then why are you sleeping with them?"

"I don't have enough time to answer that," I replied. "Poor adolescent role models, some parental neglect, bad business deals that shattered my trust… the list goes on."

"OK," she said, lowering her glasses as she typed notes into the computer.

I jumped in. "His name is Dennis Walters. He is also your patient and you can look him up in that computer. He's got these enticing blue eyes and a huge Adam's apple."

"I can't speak about other patients," she replied.

"D-E-N-N-I-S W-A-L-T-E-R-S. There will be more victims of his stupidity. Let's call him right now on speaker so I can absolve myself of any responsibility in this embarrassing debacle," I said.

"How do you two know each other?"

"It's a long story," I said. "And today marks the day it finally ends."

"I think that's a good idea," she said, smiling. Then she handed me another round of Erythromycin.

"Oh, hello old friend," I said, as I swallowed the pills.

That evening, I called Dennis over to my condo. We drank two bottles of wine and cuddled on the couch for more than three hours.

"Everything comes to an end," I said, resting my head on his chest. "And I don't even hate you for giving me an STI twice. So what was the point of you and me, anyway?"

"I don't know," he said. "That you're a maniac with a cement exterior?"

"You're projecting," I said. "And also very right."

He laughed. "Hey, I really am sorry about the whole chlamydia thing."

"Ah, water under the bridge, my friend."

Dennis paused, and asked, "So this is it?"

"This is it," I replied. "I hope I don't do this to myself again." Then my voice lowered. "I just hate that when I get comfortable with someone, it seems like they're already gone. It's like I can never grip tightly enough. Or maybe my grip is too tight. You know?"

"Jordan, you love broken guys," he said. "Everyone you've told me about has been a mess."

"Like you?" I asked.

"Yes," he said. "Like me AND you."

"I'm not a mess," I said. "I'm a work in progress."

An hour later, we got up from the couch and walked to the front foyer, where we hugged for a long time without uttering a word. I felt his chest hastily move in and out. Some of the moisture from his eyes ran down the side of my cheek.

He said, "Bye," one last time, and I stood in the doorway watching him wait by the elevator. We held eye contact. He pressed the elevator button again three times then looked down at the navy-blue carpet. He never made eye contact again.

Hey! yelled Otis, jumping off my left shoulder. ***Hey Dennis! Wait up buddy.***

Otis! I called out. ***Dude, come back here.***

He paused, then spun around, his tail whirling wildly. He looked back at me with an unmistakable smirk. ***The writing's on the wall, kid. Didn't I always teach you to leave before you're left?***

He took off running again.

Otis, I replied. ***Don't leave. Please.*** The air felt numbing. My stomach dropped so fast I felt a wave of nausea. My feet were shaking.

He was now sprinting toward the elevator, gasping for oxygen (dude was in terrible shape). Without looking back he bellowed, ***I'm not changing for anyone, Jordan! I promise I'll visit soon.***

I heard the elevator DING and watched Dennis get inside. Just before the door closed, Otis raced in at breakneck speed. The last thing I saw was his little brown tail as the metal door slid along the track and clicked into place.

CLUNK.

A year later, a mutual friend told me over brunch that Dennis had moved to Manhattan. I was relatively unfazed by the news, and it was then I realized the spell had been broken. I smirked and sipped my coffee.

But I wasn't out of the water yet when it came to my dysfunctional relationships with men.

Case in point: As we settled up the bill, my friend described the behaviour of a man that had been stalking her for weeks.

Without hesitation I replied, "Honestly, that sounds kinda nice."

A week later, I was back in therapy.

CHAPTER NINE

ELI

And now for something kind of different.

Hindsight.

Hindsight comes after an amorphous period of time brings tangible closure to our pain. Many of us hope it's the gift we'll earn after our pain begins to dissipate. But it can be brutal. It can shock your soul at 4 a.m., violently waking you up to burn the portrait of the past you once knew.

And when that portrait is nothing but a pile of ash, hindsight starts again, painting you a new picture of an unfragmented reality. And then suddenly it all makes sense. The fluorescence is blinding. You see it all. The risks that were worth it and those that were not, at a time when they are all dressed up the same.

This is my story of hindsight, of waking from a nightmare packaged like a fairy tale. So, let's start from the beginning.

Once upon a time, I had great fucking hair. Golden highlights like Jennifer Aniston. I brought in a photo of her basking in her usual sun-kissed glow to my lesbian sister Kat's girlfriend, a.k.a. my stylist. She tells me I zoomed in on a specific strand of Ms. Aniston's hair and asked her to deduce the exact colour through a pixelated and cracked iPhone screen. Truthfully, I can't recall this, but damn if it doesn't sound like the kind of unrealistic nonsense I would put someone through.

That summer, said hair was on fleek due to a strict regimen of two drops of Argan oil daily, fish oil supplements times two, Paul Mitchell extra body foam, the thinnest roller brush you've ever seen, and 15 minutes of carved-out time to form "the poof" on the front of my mane. It brought all the boys to the yard, as Kelis would say. Oh, and also my affinity for rampant promiscuity. That one never seemed to hurt.

Hello, Hollywood.

Along with good grooming, I was obsessed with improving my tennis prowess. I took lessons every Wednesday with a bald Israeli named Yosef, who had an obnoxiously aggressive bulge. He had very recently become sober and he constantly described the routine of his "new life." It was a snooze fest and a half. I told him I would rather die of alcohol poisoning than play Balderdash with my cousins on a Saturday. In retrospect, it was a hella insensitive thing to say to a man who had seamlessly christened my kick serve. I even got up at 6:30 a.m. for the lessons, which was totally uncharacteristic of me. I was hooked, and combined with gruelling CrossFit workouts, my body was shredded like cheddar.

Seven weeks into the regimen, I matched on Tinder with a man named Josh, who I knew ran in similar circles to mine, but whose genitals had never made my acquaintance. His IQ simmered in the low 100s and echoed through his incessant social media updates.

I saw his updates after he added me to Facebook and shuddered as my penis inverted into my body.

C'MON CHINA. GET IT TOGETHER, he'd post in response to a complicated sociopolitical issue, five miles above his head.

THIS IS COOL, would be his hot take on some of nature's most awe-inspiring mysteries.

I needed a tennis buddy, however, to hone my newfound skill—and plus, he had abs—so I invited him to play at a park by my house. When I arrived, he was sitting sprawled on the bench. After a quick hug, he launched into a long-winded diatribe about his ex: his ex breaking his heart, his ex's ex, his ex's former ex, and Tinder. Josh hated Tinder. Tinder was the problem. What a platform, that Tinder. Nothing good came of it. Tinder ruins lives. Tinder divides countries. Tinder killed JFK, people!

"Maybe the apps aren't the problem," I earnestly replied, before serving across the net.

After tennis, we went back to my place and took a joint shower, because well, I have the sex drive of a coked-out rabbit, and curiosity is a hell of a beast. I bailed mid-escapade and sauntered to the kitchen to make myself a protein shake.

"Hey, do you want to come to a barbecue tonight with my friends?" he asked.

"Are they annoying?" I asked. "I'm not big on humans."

"No, no, they're good fun," he said. "We can bail if you're not feeling it."

"OK, sure," I said. "But I'll need 15 minutes to style my hair."

"Really, 15 minutes?" he said. "Are you serious?"

I glared at him and downed the remnants of my protein shake.

"Yes, 15 minutes, bitch," I said. "You think I wake up looking this enchanting?"

Josh drove me to the party, which was seven minutes from my condo and not at all a "barbecue." In fact, there was no actual barbecue, just an oven and an ample supply of cocaine. It was a mid-level condo with a tiny balcony and piss-poor AC. I actually knew the host, a shrill corporate head-hunter that Ben once penetrated in an alcohol-induced haze.

("PLEASE don't remind me about that idiot," said Ben when I told him I was writing this chapter.)

There were maybe 10 attendees at the faux barbecue, four of whom were sitting on an L-shaped couch, transfixed by the Olympics on TV. It was the women's 100-metre dash, the large majority of the competitors being black women. Josh offered to make me a plate and I plopped down on the corner of the couch in my purple shorts, white fitted Zara T-shirt, and sinewy tennis calves.

"Based on our current climate, I wouldn't be surprised if the camera panned back and it was cops chasing them," I announced to the room.

The four guys on the couch erupted into laughter. *Well, that was easy,* I thought. Unprovoked, I immediately launched into graphic detail of my anal fissure surgery and concussion, my "A" material. Again, I absolutely crushed. How could I not? Fissures and concussions, the two prominent milestones in a young gay man's life. Just ten minutes in and I was the belle of the ball, golden tennis legs and all.

"Who the fuck *are* you? Just strolling in here and putting on a show," said a voice to my immediate right.

I hadn't torqued my body around to see the entirety of the man's face at this point. I was focused on delivering my vaudeville extravaganza to the other three men on the opposite end of the couch.

"Who wants to—" I stuttered and stammered as my eyes locked on the man to my right.

Tunnel vision. Time froze as my biological functions went into unimpeded overdrive. My heartbeat was bouncing out of my ear canals. *Fuck. I'm stuck.*

I could always run from this feeling, but on this day, I lost the battle within seconds. Hot blood rapidly circulated across my cheekbones. It had been almost a decade and the "Patrick" feeling was back. This blood was relentless. Down my neck. More hot blood, down my chest.

Heartbeat—BOOM—heartbeat—BOOM.

Focus, you idiot. Say something. Anything. How long has it been since you said something? My left leg went kinda numb.

"Umm, hi," I said, like a blotto teenager.

"Umm, hi," he replied, smiling nervously. I took solace in the fact that he was also a visible mess—but a cute mess, like a coy puppy. He looked at the floor, then back at me with his strong nose and pale blue eyes.

Seconds passed. Maybe five? 10? We both stared inquisitively. I'd never watched a person's pupils dilate before. He blinked. Once, twice, three times. He held his smile. I couldn't look away.

"Have we met before?" he asked.

"I don't know," I said. "I feel like…"

"Like we have?" he said. "I know, same."

"But I don't think we have," I said. "I feel like I would have remembered."

"How don't I know you then?" His eyes narrowed, and he put his hand on my shoulder. The second it hit my skin, the nerves went to work down my back.

"I'm going to get a drink." I shot up, electrified. "Do you want one?"

"I'm coming with you," he said. "Cool?"

"OK," I mumbled. "I'm Jordan."

"Eli." He smiled. "I'm happy I met you, Jordan. I wasn't going to come tonight."

"Same," I said. "I'm kind of your friend's date for this party but not actually, ya know? Not my type."

"Good." He winked. "Very good news."

There were others who wove in and out of our chats that night but I barely remembered them.

In fact, I couldn't say if I even paid any attention to Josh. I had so much I wanted to tell Eli and he hung on to every word. We were love junkies, strung out on limitless serotonin and with the pacing you might get from amphetamine pills. The natural pauses between sentences vanished. I was freefalling in screaming colour.

At three points in the night he asked me why we hadn't met and I'd remind him each time that he had already asked that. It didn't matter. We were here now. When I left to go to the washroom, he stood outside, tapping his foot.

"Missed you," he chuckled, red-cheeked, upon my exit. "Is that weird? Did you miss me?"

Of course I missed him. I hadn't been this high for a decade. It was transfixing.

"Nah," I replied.

Then we'd get high on prolonged eye contact and smile. I'd overshare as fast as I could because I was making up for lost time. All the times we hadn't met. All the time we'd missed apart. I was spinning, my words leaving my lips before I had time to piece them together. Every message from then to now trailed behind me. *You're unlovable. You don't get a happy ending. You're a broken guy from a broken home…*

I'll show them, I thought. *I'll show everyone.*

"So my sister is a nurse," I chattered. "She has a dark sense of humour like me. My other sister is a creative type. She's a great filmmaker."

"I can't wait to meet them," said Eli, smiling. "All of them."

Time moved too fast that Saturday night but I remember every moment with Eli like a haunting slideshow on old 8mm film. The moments clicked and changed but lingered just long enough to sear themselves into my mind. It was the start of something monumental and I leaned into it without hesitation. I gave up control and switched to autopilot, or whatever the hell my version of it was. *This is a thing now,* I thought. *And it's either a happy ending or another scar etched into my heart. Worth it.*

At 1 a.m., Josh offered to drive me home, seemingly oblivious to the situation at hand. Eli hugged me and whispered in my ear, "I'll add you to Facebook." Then he pulled away with a wink.

At 4 a.m., I received a message from him with his number.

At 4:01 a.m., I sent a message to Ben: *I met someone tonight and it was so intense.*

The next day I texted Eli around noon. He responded immediately and asked if he could call me. *'Cause I really wanna hear your voice,* he wrote.

We chatted on the phone for three hours that day. He pumped me for details on my upbringing, my career path, past loves lost.

Did I want kids? Well, why not?

Why hadn't we met yet?

Did I want a dog? Which breed?

Why hadn't we met yet?

Hey, why hadn't we met yet?

In retrospect, I know now that after the three hours were over, I had learned next to nothing about him. But it *was* the setting for the perfect storm.

I'm a writer. I live in the flurry of my thoughts. I replay moments endlessly, connecting them, squeezing imagery like it's the last pulp in a Florida orange. And to write about these moments I need to feel every dimension of them. And then I need them validated by a receptive ear, sometimes for three hours at a time.

Eli also had a relatable and realistic cynicism about the human condition. Not enough that it would smother you, but enough to let you know he understood how the world worked. And his humour. God, was he funny. After I cracked a joke about his horrendous fashion sense, he told me he genuinely wished that my colitis declined to the point where I needed a colostomy bag. That might sound harsh to you, but that kind of dark humour is totally my bag, baby.

We both needed humour as a crutch for survival, but his reliance was next level. It was the perfect buffer to create unwavering emotional distance between the two of us. (Again, all in hindsight.) After I got off the phone with Eli, I was spent. I called my sister Lisa to confirm our dinner plans that night. Fifteen minutes later, Eli called back. He just *had* to tell me something he forgot to bring up. I listened intently for another hour, then showered and got to work on the construction of "the poof." *First name Jordan, last name Aniston.*

I met my sister for dinner and she couldn't get a word in edgewise. I was all things Eli. She nodded as I exploded at every seam.

"That's great, Jord." She nodded some more, through undertones of concern. "I'm really happy for you."

When you really need something in life, that is the time to pause and reflect on why. That which sustains us has the power to ruin us. I hate admitting this, but at the time I met Eli, I couldn't stand alone. I was incredibly adept at reeling in men to fill the void and tossing them aside, like crustacean shells (Nathan, Dennis, Morgan, Jesse—OK, yeah, Jesse beat me to the punch. Don't rub it in). Each of them was a placeholder, telling me the things I couldn't tell myself. That I was valued. That I couldn't forge intimacy. That I was lovable. That I was enough.

It's important to understand that, like most gay men of my generation, I lost nearly 20 years of my life. I didn't have a prom date or a first kiss that I held with a level of legitimacy. I lacked role models and relationships that I could mimic. And as much as you try to swat away the darkest messaging, God, it fuckin' lingers like a stain. If you're not gay, imagine the sting of knowing that there are people dedicating their lives to making sure you don't get married, or making sure your employment could be terminated on the basis of your sexuality.

Imagine never seeing yourself represented in a relatable manner in media. Imagine knowing there are places in the world you'll never visit, and that millions wish for your death. Couples massages. Threats to your safety. Expressing love on an island resort with stares upon stares from strangers. It probably doesn't serve our long-term purpose remaining segregated in gay bars, but a safe space is simply a respite from these sorts of glares. Those glares shrink us and pull us in to a disempowered past, back to the nightmares of youth. Those glares are a reminder of our days spent hiding in the darkness.

The YouTube comments, the religious demagoguery, the most awkward medical appointments… it's a never-ending onslaught on the way you express love. And it would be the highest level of naivety to think this wouldn't have far-reaching implications on our mental health.

I felt my love was primed to fail if I didn't make concessions. I believed I was a misfit. Progress was coming, but it was depressingly slow.

I once lived my life as a ghost, stashing old VHS tapes of *Queer as Folk* (my reference point) under my bed. I'd count the hours until I could devour them in the early morning, while everyone else was asleep.

And even the show's messaging was kind of bleak. The characters reaffirmed thousands of negative messages I'd subconsciously planted in the deepest caverns of my brain. A rough road lay ahead, kiddo. Gay relationships *were* possible, but complex, and by-products of men who limped out of the closet, maladjusted survivors of unrelenting trauma. I was determined to make Eli the exception to the rule. We would be no match for any circumstances that came our way. I vowed to do it, even if those circumstances were the ones that would determine everything that would transpire.

At 6:30 p.m. Sunday night, Eli picked me up in his white SUV outside my condo on King Street West. At first blush, the man had beautiful biceps… and hideous sunglasses. White fitted tee, black jeans. His hand over mine as I shook with a visible tremor.

"God, you're nervous," he said. "Just relax. Seriously. Isn't it obvious I'm totally into you?"

My hesitation was visceral. I knew it was all real. I was terrified. I tried to feel it but my mind was still batting down the exuberance of my heart. The hesitations started to dissolve. My heart had won the battle.

"No," I playfully lied. "I'm fine. Get over yourself, dude."

Our first date was at El Catrin in Toronto's Distillery District. We couldn't keep our hands off each other. Really sophomoric, super giddy shit of the highest purity. Young(ish) love is the best. Falling face first without hesitation, not caring what lies beneath, even if it's shards of glass. We didn't really need to say much. The nonverbal cues did all the talking. Except for the following moment, three minutes into my empanada:

"So how long have you been out?" I asked.

He looked down at the table. "Umm I'm not. Like I am, but…" He trailed off.

"Explain."

"Well, like, obviously I have gay friends, you met them."

"Yeah, they weren't great," I said.

"Ha. They're alright. But yeah, I'm not out at work just

because of the profession I'm in."

"Medicine, right?"

"You remembered," he said, smiling at me. "Impressive."

"Thanks, but I don't really buy your whole excuse about being out. What about your family? Are you out to them?"

"No, I'm not out to them."

"You're 36," I said. "Isn't that kind of pathetic at this point?"

He paused and moved his entrée around with his fork. He shrugged. Then he steered the conversation back to me, my favourite subject.

Hi, it's me. A red flag. Yeah, right over here, Jordan! How much more obvious do I need to be, man?!

I wish I had run. That was my most blatant message from the universe. I was in my 30s. I didn't need this shit. But I knew gay love came with compromises and complications. This was the one I'd work through with Eli. He would come out *for me. I was worth it, right?* My infatuation didn't shift an inch. He drove me home and we made out for 10 minutes in his car.

"I cannot stop kissing you," he said. "Literally cannot. You are just so cute. Ugh."

"Samesies," I replied.

Weeks went by and we spoke all day every day, texting for hours on end. In the end I had to delete our thread in the throes of heartbreak because it felt like someone had a death grip on my heart, but here is one exchange I recall:

JORDAN: But are you freaking out? Like I'm freaking out.

ELI: Yep. I've never felt this way about someone.

JORDAN: Same. I hate the vulnerability.

ELI: I feel naked.

JORDAN: Promise you won't break my heart. I honestly couldn't handle it right now.

ELI: I won't. I won't. I am going to do my best.

Two weeks into our stay at the love hotel, I messaged a mutual friend on Facebook, just far enough from Eli that I knew it wouldn't get back to him.

Hey, I wrote. *I'm totally falling for Eli and I realize we're mutual friends. Can you give me some intel? Things feel a bit intense but I might just be a bit paranoid.*

Hey Jordan, he replied. *I can't say I have great things to say about him.*

Explain.

Well, is he out yet? he said. *Because he wasn't seven years ago and I doubted he was ever going to be.*

No, I said. *Not at work or at home.*

Listen, he said. *He has a lot of issues. He put me through hell and it's always the same story with each guy. Super committed and then he disappears and comes back like nothing happened. It's very confusing.*

Really?

I'm just saying, you're probably going to see this ugliness come to life soon, he said. *He's not a bad guy but he is not dating material. Trust.*

I ended the conversation with a strange feeling in my gut, which I quickly shook off. *What does he know?* I foolishly thought. Maybe Eli just wasn't into him and he couldn't handle it. I wasn't about to give unsubstantiated rumours a lot of weight. First, I planned a sleepover. Eli was incredibly game.

"OK, so Friday at 7?" I asked, my arms around him.

"Yeah!" he said. We were outside his apartment after five blissful hours together. "That sounds awesome."

Well, it wasn't awesome. I am actually cringing as I get ready to type this part.

I bought wine. I bought two baseball steaks. I cleaned my condo from top to bottom. I changed the sheets. Then around 4 p.m. I texted Eli to make sure 7 p.m. worked for him. No reply.

5 p.m.

6 p.m.

6:45 p.m.

Finally, I received a reply. *We had plans tonight? I'm having drinks with friends if you want to come.*

I felt humiliated, like my head was about to spin off my neck. I didn't even reply and instead went out with friends.

The next morning, I was walking home from the gym when Eli called. "Heyyy. Happy two-week anniversary," he said. "Are you so excited to be dating me? Because I think you're incredible."

It was a mind fuck. I didn't know what to say so I just replied, "Uh, yeah." Then I said, very calmly, "Listen, I'm not sure what happened last night but I know we had plans for a sleepover and you just blew me off without an explanation. What gives?"

"Oh man," he said. I could practically hear him rolling his eyes. "I'll come over tonight, OK? Just calm down."

"I am calm."

And so he did come over, with two pints of ice cream to watch a movie, with the sun still up. It felt the same. Seamless. He again tried to convince me I had overreacted about the sleepover.

"What?" I said, "No I didn't. You blew me off."

"You're so dramatic," he said. "You're like the most dramatic person I know."

"Oh whatever," I said, tickling his stomach beside the kitchen counter, and initiating a play fight. He held my wrists firm.

Then I looked up. "Stop fighting it. You're falling in love, gurl."

I'd hit a dead end I never saw coming. Something snapped in his eyes. He riotously threw me against the fridge, which knocked the wind out of me. I started to cough as my windpipe spasmed.

This was just a silly mistake, I told myself. *An underestimation of his own strength. We're two men play fighting. He already called me dramatic earlier. If I make a mistake here, I could lose him for good.* I coughed some more.

"Are you OK, Jordan?" he asked, filled with what looked like unmistakable concern. He was blinking so fast. After a few seconds, I nodded.

"I'm fine," I lied. I tried to catch my bearings and put my hand up to fend him off temporarily. I coughed again. *Just relax. He's made a stupid mistake.*

"Good," he said, then kicked me right in the balls, laughing.

I fell to the ground, clutching my abdomen. I was nauseous and confused. *Who the fuck was this maniac? What was he doing? Was more coming?*

That wild swing in a person's mood. I'd seen it before in Dennis, and even worse in my dad. It was midday sunshine to pitch black in mere seconds. Was this Eli's normal?

"Are you OK?" he repeated, feigning concern. "Jordan? Jordan? Are you OK?"

I nodded again, still on the floor. Then he started laughing maniacally.

"OK, I gotta go," he said, putting on his shoes and kissing me on the forehead. "Love you."

"Bye," I said, utterly confused as the door slammed.

I considered telling Lara or my mom. Maybe Beth. All women. Women can be trusted. But I knew what they'd tell me. *Get the hell away from him. What are you doing? When are you going to have enough?*

But as much as it felt psychotic, it felt expected. It felt familiar. The concessions I needed to make to get what I wanted in life—I saw them all in front of me. I knew love was harder for me. It felt ingrained deep in my flesh. That message flooded my brain at least once a week. *Gay guys don't get happy endings, but especially you, Jordan. Take what you can get.* Then another side of my brain kicked in to offer another take. *But remember Patrick? You need a Patrick.* My mind flashed to the potted plant and the day of the mental hospital. I'd thought Eli was a Patrick.

Aren't you sick of this yet? I asked myself. *You're lying on the floor. You're back in confusion and chaos. Walk. Walk away. You're not just nauseous from the kick to the balls. You're lovesick.*

No, I thought. *I've waited ten years to find love again.* Others had moved on. I was stuck. I felt it slipping out of my fingers. I pictured Eli getting into my elevator to the ground floor and my stomach sank. I asked myself, *What are you doing wrong? He's perfect. It fits. Toss out everything you've learned in the past decade. This is a once in a lifetime opportunity.* I took a deep breath and pictured our future house and rescue dog in my head. It was all so close I could touch it. My perfect ending, just over the horizon. Just one last hill. I got up and took a long shower.

The next morning, I got a text from Eli that said, *Hey, remember when I came to your house last night to watch a movie and beat the shit out of you?*

Yep, I replied. *I have a photo as proof.* I sent him the famous photo of Rihanna, post encounter with Chris Brown.

Hey, red flag here. Seriously, dude?

I wish I could say that was the only time I remembered aggressive shoves, but all were tied to the prospect of long-term intimacy. Once, Eli tripped me in a park out of nowhere, my lower leg sliding across gravel on contact and removing a layer of skin.

My friends loved Eli at first. He once came to Patrick's house to squeeze in 20 minutes with me before bed.

"He's funny," said Patrick. "He's good for you."

"I really like this one," said Patrick's fiancé, Dom. "Don't screw this up."

Even Ben, a harsh critic, loved the guy.

The three of us went out one night to Wrongbar in Toronto's West End, with Eli footing the bill.

"The man is literally obsessed with you," said Ben. "I haven't seen anything like this."

I wanted to show him the 3-inch bruise on my shoulder blade but instead I just said, "I know, he's really special."

Here I am that night. Smiling through the pain with Patrick.

Then on the night of my 31st birthday, when he was due to meet all of my friends, he was a complete no-show. I gave him a buffer of 10 minutes and then blocked his number for good in my iPhone. I could feel everyone pitying me. Ben even put his hand on my shoulder, offering to chat privately. I struggled to find the words amongst their sympathetic eyes.

"I'm fine. It's honestly for the best." I repeated, even though it wasn't. It was the most brutal low after riding high on flood after flood of ecstasy. When I got home that night, I binged on all my leftovers and cried gutturally on my couch. Then I took a shower and noticed the bruise in the mirror. I sent our mutual friend a message on Facebook.

It's happening. Everything you said would happen is happening. I'm such an idiot.

And that was the point I should have ended it. You see it. I see it now. But I never saw it then. I still couldn't get out of my own way. How did this guy own my heart even though he'd done nothing to earn it?

Three weeks went by with Eli still blocked in my iPhone. I had assumed he was trying to contact me but I held strong until the first snowstorm mid-fall. I was nearly through a bottle of cab sauv, solo, when I unblocked him and wrote, *I just don't know why you did this all to me. I only wanted to fall in love with you. That's all. Just tell me why?*

He replied within seconds. *I can't believe you're messaging me.*

I wrote back, *What?*

He played the victim. *I've been worried sick about you, Jordan. Calling and texting and you haven't replied for weeks.*

I wrote back, *I blocked you. I don't want to speak to you. I just need to know why. I can't make sense of any of this. I've never seen someone so in love with me and then pull stunt after stunt. Just explain.*

Jordan, please come to my house. I want to talk to you and explain everything.

No. I knew if he got me alone and in person, I'd cave. *Just type.*

But he persisted. *I have a lot to say. Please just come. I'll order pizza.*

Every fibre in my being told me to stay put. I had to stop the endless loop of gaslighting and emotional abuse. But what grand explanation awaited me? I had to be missing something. At what point is love still worth fighting for if you're really only fighting yourself? The fact that I immediately took an Uber to his house, only an eight-minute walk from mine, at his command is picture proof that I was still a puppet on his string.

I was already drunk when I arrived at his apartment. He motioned me in like no time had passed and I sat down on the couch. He launched into a litany of banal topics. He'd seen that article I'd written (not about him) and it was "so depressing." After two minutes I put my hand over his mouth and said, "I didn't come here for that. Talk. I've said everything I need to say. If you ever want to see me again, you'll talk."

"What do you want me to say?"

"If you have to ask then it was a mistake coming over here," I said. "I'm giving you one more chance to explain." The alcohol had lowered my inhibitions, but only to my regular, baseline personality. Unapologetic, ball-busting, fearless… a tough cookie who knew his self-worth.

"OK," he said. "I'm a messed-up dude, but you already know that. I do this all the time. I go hot and then I go cold with men and it's always the same story. I've had a rough time growing up being gay."

I interrupted him. "We all have, Eli. But you don't get to run around like a bull in a china shop smashing down the rest of us who are already on a shaky foundation. You're an adult. And you're abusive. Thanks to you, I now know what it's like to be gaslighted, and it's fucking horrible."

"No, you don't understand, Jordan."

"Well, then, make me understand. This is your chance. There are very few men I would come here for after what you put me through. But here I am. I'm willing to help you. Let me help you. Please."

"My childhood wasn't normal. I'm not sure I recovered. I'm not sure I can love someone truly." He paused. "And you're great. Honestly, there is nothing wrong with you. It's all me. I'm fucked."

His eyes went red and he wiped away the accumulating moisture.

"Seriously man," he said. "You deserve better. Go out there and get better. Please."

I paused, gutted over his words. They were words I wished I could have told myself for the past decade and deep down I was finally starting to believe them. *I do deserve more. How did I get here? I knew better. Didn't I?*

But my mind flashed to our happy ending.

"I don't connect with people like this," I said, resting my head on his couch cushion. "Can we even fix this?"

"I want to. I really want to."

"All my friends hate you," I told him.

"I know. How can I fix things?"

"You need help, man. Real help. Not the kind I can provide over bento boxes. And if you get help, I'll try this again. But only if. We need time apart, like a few weeks at least, and if you want this enough, you'll go," I said. "So go. Get help. And then we can fall in love. I don't want to wait anymore."

"I want to fuckin' marry you," he said, rubbing my arm.

"I'm sorry."

Then I uttered the most heartbreaking words I've ever said to another person.

"You want to know something?" I said. "I've lived my days waiting to go to sleep. Because when I was dreaming, I would get to see you again. I just thought you should know that."

"I'm sorry, Jordan," he said, hugging me. "I am really sorry. I love you, man."

We lay on his couch for two hours as I consoled a soul even more broken than my own. After I left, he sent a text that read, *Thank you for coming here. I know that wasn't easy for you. And if you want someone better than me, like someone who isn't crazy, well then I completely understand. Xo*

I wrote back, *I'm not going anywhere.*

But Eli did not respect my mandate of temporary emotional distance. The very next morning he sent me a text that read, *Rainy days, perfect for cuddling and watching a movie.*

Then the next day, another: *Watching How to Lose a Guy in 10 Days. You remind me of Kate Hudson. Her spirit. And she's funny. Miss you.*

I wrote back, *Distance, man. I said distance.*

He replied, *I know, sorry. I'm waiting for my emergency therapy session.*

Four weeks passed and it was nearly Christmas. I bought him a mug with a photo of me on television, an appearance he said he watched three times, with a caption on it that read, "My Hero." I was so amused with myself that I bought nine more for my friends and family.

We agreed to meet for dinner at Fred's Not Here, a steakhouse steps from The Royal Alexandra Theatre. I gave him the mug with some swag I'd stolen from work. I asked him how therapy was going and he said, "Fine, good." I didn't press further as I know the process is predicated on confidentiality. *But can I honestly say I ever believed he actually went?*

"So what are you doing for the holidays?" I asked.

"Nothing," he said. "My family is going to Mexico and I don't feel like flying down so I'm just going to spend it alone."

"Why?" I said. "It's your family. Just go."

"Honestly, they hate me."

"No, they don't," I said. "Don't say that."

"It's true." He dropped his head.

"You know, ummm." I hesitated. "I really don't want you to spend the holidays alone. Especially knowing the state you're in."

"Then I'll come to yours!" he said. "Parents love me."

Then I lost my mind, again, and agreed. "I guess that would be fine. We have lots of room. But platonically. You're my friend—" (*Jordan, you're a terrible liar.*) "—and we need to keep it there." (*Yeah, sure, buddy.*)

"Yes!" he said. "I'm so excited. What should I bring?"

Do I even need to tell you what happened next?

Do I even need to tell you that history repeats itself, often in more egregious ways?

There I was, staring glumly at an empty place setting on Christmas Day at my sister's new house outside of the city. Looks of pity from everyone I loved as I saw the text on my phone that read, *I'm sorry, I can't. I know you're not surprised. Please don't hate me.* But now I really did. My empathy had gone to the wayside. When I got back to Toronto, I was riddled with uncontrollable rage.

The texts from Eli continued hour by hour, but even his gaslighting attempts could no longer penetrate.

ELI: Hey! How was Christmas?

ELI: Hey I want to give you a gift.

ELI: Let's go to that illusionist show. Looks so good.

ELI: Hey.

Finally, I replied, *Dude, just stop. Please just stop. Forever.*

Eli did stop… for four months. I thought about him almost every day. Because we lived less than six blocks apart, sometimes I'd walk by his building and look up at his window. I'd see his light on and be transformed back for a passing moment. I'd put on a Taylor Swift song and marinate in the sadness. It was oddly satisfying. My heart still felt like it was decaying, but a little less every week. Then he joined my boutique CrossFit gym. There he was, at a 10 a.m. class, bright-eyed and bushy-tailed, waving me over like nothing had happened. He knew I loved that gym. I was there almost every day for over a year. It was *my* thing, my method of restoration for my mental health after he chipped away at it for the better part of six months. I knew all the instructors and I almost always went alone. He didn't care and, because he was a professional bulldozer, he'd found a way to see me. But I had to admit, he seemed different. More thoughtful. As my anger began to fade, we started to chat again. Sometimes we'd even partner up on exercises. Over the course of two months, the cycle pulled me back in at such a glacial pace I barely noticed.

Twice, two of my CrossFit friends asked me how long I had been living with my boyfriend. In fact, everyone assumed we were together because our connection was so palpable.

"We're not together," I'd correct them. "I'm just trying to stay civil. He put me through a lot."

"You guys are totally in love," one said. "It's seriously adorable."

We saw each other, rather sparsely, for brunches and lunches over a couple months. Once, we made out in his car after class. (*Yeah, I know.*) Sometimes he'd text me to see if I was going to class, and if I confirmed it, he'd say, "Good, because I'm only going if you're going."

But I *was* healing, and I was even seeing someone else. It felt incredibly tame after emerging from the cyclone. I learned not to confuse intensity with intimacy, the wise words of a former therapist. Eli often found reasons to insult the new guy, and asked me on two different occasions if the guy was "crazy like him."

"Not even close," I replied, and really meant it.

One day, enough was enough. The lingering spark that once let me destroy myself flickered to a slow death. I wrote him this text: *Listen, I think it's clear we can't be friends. Well, I can't, anyway. It's too painful. I'm going to start going to other classes at the gym. No hard feelings. I'll always love you.*

I dodged him for five weeks until one day our schedules collided. There were 19 people in the class and we couldn't avoid each other, so I walked over to catch up. I put my hand on his shoulder and was immediately greeted by the sinister gaze of the man who once threw me against a fridge.

"GET THE FUCK AWAY FROM ME!" he screamed.

"What?" I looked into his eyes but they seemed unrecognizable. Darker. Uninviting. I was just trying to be civil. *I* was the victim of *him*. He couldn't possibly think it was the other way around.

"Are you joking, Eli?"

"SERIOUSLY, JORDAN. GET AWAY FROM ME RIGHT NOW. I DON'T WANT TO SPEAK TO YOU."

Everyone in the class stared. I shrugged and retreated into a corner. I no longer needed to practise civility. That day, the train of Eli, which had dragged me senselessly across the city for almost a year, ground to a final halt.

The mental souvenirs tapered off over the months that followed. His laugh, the way it jumped in pitch. The times he'd get up in the middle of my sentence to kiss me. Slow dancing with a blanket wrapped around us in his living room. These were moments I'd meant to last forever. It was all a cruel trick, a nightmare, a flash of time that stole hope from a dwindling supply.

Last July, I met up with Eli as a test. I needed to know how far I'd come and if time had taught me self-respect. For two hours over lunch, I saw myself floating above my body, far divorced from my former self. I was overcome with a bevy of emotions, but the only one that lasted was sheer pity for him. And I was spent, devoid of unconditional empathy for someone who eroded my trust in anyone who came into my life. So, days after our lunch, I drove across the city to meet a person who had the highest potential to help Eli. I told him everything, including the time Eli hinted his time on Earth would be short. That person wasn't surprised and vowed to do his best to stage an intervention. It was an emotional handing of the reins and a humbling reminder of the limit I always had over the situation.

One of the biggest mistakes I made with Eli was believing our time together was like a labyrinth. Labyrinths come with twists and turns but there is only one path in and out. Relationships, like labyrinths, can be long and difficult to navigate, but they shouldn't send you down a baffling pathway of broken branches and dead ends. Hindsight has taught me that Eli was my maze. He trapped me into what felt like perpetuity, shattering my bearings so I was unable to pinpoint where I stood. Yet if you asked me honestly, I'd tell you I still don't consider him to be a bad person. His sins are redeemable and I need him to be OK, even if I know that's a wish that comes from the blindest hope.

If I had to give you a specific moment that woke me from

the circus of the past decade, it would be in that gym class, being yelled at by Eli. That frozen moment in time cleared my system and showed me what I never wanted to feel again. I promised myself I'd start to wind down all the drama in my life. Never again would I destroy myself for someone who never even deserved me in the first place. Could I blame him though? He once told me that right to my face.

These stories we think are all about others can sometimes be a 30,000 ft. look at ourselves and what we'll do to be loved. Sometimes we need to see and experience the worst versions of ourselves in order to start the transition toward our best. I never got that "great love" from Eli, but it was a period of time that helped form my future self. And I refuse to force a future lover to pay for his sins.

We all have our "Eli"—some of us are still dating them. It's up to us to learn when to walk away before we leave another scar on a frangible heart. It's also on us to stop imagining those we could love as what they could become in the future, rather than who they are now. Now has to be enough. We can't exhaust ourselves moulding others into the kind of love we're missing from our emotional core.

Today, I feel like a rescue dog, learning to trust again. The party is not over but it feels like people are starting to get their coats and cabs. I'm writing my own story, taking my time, day by day. I've learned boundaries and I have surrounded myself with loving relationships I hope to model one day. I'm not sure if you picked up on it, but somewhere buried in this book, among the avalanche of cock, is a closet romantic. There are two men who could tell you all about that secret side of me. They're the bookends of this memoir.

The truth is, I'm remorselessly guarded and so reliant on

humour because I've survived all kinds of abuse in my life. I've watched allies transform into enemies overnight. I've been discarded in metaphorical ditches. I watched my dad leave our family behind without even looking in his rear-view mirror. I've watched my childhood heroes become the monsters that still live under my bed. Sometimes I lie awake staring at the ceiling for hours, sensing them so close by.

Don't get me wrong; I'm grateful for the uniqueness of my experiences in my life. For one, I learned no one can break me if I believe I can weather the storm. I've also learned when you make everything a joke for years, your life can sort of become one. And when you stop entertaining people, they wonder why the monkey isn't dancing for them anymore. Those people in your life, well, they gotta go. So, I told them to. Several of them. Because even without humour, I know I still have a ton to offer the world. Writing this book has taught me that in a lot of ways. (Thank you to my editor, Emily, who made me realize this book is actually about my love story with myself.) The book you're holding is a story of how I'm my own worst enemy at times. How I pretend I'm not looking for love, even when I am. How I try to get love. How I process it. How I brush it off. How I distill it. On stages. Through microphones. Yes, even from you, the reader. I guess this monkey can never stop dancing.

Ironically, it always felt like I experienced love on a deeper level than most. I still do. That will never change. You might love my metaphors, but imagine feeling them! Now I'm crying as I type this. Ugh, emotions. (Thanks, Emily!)

My hindsight is a reference point for what I won't settle for anymore. In such a declaration, I find myself moving closer to the kind of real love I've needed all along, guys like Patrick. And as such, maybe I owe Eli, the man who broke my heart, both nothing and everything at the same time. He slowed down my world and kickstarted my search for normalcy. I thought he would be the one to rescue me from the chaos of the previous decade, but he just taught me how to rescue myself. So, thank you, Eli. I forgive you. Even after everything, I hope you find love, too.

Listen, if you're young and idealistic, hold onto that bright light as long as you can. But here's the truth: Love is not going to save you. I should know. I chased it for a decade, albeit with shitty tools and under the guise of fun.

OK, I'll admit, love will sustain you. It will enrich you. It can be the metaphorical hand that holds you above the fray when you need it the most. But all the bullshit *Sex and the City* spewed about putting your relationship with yourself above all others… well, frankly, it's kind of true. It's your job to heal yourself, to eventually enter relationships when you're whole and only when you're whole. Don't bring your baggage, slumped over your shoulder, to the next person and ask them to make sense of it.

It has been exactly a decade since that day outside my apartment when I told Patrick I would find a way to be OK. And I finally have, just in a different form than I thought at the time. I'm writing this on the island of Ko Lanta right now, all alone, but not feeling lonely at all. My days aren't filled with the thrill of the chase anymore, only a kind of newfound peace.

I haven't seen Otis in a while. I hope he's doing well. I try to tell myself a little boredom in your everyday life is a good thing. We all know he thinks differently. That damn Otis. He's in all of us.

I still feel like I'm living in a wild movie at times, but this time I'm not driving the bus. It all kinda got old shockingly fast. And when I'd flushed the system, I decided to write new rules to last me a lifetime. I wrote them on a pad of hotel stationary—here they are:

1. Stay thin-skinned and open to real love, the kind that allows me to run into the arms of another without losing myself.
2. Stop trying to change others to be what I need.
3. Distance myself from those who pull me back toward the past, even if I have most of my favourite memories with them.
4. Reflect on what I've learned every day.
5. Ignore Otis… most of the time.
6. Know that just because I'm OK with oversharing doesn't mean others want to (OK, I'm definitely gonna mess this one up).
7. Know when to cool the laughs, drop the shield, and let the pain rush in.
8. Learn to trust again in the face of a world that often gives me little reason to do so.
9. Let others fill brunch with their wild tales.
10. Avoid shutting down. Shutting down is shutting the world out, and if I do that, I'll miss the most beautiful glimpses of what it means to be alive.
11. Be kinder to myself.
12. Show up for people, even if they never did the same for me.
13. Remember that most people, even Eli, may just be doing their best.

I watched the sunset on the beach today. I watched it without a mind-altering substance in my stomach. I watched it fall below the waterline (God, it was gorgeous) and I thought all about hindsight.

Hindsight has sparked new non-negotiables in my life and manufactured unwavering self-worth. Hindsight can show you the sedated pace at which your darkest days migrated to the brightest of white. Hindsight shows you how far you've come and how limitless the future can be, if you want it to be.

Sometimes I don't recognize the guy I am today. He would have spotted Eli from a mile away and run in the other direction. This guy is different, but only in a few distinct ways.

I feel sexy. I feel powerful. I feel confident, something I earned from personal accomplishments and overcoming obstacles, instead of trying to find it in men. I can stand on my own two feet even when they're shaking. I swat away the darkness of doubt and the fear of loneliness that once controlled my mind. I found a courage I never thought I could have and I feel higher than I ever have been before.

Even here, at my highest point, I feel the least afraid to fall.

And maybe that's because I know that if I did, I wouldn't need anyone to catch me.

AFTERWORD

I hate to break it to you, but most celebrities you love aren't their real selves. Their high-powered publicists carefully craft an image that won't make waves and in turn maximize their earning potential. You don't know Beyoncé, you know Beyoncé the brand.

The route I've chosen is the farthest thing from that. Sometimes I wish I had that luxury. The readers of this book and the tens of thousands of listeners of my podcast, *Shame On You*, know me inside and out.

Shame On You was launched March 19th, 2019 with my friend "Ben" as a journey to zero gay shame. The first week we had 200 downloads in four countries. At the time of this reading we will have posted millions in over 100 countries, including many where it is illegal to be gay.

The podcast was always envisioned as an audio diary of our lives with little to no filter. Our competitors played it safe with apologetic undertones. We spoke in an unfettered manner and took a leap off a cliff into the many undignified aspects of gay existence.

We've interviewed multiple men I've had sex with, a gay priest, a stripper I went on a date with, two porn stars, a meth addict, former professional athletes, our family members, and more.

At times I wonder if I have a sickness inside me. Who would

open themselves up to the vicious scrutiny of the online mob? Who would render themselves radioactive with possible dating prospects? Who would overshare on such a level that it would create an army of fuming enemies?

Ya boy, JP, would.

In ways, I feel like Ben and I were sacrificial lambs. Slaughter us if it creates change.

The podcast was created because I searched high and wide for the content I needed as a young gay kid. I needed someone to give it to me straight. To fill my ever so curious ears with their carnal tales. To take unprecedented risks. To show me the many lessons they learned through all their missteps. To be a proud, unapologetic gay man.

In the months since launching the podcast we've had thousands of messages come our way, including men who came out of the closet, divorced their wives, went on PrEP, left an abusive relationship, and even a closeted priest who left the church. We've also received an onslaught of hostility. One man told us that we're "everything wrong with the community," while another told us we're "everything the gay community needs right now." To each their own, I guess?

Every single podcast fan I've met has made me smile. These fans are reflective of the messaging we are outputting, and I'm proud to fight for them in my own special way, with my famous anus and the power of my words.

Starting September 2020, I'll be pursuing a new project alone (and with some superb surprise guests). It's a podcast called *Unmentionable*, which I see as a new chapter in my life and something I hope I can host for the next 30 years. It will be broader, and will reflect a maturation process I went through over the past year. It's been a process with a lot of self-reflection and psychoanalysis, but don't worry, it will still be silly as hell. And Otis will make a few visits.

Even though I'll miss *Shame On You*, I know it's time to move on. I hope everyone knows I gave it everything I could, and that it was such a rewarding experience for both of us. Sometimes decisions in our lives just sort of make themselves. We can choose to fight them or move in tandem with the wind. It feels kinda nice to do that. I'm not sure what "Ben" has planned next, but he's capable of greatness and I'll be rooting him on.

Luckily, the podcast was always the perfect launching platform for a memoir, which was originally titled "My Therapist Sent Me Nudes."

I shopped the book around to publishers and agents across the spectrum and was told, in no particular order:

- "gay men don't buy books" (from a gay man)
- "write a book for young women"
- "write an inspirational, non-comedy book about gay shame" (What?!)

I knew in my gut I was fighting an uphill battle, but I couldn't cede to heteronormative ideals that are dominating the marketplace. I also knew the podcast was the perfect market research illustrating the demand for a book of this ilk. Plus, something beautiful was happening. The gatekeepers of the entertainment business were dissolving at a faster rate than ever before. Over 80% of readers now buy their books online. That stat alone made me realize that this was always a digital marketing play.

So, I self-published this book, which allowed me total creative control and far superior royalty payouts. I handled my own press, digital marketing campaigns, cover design, pricing, editor selection and layouts. In the span of 30 days I devoured everything I could about the book publication business to maximize my chances of success, whatever that means.

The new title, *Famous Anus*, was a rebellious move I decided on after two major execs told me "a book of that title will never sell." I get their position. They play it safe. They recycle what works. But playing it safe is synonymous with being forgettable. I went for broke.

Each time I felt the urge to delete a story in this book, I resisted. I resisted the erasure of any part of my life story and I always will. If I hide these tales, I'm sending a message that they should only live in the darkness, like I did for the first two decades of my life. I want to be remembered as brave after I die, the guy that danced onto the plank with ravenous sharks circling below. I'll always give you the purest version of myself in both my current and future art.

By supporting my work, you've sent a message that queer stories should live in the open. That we are commercially viable and valid. I hope we can all spark a ripple effect that changes the entertainment landscape in the many years to come.

I can't wait for you to read the next book. It's already in progress.

Please go and write the tales you've always needed as a queer kid. I promise to support you all along the way.

Love you long time,

Jordy P

Acknowledgements

Not everyone below helped me write this book, but they did play a part in forming the person I am today. Some didn't mind me writing about them. Some even begged me to feature them more. No need to worry; I have at least two more books in me. There is plenty of time to humiliate you all. Thank you to the following people (in no particular order):

Jennifer Bill - my first editor, who once believed in me enough to give me a nationally syndicated newspaper column. Thank you for your help and for making me realize I know very little about grammar and syntax.

Emily Krempholtz - my second editor and the person who dragged me across the finish line. You pulled something out of me that I didn't think was possible. You are a true talent. Thank you for coming into my life. Also thank you for making me cry on my keyboard at three in the morning… twice.

Mom - My greatest cheerleader. Thank you for teaching me that what makes me unique is what will make me successful. I couldn't have finished this without you housing me and pushing me as a writer. I hope you didn't cringe too much.

"New Dad" - for being more of a father to me in three years than my original one. Also, for calling me "famous anus" in public. That never gets old.

Marijuana - the silent co-writer of this book. You never let me down.

Mushrooms - you helped at a few parts, too.

The listeners of *Shame On You* - I love you all. OK, maybe not all. There are a few a-holes in the mix.

My sisters - who understand that as our life gets shittier, we become funnier.

Stefen - I'm still going to bang your brother.

My nephew, Cole - you have a publishing company named after you and you can't even talk. How cool is that, little buddy? If you're reading this right now, I hope to God you're 18.

"Patrick" - the only boyfriend I said "I love you" to and actually meant it. Jerky Jerky.

"Ben" - my partner in crime. How are we alive?

"Jesus"- for being stronger than all of us and floating to Canada on fraying driftwood.

"Lara" - my very first and oldest friend. Thank you for helping me out of bed when I was so depressed I couldn't even wear underwear.

Abz Hakim - for nailing the cover on the first try. Yes, I sent you very weird instructions.

Britt - for all those stoned midnight phone calls, giggling over passages from this book.

Britt's dad, aka the president of my fan club - Yes, I am actually this cool. It's a lot of work.

Chris P - for keeping food on the table and supporting the GDP of India.

Sandra Z - for teaching me my worth in a single text message. What a ride we've had.

And to everyone else in this world… you were absolutely no help whatsoever.

About the Author

Jordan Power is a writer and comedian who has sold out live shows across North America. He is also the co-host of *Shame On You*, a podcast with listeners in over 100 countries that explores his journey to zero gay shame. For podcast updates, tour dates, and more, he can be followed on all social media at @JPowercomedy.

His next memoir is already in progress. It might just be even wilder than this one.

Made in the USA
Middletown, DE
25 July 2020